Why Politics Fails

Ben Ansell is Professor of Comparative Democratic Institutions at Nuffield College, University of Oxford. Following a PhD at Harvard he taught at the University of Minnesota for several years, becoming a full Professor at Oxford in 2013 at the age of thirty-five. He was made Fellow of the British Academy in 2018, among the youngest fellows at that time. His work has been widely covered in the media, including in *The Times, The New York Times* and the *Economist*, and on BBC Radio 4's *Start the Week*. He is the Principal Investigator of the multimillion-pound ERC project 'The Politics of Wealth Inequality', co-editor of the most-cited journal in comparative politics and has written three award-winning academic books. This is his first for a general reader.

D1339220

Why Politics Fails

*The Five Traps of the Modern World
and How to Escape Them*

BEN ANSELL

VIKING

an imprint of

PENGUIN BOOKS

VIKING

UK | USA | Canada | Ireland | Australia
India | New Zealand | South Africa

Viking is part of the Penguin Random House group of companies
whose addresses can be found at global.penguinrandomhouse.com.

Penguin
Random House
UK

First published 2023
002

Copyright © Ben Ansell, 2023

The moral right of the author has been asserted

Set in 12/14.75pt Bembo Book MT Pro
Typeset by Jouve (UK), Milton Keynes
Printed and bound in Great Britain by Clays Ltd, Elcograf S.p.A.

The authorized representative in the EEA is Penguin Random House Ireland,
Morrison Chambers, 32 Nassau Street, Dublin D02 YH68

A CIP catalogue record for this book is available from the British Library

HARDBACK ISBN: 978–0–241–51762–8
TRADE PAPERBACK ISBN: 978–0–241–51763–5

www.greenpenguin.co.uk

To my parents

Contents

Introduction: Simple Problems,
Impossible Politics

The headline in *The New York Times* was stark: 'Warmer Climate on the Earth May be Due to More Carbon Dioxide in the Air.' The author, Waldemar Kaempffert, highlighted a theory originally developed back in 1861 but which was only now being taken seriously again – mankind's emissions of carbon dioxide might be permanently heating the atmosphere.

Kaempffert argued that seemingly small increases in CO_2 could have grave consequences, converting 'the polar regions into tropical deserts and jungles, with tigers roaming about and gaudy parrots squawking in the trees'. Florid description aside, the scientists Kaempffert spoke to argued that the rise in global temperatures of 'the last sixty years' was due to 'man increasing the carbon dioxide content of the atmosphere by 30 per cent – that is, at the rate of 1.1°C per century'.

The *Times'* prescient article was published on 28 October 1956. The 'last sixty years' of globally rising temperatures Kaempffert referred to was the time since the start of the twentieth century. The science on which these predictions were based was already a century old.

More than six decades on, the warnings feel much more real to us. Global temperatures are another degree Celsius warmer. And the pace of change is accelerating. The current best-case scenario is another 1.5°C increase, which brings us ever closer to the prospect of squawking Arctic parrots. But more likely is the desertification of much of Southern Europe, India and Mexico, endemic flooding and billions of displaced people.

The scientific jury was still out on why global temperatures were rising (or even with much confidence whether they were) in the late 1950s. We no longer have the excuse that 'we really don't know what's happening', despite the special pleading of climate sceptics. The debate has moved from whether humans are responsible for climate change to what, if anything, we can do about it. Progress of sorts, but it raises a crucial question. If disaster is about to hit us, what the hell have we been doing for the past seven decades?

Climate change is a simple problem with impossible politics. By simple, I mean that the road from A to B – carbon dioxide emissions to global atmospheric heating – is direct and well understood. Carbon reduction – removal even – is an obvious solution. We understand the science. What we don't understand is how to get anyone to do anything about it, even though it affects us all. Why, despite knowing for decades that climate change is a fundamental threat to humanity, have humans been so passive?

Carbon dioxide is a global problem but our politics is helplessly domestic. If I pollute more, my emissions cannot be contained within my national borders. They are your problem too. And vice versa. And if I'm just a small country, then it probably doesn't matter much if I pollute – I can't change the global climate on my own. Of course, that's not just true for me – it's true for most other countries. We'd all prefer to carry on as normal and hope someone else will pay the costs of carbon abatement. There's no world government that can effectively sanction us. And so, in the absence of effective international agreement, we all blithely continue to heat the atmosphere. Our politics doesn't seem big enough to respond to even an existential threat.

But maybe it is. Over the past few decades, since at least the Earth Summit in Rio in 1992, there have been concerted political efforts to wake us from our inaction. They have not always been successful. The Kyoto Protocol of 1997, which set binding targets for rich countries, was either unsigned (America), non-binding (China) or abandoned (Canada). The Copenhagen Accord of 2009, attempting to resuscitate Kyoto, was an abject failure. But the Paris Agreement of 2015 does seem to have been effective so far, despite the Trump administration's brief exit from it. Its success is a product of flexibility, deliberately vague wording and pushing decisions off into the future. Though imperfect, it shows that politics doesn't have to fail.

Climate change presents us with five core political challenges. It tests our vision of *democracy* – can we really assemble a stable global consensus on how to reduce emissions, one that doesn't break down into chaos or polarization?

It raises fundamental questions about *equality* – should richer countries pay more to resolve climate change; does each country have an equal 'right' to pollute?

It forces us to consider questions about global *solidarity* – what do people in developed countries owe those in poorer countries; are we willing to financially bail out people whose coastal villages or beach-front properties are threatened by rising oceans?

It potentially threatens international *security* – how can we cope with mass exoduses of climate refugees; how do we enforce international climate rules in the absence of an international police or legal system?

And, most fundamentally, it threatens our collective *prosperity* – by despoiling the environment for short-term gain, are we not only risking the costs of drought, famine and pollution but also threatening our long-term ability to eke out existence on a rather lonely satellite of the sun?

These are existential political problems. But they are not new ones. We have struggled for millennia as a species to reach our collective goals of democracy, equality, solidarity, security and prosperity. And other great challenges await us beyond climate change: from poverty to polarization to pandemics. We need solutions. While politics is imperfect, it may be our last best hope to reach common ground.

Common ground

Politics. A fraught word. For some of us it signals the distasteful, venal conniving of politicians. For others, it invokes possibility – a chance to collectively accomplish what none of us alone can. Or perhaps both. Politics, at its root, is how we make collective decisions. It's about how we make promises to one another in an uncertain world. And it is essential to resolving our common dilemmas from climate change to civil war, from global poverty to the COVID-19 pandemic.

But politics is a double-edged sword: it not only promises to solve our problems but creates new ones for us as well. We need it but we often hate it. We look for alternatives – efficient markets, advanced technology, strong or moral leaders who can get things done. But without politics these are false gods. Any technological quick fix, any perfectly designed market, any virtuous leader speaking 'for the people' will run up against us humans and our tendency to disagree, dissent and defect.

Politics is how we manage these inevitable disagreements. We can't avoid politics or wish it away. Elections have winners, and so they also have losers. Spending money in an unequal world requires some people to pay more than others. Having police or armies protect us simply raises the question of who protects us from them. When we try and push politics down in one place, we find it pops up in another, like the proverbial paste in the toothpaste tube. So, loathe it or love it, we're stuck with politics if we want to achieve things beyond our own backyard.

Are there things that you and I both want, despite all our ostensible differences? Most people – no matter how polarized we might seem to be on the surface – do agree on some things. Five, in fact. Five things at the heart of conquering our most existential challenges, such as climate change. Five things that also present a series of traps that we need to escape from. Let's take them in turn.

Democracy

A contested concept for sure. But let's take it as the right and ability of the mass public to choose and replace their leaders. Around half of the world's population currently lives in countries that are broadly speaking 'democratic'. Even if only half the world lives in a democracy, the idea is attractive to far more, including those stuck in authoritarian countries. Eighty-six per cent of people in the World Values Survey, which surveys people in democracies and non-democracies alike, think having a democracy is either a 'very' or a 'fairly' good way of running a country. In fact, over 90 per cent of people in China, Ethiopia, Iran and Tajikistan also agree with one of these statements. Democracy appears more popular in these four authoritarian countries than it is in the United States. Perhaps people mean different things when they say 'democracy', and scepticism might be higher when you live in one. But rule of the people, by the people, maybe even for the people, remains alluring to us.

That said, the past decade has been a challenging one for democracy. The 'third wave' of democratic transitions, which began in the mid 1970s and washed away most Communist regimes in the early 1990s, had petered out, perhaps reversed, by the early years of the twenty-first century. Authoritarian powers from Russia to China have increasingly flexed their military muscles. The 'homes' of democracy from Greece to the United Kingdom to the United States have been roiled by controversial referendums, the success of populist parties, and attacks on mainstream media, the bureaucracy and expertise.

Democracy may be a widely held ideal but it's clearly one under increased pressure. Sometimes we bemoan the chaos and indecision when democracies can't seem to decide on anything. At other times, we fear the anger and venom of political polarization as political parties denounce each other. But, for most of us, democracy remains essential, despite its flaws. Figuring out what makes it work effectively is a crucial challenge of our era.

Equality

Like democracy, the concept of 'equality' means different things to different people. But at its root is the idea that everyone should be treated the same, without favour, impartially, 'equally'. Very few people openly argue that people should be treated systematically unequally, though clearly racism and sexism still fester throughout our societies. But equality extends beyond processes and fair treatment to opportunities and outcomes. Here there is more heated public debate. Standard 'left–right' politics in wealthy countries often hinges on whether affluent people's incomes should be taxed and redistributed to the less fortunate.

Even here there is, perhaps surprisingly, a large amount of popular consensus. In 2019 just 7 per cent of people in wealthy countries disagreed with the statement that 'differences in income' in their country were too large. Seventy per cent of people wanted the government to do more to reduce this gap. And, sadly, 70 per cent of them also agreed that politicians in their country 'didn't care' about reducing income differences. It's unlikely that most people want everyone to have exactly the same income. But these survey data suggest a wide unhappiness with the levels of inequality we do experience in our day-to-day lives.

People may dislike inequality but that clearly hasn't prevented a resurgence of income and wealth gaps across the industrialized world. We live in an age of an apparent inequality paradox – global inequality has declined overall as billions of people in China and India have been brought out of poverty, but in wealthy countries inequality has risen dramatically since the 1980s. Closing factories and stagnant wages in rich countries have produced a backlash against both wealthy urban areas and trade with poorer countries. The political effects of this backlash have been profound, upending traditional left–right politics in America and Europe, as populists denouncing 'globalists' have won election after election. Equality, or the lack thereof, has taken centre stage once more in our political life.

Solidarity

None of us is immune from the vagaries of fortune. We will eventually become ill and die. Or get hit by a bus tomorrow. Our working lives are rarely a straight uphill ride from A (rags) to B (riches). Sometimes we are unlucky. We hope that others currently experiencing good times can help us when we're down, just as we might reciprocate. This is solidarity – support for your fellow citizen going through a tough period. We often debate who should provide solidarity and how much. But whether it comes from the state or the church, starts at home or among the poorest of the world, it has always been a widely shared human impulse.

In wealthy democracies today, some of the most popular policies – the electrified 'third rails' of politics that will fry an unwary politician who tries to cut them – are solidaristic ones: Social Security in the United States, or the National Health Service, Britain's alleged 'national religion'. Across wealthy countries, almost 95 per cent of people think the government should be responsible for providing healthcare for sick people. Even in America, where the government's role in healthcare is fragmentary to say the least, 85 per cent of people want it to be responsible for health.

And sometimes global solidarity strikes closer to home than we had imagined. Global public health has often seemed a rather esoteric topic: something that happened to people 'over there' – the target of foreign aid and international charity but nothing to provoke real existential worry. The COVID-19 pandemic has changed that balance of risk dramatically. The ill and well are tied together across rich and poor; the wealthy West and the global South. Pandemics don't recognize national borders. COVID-19 also exposed stark disparities in access to health across the world. Who we feel solidarity for has become more important than ever, as a virus in a neglected tropical slum can travel invisibly to gleaming Manhattan penthouses. Or, indeed, in the reverse direction.

Security

Perhaps our most basic desire as humans is to be safe, to survive. If we can agree on anything, it's surely that we all wish to remain alive and well. In worldwide surveys, 70 per cent of people stated they preferred security over freedom, with the number highest in those countries with recent experience of war. For most of human existence, the violence of war has been a tragic fact of life. But, until the Ukraine War broke out, interstate war had become scarce in recent decades.

Day-to-day life is also safer than it was. Keeping peace was largely achieved through 'self-help' for most of human history – we caught our own criminals. Today we have professional police services that, though often far from unbiased, are broadly able to keep public order. Trust in the police is generally high: well over three quarters of people have 'high' or 'very high' trust in the police in the United States, United Kingdom, Germany and Japan. It is in those countries where homicides and crime more generally are highest – Brazil, Guatemala, Mexico – that trust in the police is understandably low and the demand for security over freedom especially high.

The past few decades have seen growing levels of violence *within* states, from civil wars and terrorism to human rights abuses. Police violence is now a core political debate in many wealthy countries. By some accounts, 2016 was the most violent year since the Second World War. Can we avoid the endemic violence that pervades countries from the Democratic Republic of the Congo to Afghanistan? Can we make sure that the police and soldiers we employ to protect us don't prey on us? And does the Russian invasion of Ukraine mark a return to the 'bad old days' of interstate war?

Prosperity

We all want enough money to live on. Most of us would like at least as much as we have today. And many of us have been lucky: each of us in the industrialized world lives a life of luxury beyond the wildest dreams of our ancestors ten generations ago. Even in a single generation, we have become used to getting wealthier. Around the world, 80 per cent of people think they live a life as good as or better than that of their parents – in China, 90 per cent think they are better off.

But endless economic growth is not without its detractors. We cannot simply extract energy without consequences. We are warming the planet, potentially beyond its carrying capacity. And we need to act quickly. The Intergovernmental Panel on Climate Change currently estimates that global temperatures will rise above the 'tolerable' level of 2°C by sometime around 2040.

The consequences in terms of drought, flooding and sheer heat exhaustion are hard to wrap our heads around, though the increasing frequency of 'once in a century' landslides, floods and other natural calamities is providing us with unnerving glimpses of our future. In many wealthy countries, such as Australia, Germany and Italy, twice as many people value protecting the environment over economic growth. This trade-off is beginning to bite. We may all want global prosperity but maintaining it depends on halting, or at the very least massively mitigating, the destruction of our planet.

Political economy

Democracy. Equality. Solidarity. Security. Prosperity. Fine things. Goals that most of us can plausibly agree on, even if we debate the means to these ends, or even the finer variations of these ends. Collective goals such as these ought to be within our reach – and even if we can't ever fully attain them, we should at least be able to travel in their direction.

So what is stopping us from striding purposefully towards our goals? And what is putting them in jeopardy? We are. Or, rather, our politics is. Political life is where our individual self-interest and our collective goals clash. And self-interest often overwhelms a collective goal. We continue, for example, to demand cheap oil to fuel our SUVs and flights to Paris for the weekend, even as we slowly cook the planet. I will show throughout the book how this gap between self-interest and collective good plays out and what we can do to harness politics and make it work effectively towards our ends. In other words, to stop politics from failing.

My arguments and evidence are based on political economy, the school of thought that takes seriously how the individual and society interact. By starting with a model of each of us – what we want and how we plan to get it – and then panning out to view society at large, we can see how our best-laid plans can be undermined by . . . well, us. We'll look at how our own private interests culminate in collective chaos, and then how to escape the traps we've created for ourselves.

I came to political economy from a background in studying history. Like the other social sciences – but unlike history – political economy seeks to find general laws or patterns that explain human behaviour in the past and present. And, like many a convert, I found myself drawn away from my previous training – from the contingency and specificity of historical analysis to the universality, simplicity and just plain usefulness of political economy.

Political economists start with simple models of self-interested individuals and then see how those individuals interact with and constrain one another. We derive and develop mathematical models that explain and predict behaviour. We don't do so out of a misguided physics envy but because these models force us to think through the consequences of the assumptions we make about people.

Political economy lets us ask and answer questions from the micropolitics of our everyday life – how will I feel about funding public pensions when I buy a house? – to the macropolitics of everyone's life – does rising inequality threaten our political stability? It does so by assuming people are broadly the same – politicians and voters, rich and poor alike – and face the same temptations and traps. This book will show you that this way of thinking about the world is powerful and insightful, and sometimes even beautiful.

The basic model underlying political economy is that everyone is selfish, or at the very least self-interested. You have a set of things that you want, and you'll do your utmost to get them. Self-interest is everywhere. It explains why we do what we do. And why we should expect others to do that as well.

You might say, isn't this a highly cynical way to look at the world? But to study self-interest is not to condone it. It's certainly not an ethical guide about how to live your life. Instead self-interest is a useful analytical tool; the basis of the theories we create to explain human behaviour. Political economists use this model of self-interest not just to describe, explain and predict individual behaviour, but also to recommend policies for governments. Policies that might make things better for us all, even though everyone is self-interested.

Focusing on self-interest means thinking about the world as individuals. Rather than talk about classes, or cultures, or some other group, we begin with individual people first and build up from there. In fact the very concept of a group of people having 'interests' is dubious – why would individuals in a group all behave in the same way? How can a group be said to have any preferences of its own? After all, it doesn't have a single mind.

But individuals do have single minds. We have preferences about the world. There are some things we like and some things we dislike, and we can order these preferences. Given those preferences, we try to calculate how to achieve our favoured outcome. In an ideal world, we make the *best* possible choice. In mathematical terms, we 'maximize' our happiness given our options by picking the choice that gives us the highest 'utility'. So we have a set of preferences about things that might happen, or we might get. And we have a way of choosing the one we most like. That's the idea of self-interest.

The core insights in political economy don't come from just assuming people have preferences and choose their favoured option. This would lead to a rather dull answer that people will choose to have as much of something as they can get. A higher income makes me happier. And I keep on getting happier, the more income I get. To infinity and beyond. Something presumably stops us from just getting ever higher and higher utility. That something is the world around us.

People always face some kind of constraint preventing them from getting exactly what they want. The constraint could be physical – there is only so much natural gas or gold on planet earth. It could be institutional – I might maximize my income by robbing every bank in the country, but the law is eventually going to be enforced and prevent me attaining that goal. And in many cases it will be social – other people's own behaviour will constrain what I can achieve.

Constraints force us to face trade-offs. We can't get everything we want and so we will have to make decisions about what we are willing to sacrifice. The existence of trade-offs is a regular, mundane part of our lives. When we go to the shop and choose to buy a particular brand of coffee, we are making several trade-offs: we are choosing one brand over another; we are choosing to buy coffee and not tea; and we are exchanging money for the benefits of getting coffee. And since money comes from working, the benefits we get from coffee are being traded off against that most basic element of our existence – time.

Political life is all about trade-offs. When I'm in a polling booth, I make a decision between one candidate or another. Implicitly, I am also trading off things I like about one party against things I like about another. For example, I may want lower taxes but be socially very liberal – across different countries, whether I vote in the UK for Labour or the Conservatives, in the USA for the Republican or the Democratic Party, in France for the Parti Socialiste, En Marche or Les Républicains, depends on how I weigh those preferences together.

I have also made a trade-off by coming to the voting booth in the first place. Voting costs time and effort. There might be benefits to your preferred party winning and those may outweigh the cost of standing in line to vote. But your own vote is very unlikely to be the deciding one. Once we weigh those benefits of your party winning by the tiny probability of your vote being decisive, the cost you incur for sure from voting will loom far larger. Which means it might not be rational to vote. Hence, political economists argue that there must be an element of 'duty' in people's preferences that makes up for this and so helps predict who will actually turn out to vote. If I enjoy the feeling of making a difference, or I am especially interested in politics, or I can take time off work, then I will go out and vote. By contrast, turnout will be low among the apathetic, the apolitical and the impoverished, who can't afford to take time off work.

Politicians also act in a self-interested fashion. US congressional representatives often complain that they spend a huge amount of their time phoning would-be donors rather than on policy. Why don't they put down the phone and do the real work of a legislator? Because you can't make laws without winning elections. And to win elections you need support from voters. How do voters know how to vote? Because they watched campaign ads, which cost money for both incumbents and challengers. Hence, both candidates are driven into a campaign arms race because they want to get elected. It's not that politicians are venal or stupid (though some are) – it's the choices and trade-offs forced on them to get elected that explain their behaviour.

Forcing ourselves to consider self-interest when we look at political life might seem one-dimensional. But I'd argue it's quite liberating. We don't have to assume that some people act for nobler reasons than others. Or that some people simply can't be understood. There's often a self-interested logic underlying the behaviour of the most apparently selfless people, or what appears to be a charitable, enlightened public interest.

Take education. Most opinion surveys find a high level of support for government spending on public education. Perhaps this is because people really do want more spending. Or perhaps they feel bad telling interviewers that they don't really care about school funding. If we dig below the surface, however, we find some quite sharp differences among people, and they accord closely with base self-interest. In particular, richer people are threatened by expanding public education. Not only must they pay more in taxes to educate other people's children, but those newly educated children also provide competition for their own children in the job market. Education funding is a 'double bad' for the rich.

Self-interest plays out everywhere in education. We'd expect authoritarian regimes run by the rich to restrain public spending and refrain from compulsory education – which is true in cases from Franco's Spain to Marcos's Philippines. We'd expect right-wing parties to be less likely to spend more on education or to talk about it in their manifestos – which occurs in countries across Europe from Germany to the UK. And, finally, we'd expect rich people to be less supportive of government spending on education, which we see in public-opinion surveys of people in wealthy countries. Indeed, rich people are most opposed to government spending on low-income students when university enrolments are already high. Precisely because mass higher education might 'devalue' the degrees their own children receive.

Self-interest is a useful way to make sense of how people behave. But what happens when self-interested individuals get together? Then we enter the world of the collective action problem.

One of the few laws of political science is that democracies don't fight each other. The 'Cod Wars' between Britain and Iceland – NATO allies no less – are an odd exception. These conflicts, from the 1950s to the 1970s, were about that once bountiful fish, the north-east Atlantic cod, and Iceland's desire to expand its exclusive territorial rights for fishing it. Over the decades, cod stocks collapsed dramatic-ally, and as the number of fish plummeted, tensions rose between Icelandic and British fishermen. The wars led to one accidental death by electrocution, shots were fired, boats rammed, frigates launched and jets used for reconnaissance. The Icelanders even equipped their coastguards with wire-cutters to cut the nets of British trawlers as they passed by.

Why were exclusive fishing rights so important to Iceland? The problem was that the self-interest of British fishermen directly affected Icelandic fishermen and vice versa. Fish are an odd form of resource – they are limited in supply but hard to prevent others from catching. If you own a dairy farm, you also own the cows that live on it and the milk they produce. If someone else wants access to the farm, your property rights stand in their way. To get hold of your cows or your milk, they must pay you some mutually acceptable amount.

The sea, on the other hand, is hard to own and hard to monitor. In the deep sea, outside 'exclusive fishing zones', no one has the right to charge anyone else for fishing, so it's basically a free-for-all. Even if I claim exclusive territorial rights, like the Icelanders, the sea is hard to patrol for fishing boats, so I still can't effectively exclude you. Conse-quently, we both end up fishing in the same sea, and with too many fishers we end up depleting the stocks rapidly.

Fishing is a classic example of 'the tragedy of the commons'. With-out private ownership, anyone can fish to their heart's content. Which sounds great, but the more I fish, the fewer fish there are for you. My self-interest ends up hurting yours and vice versa. If we could bind ourselves to an enforceable agreement where we each got a decent share but prevented overfishing, then we could both end up happier. We would have a collectively better outcome. But if we can't enforce this agreement – which is hard in the stormy North Atlantic ocean – then we will just follow our individual self-interest in the moment and catch fish until there are none left.

Economists refer to the effects that the fishermen have on each other as 'externalities'. An externality occurs when a third party – an Icelandic fisherman – is affected by a market transaction between two other people – a Scottish fisherman and a Glaswegian restaurant-owner who buys his fish. Political life is also full of externalities. Most of them are negative. A government policy that subsidizes energy production leads to pollution that ruins a local beach and the livelihoods of people operating hotels and restaurants in the area. A low-traffic zone in one London neighbourhood leads drivers to clog up another. Sometimes, more happily, there are positive externalities. A new rose garden dug by a green-fingered neighbour raises the value of properties with an unspoiled view of it. But, in all cases, self-interested behaviour by one set of people can spill over into the lives of others.

These 'collective action problems' emerge any time a bunch of self-interested individuals interact in ways that, perhaps inadvertently, undermine some broader collective goal. Collective action problems emerge because we are *interdependent*. What I choose to do affects the environment you face and hence what you choose to do. And the problems we encounter throughout this book in getting things we all want boil down to this tension. We can't commit other people to ignore their self-interest and 'do the right thing' – stop fishing, stop driving, stop polluting – and so we can't commit ourselves either. It's the making of a tragedy.

Politics as a promise

What makes political economy both fascinating and challenging is that the things we study – people – can respond to what others are doing. Not just that, they can anticipate what others are going to do. Collective action problems emerge *because* we are smart. We can't blame them on people acting 'stupidly'. But that raises the stakes. We will have to outsmart ourselves if we want to solve them. And we'll do that through politics.

What is politics? Superficially, it's parties campaigning in elections. Or legislators passing laws and implementing policies. Or countries forming alliances or signing treaties. But more fundamentally politics is about making *promises* to each other.

You and I make promises all the time. We make an agreement with someone else that we will do something. We promise our spouse we will go on a relaxing holiday. We promise our boss that we will complete an assignment on time. Promises aren't always nice. Gangland bosses also make promises – to kneecap a shopkeeper who refuses protection. But all of these are individual promises. Politics is about how we make collective promises to each other – politicians to voters, presidents to parliaments, allies to adversaries.

A promise is an agreement to do something in the future. What differentiates a promise from a contract, however, is that a promise cannot be legally enforced by some third party. A promise might not be fulfilled and, if so, there's often no recourse. If your partner reneges on a promise, well, you're on your own.

In political life, there is no guaranteed recourse for a broken promise either. If a government fails to enact its manifesto, you can't sue it. If a political party decides to bail out of a coalition, the other parties are out of luck. If an ally shies away when you are attacked, there's no international court you call on to summon them. Promises cannot be enforced. They rely on trust and expectations. They come with a degree of uncertainty.

Politics is built on uncertain promises because there is no higher power than politics itself. Politics can create legal systems that enforce our economic and social interactions. But we can't effectively do the same for politics itself. At root, every decision we make about who should exert power, who has what rights and obligations, is another set of promises we've made to each other. Nothing outside politics can force us to abide by those promises. What's more, politics is socially constructed and contingent. Political decisions cannot be permanent. Just like promises, political choices only have meaning in our minds, and they can be made and remade.

Think back to the problem of fishing in the North Atlantic. Nobody owns the oceans. And even if they did it would be near impossible to monitor any trespassers. Any legal contract we drew up would be unenforceable because we can't observe every infraction.

There's no international police force, jury or judge that can catch or punish any wrongdoer. Instead, countries must make political promises to one another on behalf of their fishermen. These agreements can help set expectations and stop overfishing in the short run. But as we saw with Iceland continuously extending its fishing rights, it's impossible to prevent people from reneging on promises if they think it's in their interest. And because of this new promises will need to be made. Politics never ends.

We'll see throughout this book that politics can make promises that will help us achieve our five goals of democracy, equality, solidarity, security and prosperity. But these promises may be fragile and temporary.

With democracy, we can develop electoral rules and legislative institutions that can constrain our chaotic preferences; but these rules can be dismantled by their political enemies.

With equality, facing revolution or mass discontent, the wealthy elite can promise to redistribute to the people; but once the people acquiesce, the elite may renege and repress them.

With solidarity, when times are hard, we may be willing to vote for social insurance programmes; but when times are good, we may undermine them by not supporting the taxes needed to pay for them.

With security, we want a police force that is strong enough to protect us; but any force that powerful may also be able to take advantage of its power and turn its force on us.

And with prosperity, we want everyone to cooperate on challenges as fundamental as climate change; but we'd also like to have cheap fuel for our car.

We make each other promises all the time. And then we try and skip out of them. So how can we make our political promises more effective? Why does politics fail? And when can it succeed?

Political promises succeed when they are self-enforcing. When we are trying to solve collective action problems, we need our promises to have the seeds of their own stability. We need to make reneging on them difficult. And the best way we can do that is to try and grant them some permanency by establishing political institutions – formal

rules and principles – and developing social norms – informal expectations about how we should behave. These institutions and norms
will live on beyond the moment of their creation: they are the flour-
ishing forest grown from the seeds of previous political promises.

Political *institutions* are the formal laws, rules and organizations
that make decisions stable and long-lasting. We often associate them
with the people who write and enforce them, and the buildings they
work in, from courts to parliaments. But what matters about an institution is not its bricks and mortar, but the formal writing down of
political promises. Institutions bind us into choices we make. They
allow us to fix our expectations of what others are likely to do, so
that we can make effective choices ourselves. Because institutions are
the legacies of past promises, they may not perfectly match our current needs. Politics moves on. But even if the shoe doesn't quite fit,
we should be careful about throwing it out.

A telling example is the filibuster rule in the US Senate. The filibuster allows just forty out of one hundred US senators to stop
legislation. Initially, the filibuster permitted individual senators to
continue speaking to block the passage of a bill, which could bring all
business to a halt. But in the 1970s an agreement was made to let
either party filibuster particular bills by simply issuing a note of
intent. Since then, passing most bills in the Senate has required a
supermajority of sixty senators.

The filibuster is flawed in all kinds of ways – it over-represents
small rural states and was responsible for the continued blocking of
civil rights reforms in the 1960s. But removing it is not risk-free.
Between 2009 and 2015, Democrats insisted that the filibuster be
removed to prevent the Republican Senate minority blocking President Obama's reforms. Ultimately the Democrats removed the
filibuster for all executive orders and judicial appointments, except to
the Supreme Court.

But before long the shoe was on the other foot. When the Republicans took control of the Senate, House and presidency in 2016, they
were able to remove the filibuster for Supreme Court appointments
too and quickly approve three successive Supreme Court nominees
with just over fifty votes – a very slim majority. In 2022 those same

judges were able to rule against Americans' long-standing federal right to abortion. Institutions may often be dysfunctional, but they do structure expectations and behaviour across politicians in and out of political office. In their absence, we often just end up with 'might makes right', as those with power exploit those without.

Political *norms* are informal patterns of behaviour that others follow, and we too decide to follow. This can be for positive or negative reasons. We might accept norms because seeing what others are doing helps us understand what's best for us. Alternatively, we might do so because if we don't follow the norms, others will punish us. Norms guide how we think, how we perceive the world, who we trust. They are invisible but highly effective at driving collective behaviour – potentially much more so than edicts from formal political institutions.

Norms are also vaguer and harder to enforce than formal rules. They can be difficult for politicians to encourage and invoke. Not every President is a Kennedy or an Obama – able to persuade many citizens to see the world through new eyes and shift their behaviour accordingly. Nor was every citizen particularly enamoured of Kennedy or Obama. So while norms will be an important part of understanding effective political solutions, they can't solve problems such as climate change, police violence or political polarization, without the starker strength of laws and institutions.

Because politics depends so much on institutions and norms it also plays out differently around the world. Clearly democracies have norms governing behaviour that are sharply different from those in dictatorships. Citizens of authoritarian countries have strong incentives to falsify and misrepresent their true preferences and are unlikely to have strong levels of trust in either government or their fellow citizens.

Across democracies we also see radical differences. Many scholars highlight the success of countries such as Denmark and Sweden with their inclusive electoral systems, high social trust and low corruption. But these are not God-given tendencies of the Nordic world (please note the Viking era). They are long-standing patterns of political behaviour that might be hard to replicate elsewhere and depend on a web of interlocking institutions and norms. We'll explore a wide array of cross-national and historical experiences in this book that shed light on how institutions and norms underpin whether politics succeeds or fails.

Democracy, equality, solidarity, security and prosperity are admirable things. But in each case we will face a political trap, triggered by our self-interest, that stops us from reaching our collective goals. These traps are not our tragic destiny. But they are insidious, pervasive and sometimes even enticing.

So we have a couple of options. We can learn to identify the traps 'in the wild' and carefully step around them. Alternatively, and more unfortunately, we might already have been caught in the traps. And then we need to learn how to escape them. Only if we can understand why politics fails can we figure out how to make it succeed.

PART I
Democracy

There's no such thing as the 'will of the people'

1. Westminster: Wednesday, 27 March 2019

We arrived at the entrance to the House of Commons in London an hour early. We had expected long lines. The media had been in a frenzy ever since Prime Minister Theresa May's third attempt at passing a Brexit bill had been emphatically defeated. British political circles were abuzz about next steps, next moves. British political parties had lost control of their own Members of Parliament (MPs). Democracy didn't seem to be working. And chaos was ensuing. Was there a way out of the parliamentary gridlock? Surely Parliament must be able to agree on something?

Iain McLean and I had been invited to Parliament to provide advice to MPs seeking to find a solution. We made our way past statues of long-dead leaders to the committee rooms, upstairs. Here we sat on green suede chairs in an empty corridor, waiting for our hosts. Iain is probably Britain's leading expert on electoral rules, the author of a book titled *What's Wrong with the British Constitution?* If anyone could devise a system that might break the logjam, it was Iain. I was there as backup, as a specialist on political institutions. But what if even Iain, with or without my assistance, couldn't find a solution? What if Brexit was too complicated for any system to resolve?

Shouldn't this all have been simpler? The EU referendum of 2016 was a momentous event in British political history. 'Brexit', as the unexpected decision to leave the European Union has become known, was a simple vote over a seemingly simple question: 'Should the United Kingdom remain a member of the European Union or leave the European Union?' Leave won by 52 to 48 per cent – a sign perhaps of a divided country, but a clear victory nonetheless. Democracy at work.

The trouble came when politicians had to decide what kind of Brexit should be implemented. The people had spoken. But what were they saying? There are lots of countries in Europe that are not members of the European Union: from Norway to Switzerland to Turkey and Russia. Some, like the Norwegians and Swiss, have very close relationships, mirroring European Union laws and allowing free immigration of European nationals. Others such as Turkey have the same trade policy as the European Union but precious little else. And still others – Russia, Armenia, Azerbaijan – are kept very much at arm's length from the European Union. So 'Leave the European Union?' – Yes. But how?

For the past three years Theresa May had tried to come up with an answer. Moving from the simple binary question to exactly how to disentangle the United Kingdom from an organization it had been part of for over forty years proved nightmarish. All kinds of decisions had to be made that were not on the ballot. Should the UK remain part of the EU's 'single market', which would prevent limits on EU immigration? Should the UK remain part of the EU's 'customs union' and forgo the chance of having its own trade deals? Or should the UK abandon all cooperation with the EU and strike out entirely alone, economic repercussions be damned?

A particular problem lay with Northern Ireland. After generations of violent conflict, the Good Friday Agreement in 1998 had ushered in two decades of peace between Catholic and Protestant communities. But it relied in part on the European Union – membership by both Britain and Ireland meant that there was no economic border between Ireland and Northern Ireland. The British public had voted to leave the EU. But that in turn meant the prospect of a 'hard border' with Ireland, which might destabilize peace. The simple Brexit vote again turned out to have rather more complex consequences, many of which voters – and politicians – had not anticipated.

May's own solution tried to straddle these challenges, balancing uneasily like a polar explorer standing on ice floes drifting apart. She would exit the single market to control immigration. She would exit the customs union so Britain could strike trade deals. But she also offered a 'backstop', which postponed Britain diverging from EU rules or trade policy until some solution to the Irish question could be found. The backstop meant Britain would remain in the EU's legislative orbit for untold years to come.

It was a compromise that satisfied few people. May tried to pass her Brexit bill three times in early 2019. Each time, it was defeated by a rather odd coalition. Some Brexit-supporting Conservative politicians voted against it because it was not 'proper Brexit'. They wanted to leave the European Union completely – do or die, come what may. Brexit-opposing Labour politicians voted against the bill because it was, well, Brexit. They wanted a second referendum, presumably to get a new answer.

A simple popular vote among two options had become an almighty mess once it became clear that there were many more than two ways of 'Brexiting'. Theresa May's bill did indeed guarantee the UK formally left the European Union, as the public had demanded. It was the 'how' that was the problem. Democracy was proving difficult.

Iain and I walked up the silent corridors to a horseshoe-shaped table in the parliamentary committee rooms where just two MPs, one Conservative and one Labour, were waiting. In British politics it's very unusual for a Conservative MP to side with a Labour MP over their own government, but they had both recognized the need to cooperate on this issue. With the government bill defeated, and at least five different potential Brexit bills floating around, plus a referendum on whether to call the whole thing off, they wanted to know if there was any method for Parliament to choose among them. In other words, could democracy be made to work?

We presented a series of different voting systems that Parliament could use to come to a choice. Each had its own merits. Some favoured compromise options. Others would produce a clear, if polarizing, decision. And still other voting systems explored whether any option could even meet with the vague approval of a majority of MPs.

After we had set out the pros and cons of each of these voting rules, the Conservative MP stopped us. He had figured out the obvious conclusion: MPs couldn't agree on anything, so they also wouldn't agree on a rule to agree on something. Each voting system would favour different ultimate outcomes. So choosing a voting system became a proxy for the debate at hand. We were back to square one.

But they did have one plan already up their sleeves. That evening a series of 'indicative votes' over Brexit options were scheduled. The simplest possible procedure was adopted – 'approval voting', whereby each option was considered on its own and MPs were asked simply to say whether they approved of that option. Surely, this would help figure out the set of options that MPs could abide and then leave the trickier task of choosing among them for another day.

The approval votes were cast as we were leaving Westminster. Division bells rang out and MPs scampered off to mark down which options they could live with. As Iain and I grabbed a post-meeting drink and debriefed at a pub opposite Parliament, where Big Ben had just struck nine, I looked at my Twitter feed to see the voting numbers roll in. One by one the different policies met their fate. Not a single policy was approved by a majority of MPs. Faced with a myriad of different options, parliamentary democracy had frozen in stasis.

By and large, we want democracy in principle, but it's often impossible to deliver in practice. And this is the heart of the democracy trap: *there's no such thing as the 'will of the people'*. The British public had spoken. But Parliament couldn't deliver. Even when democracy had been boiled down into a Leave/Remain binary, it seemed to be impossible to actually figure out how to implement it in practice. Life is generally more complex than simple 'yes'/'no' questions – there are multiple trade-offs, different ways of carrying out an instruction. So when it came to actually carrying out Brexit, was there really any clear 'will of the people' at all? Apparently not.

2. What is Democracy?

Democracy seems to be a goal we can all agree on. Even those of us who don't live in democracies. The World Values Survey regularly asks people: 'How important is it for you to live in a country that is governed democratically?', scoring their answer from 0 to 10. It's not surprising that in established democracies, such as Denmark and Germany, three quarters of people give democracy the full 10/10 score. But in many countries that are very far from democratic – China, Egypt, Zimbabwe, Venezuela – around two thirds of people give the importance of democracy at least 9/10. It's possible people view democracy through different lenses; perhaps even that Chinese citizens think that their one-party state is a 'people's democracy'. Not everyone might want 'Western' democracy. But in principle most people seem to want a say in how their countries are run.

The idea of democracy – quite literally, 'rule by the people' – is a powerful and universal one. And although social scientists differ in their precise definitions of democracy, it's this idea of self-government that is at its core. All of us should be involved in the making of political decisions that affect us.

Yet democracy regularly produces outcomes that aren't consensual. Often people disagree. And it is this disagreement that is at the heart of the democracy trap: *there's no such thing as the 'will of the people'*.

As we saw with Brexit, when people don't agree, the results can be chaotic. To get what they want they will strategize, they will manipulate and they will misrepresent. Our individual incentives to try and get the outcome we want will end up overwhelming our ability to come to any kind of stable collective agreement. Every time we look like we have consensus, it can be derailed by a new proposal from someone unhappy with the outcome.

Even if we avoid chaos and finally make collective decisions, that doesn't mean we've resolved our disagreements. Democracy often devolves into a shouting match between winners and losers, pulling apart friends and neighbours, polarizing us. Making democracy work – stopping politics from failing – will force us to balance on the knife-edge between chaos and polarization.

Even democracy's strongest defenders have recognized its imperfections, as with Winston Churchill's famous aphorism that 'democracy is the worst form of government except for all those other forms that have been tried from time to time'. But what do we mean by 'democracy'? And why, given its imperfections, is it desirable? Generations of political scientists have furiously debated these questions – which gives a sense of how contested democracy is, as well as of the ability of academics to argue endlessly for the sake of it. Buried at the core of this debate is some consensus. The most famous – and for us useful – definition comes from Joseph Schumpeter, an Austrian, born in 1883 in what is now the Czech Republic.

Schumpeter was very sure of himself. His stated ambitions included being the greatest economist in the world, the best horseman in Austria and the finest lover in Vienna. He claimed to have succeeded in two of these goals but was ambiguous about which. Schumpeter was rather clearer about how we should think about democracy. For Schumpeter, whatever else might be important about democracy, its core is acquiring 'the power to decide by means of a competitive struggle for the people's vote'.

This simple sentence has three big implications. First, 'the people's vote': the mass public is the final arbiter of who rules. Second, 'competitive struggle': there's no point in the public voting if there is only one option to vote for. And third, 'acquiring the right to decide': there's also no point in voting if the successful candidate can't actually do anything.

Notice there's nothing here that guarantees democracies get good politicians. But at least 'the people' will be able to throw them out if they're terrible. That doesn't sound brilliant, which explains Churchill's wry aphorism. But think about what happens if we violate any of these three maxims of democracy.

If we remove 'the people's vote', who has the right to decide?

Presumably some small elite – what Aristotle called an 'oligarchy'. Elites often have rather partial interests: wealthy people generally don't like being taxed or having ancient privileges removed. Moreover, without 'the people' as a whole being able to decide, whole groups are excluded or oppressed: women in Britain before 1918, African Americans in the US until 1965.

Of course, this raises the highly contested question of who 'the people' actually are. Some countries, such as Romania, allow all their citizens living abroad to vote; others, such as the UK, allow some immigrants to vote (those from the Commonwealth), but not others (EU citizens). Until quite recently, people under the age of twenty-one were deprived of the vote. Nonetheless, universal suffrage is something that (almost) all of us agree is crucial to 'democracy'.

How about if we remove the 'competitive struggle'? Well, then we end up with the kinds of mass elections where 99 per cent of people just so happen to vote for Saddam Hussein. When we look at leaders around the world winning supermajorities of the vote, most of us don't think 'wow, that leader is so popular, if only we too had a leader that 90 per cent of us wanted'. We tend, justifiably, to be more sceptical. And though people in democratic countries often complain that they have no real choice and that parties are a cartel, compared to a country like Russia, where elections are a foregone conclusion, these claims are exaggerations. People on the left in the United States often bemoan a perceived choice between a right-wing party and a centre party. But those two parties at least fight tooth and nail to win. They compete. They offer alternative solutions to common problems.

Finally, what if we remove 'the power to decide'? Many monarchies in nineteenth-century Europe kept ultimate power even as they permitted elections and legislatures. The nobility and the church often gave themselves a veto over elected politicians. The aristocrats of the House of Lords in Britain kept this right until 1911, using it to block taxation of their land. Kaiser Wilhelm in late nineteenth-century Germany was able to ignore the elected parliament – and, with his Chancellor, Otto von Bismarck, to prevent the threatening socialist movement from gaining power through elections. Even today, in countries such as Thailand and Morocco that have the ostensible trappings of democracy – parties, legislatures, elections – monarchs retain the right to punish criticism, however meek.

So, at its core, democracy is about the people voting, competition among prospective leaders and elections actually mattering in terms of what policies get made. You might find this kind of definition too minimalist, but even once we have established the basics – free, fair and competitive elections to decide who rules – an enormous number of differences remain *among* democracies.

In particular, we might care about how well democracies protect individual rights and freedoms and thereby prevent elected majorities from overriding the interests of minorities. Guaranteed freedoms of speech, association and conscience; protection of property from arbitrary expropriation by the government; legal systems that can enforce these rules; and respect for long-standing norms in parliament – all of these are keystones of *liberal democracy*.

Liberal democracies are like a strengthened version of the kinds of electoral democracies that Schumpeter advocated. They are not simply 'rule of the people' – indeed, they often constrain 'the people' by preventing victorious parties from carrying out all their wishes. They chain up winners to make sure they don't exploit losers. And they do so by creating or sustaining institutions that are not always themselves democratically elected – courts, ombudsmen, central banks, religious associations, newspapers, trade unions. They develop norms and procedures that prevent election-winners from shutting down legislatures or extending their time in office.

There is, then, a paradox at the heart of the liberal democracies that are home to most readers of this book. To escape the democracy trap, we have to tame democracy with institutions and norms that don't just give the winners of elections what they want. Rule of the people can't be entirely unconstrained. In fact, to make democracy work, we have to constrain it. These norms and institutions can help us prevent the chaos and polarization of the democracy trap and stop our politics from failing.

Democracy may be a popular idea, but does it actually produce good outcomes? Breathless journalistic accounts of China's economic rise have often had an implicit critique of liberal democracy – 'Look at how an authoritarian state can build glistening new infrastructure without having to worry about following pettifogging rules.' Similar stories have been told innumerable times – about Stalin's industrialization of the Soviet Union, Brazil's economic 'miracle' under military government in the 1960s, the 'Asian Tigers' of Taiwan and South Korea booming under authoritarian leadership in the 1980s.

But for every authoritarian boom there are several busts. And, save for the oil-rich Gulf states and perhaps contemporary China, almost all wealthy countries today are democracies. Economic growth tends to be more sustainable in democracies because they can course-correct. In authoritarian countries, bureaucrats and local leaders may fear giving the ruling regime bad news, so they lie, misrepresent, or hide unhelpful information. The disastrous performance of the Russian army in the invasion of Ukraine arguably reflected an unwillingness of army leaders to accurately state their preparedness to Vladimir Putin. A similar pattern plays out in economic development. Amartya Sen has argued that democracies don't suffer from famines because the press is able to warn of their impending arrival and leaders need to respond to their citizens.

Finally, democracies, ruled by the people, are more likely to legislate on behalf of the people. In particular, middle-income voters are likely to demand universal services and benefits. Democracies are incentivized to provide those policies because elections both force parties to make popular promises and hold them accountable if they fail to deliver. As an example, when countries democratize, they tend to spend around a third more on public education and to shift their focus from spending on universities that benefit the elite to primary education for the masses. Democracies also produce better human outcomes – they reduce infant mortality and raise literacy and immunization rates. Despite the challenges of the democracy trap, democracies are better able to provide for their citizens than their authoritarian rivals. It is no coincidence that the historical rise of democracy has produced an era of unprecedentedly high global living standards. Let's now turn to that history.

The history of democracy

The history of democracy has been a history of the democracy trap. The stable liberal democracies that many of us live in today are survivors. They are those democracies that have the layers of institutions and long-standing norms of rule-following that fend off the democracy trap. Democracy may have originated in classical Athens but even here it did so only fleetingly. For centuries, rule of the people has been fragile, easily descending into chaos, demagoguery and ultimately tyranny. Stable, consolidated democracy is less than a century old.

Democracy's relative youth might be surprising. Folk wisdom often dates the origins of democracy to ancient Greece, or perhaps to the American Declaration of Independence, the French Revolution or Victorian Britain. But if we insist on Schumpeter's three maxims – the people's vote, competitive struggle and the right to decide – we discover that many famous examples of 'democracy' don't necessarily qualify.

Take Britain for example. Despite the former Prime Minister Boris Johnson's claim that Britain is the 'home of democracy', that home was constructed gradually, room by room. The signing of Magna Carta in 1215 placed limits on the power of the monarchy. But the winners of that agreement were the people who owned land in medieval England, not the far greater number of people who ploughed it. In England the right of the winners to 'decide' was only guaranteed when the hereditary House of Lords lost its power to block legislation in 1911. And it was only by 1928 that universal suffrage was expanded to place men and women on equal terms. Even then, business-owners got two votes – one for their home, one for their business – as did graduates of Oxford and Cambridge. This double-counting lasted all the way until 1950. On this measure Britain has only been a democracy for seventy-odd years.

We can tell a similar tale with another long-standing democracy: America. It is certainly the case that America had a wide electoral franchise following independence in 1776. But it applied only to free men. Women were not enfranchised until the Nineteenth Amendment was ratified in 1920. And African Americans, despite the emancipation of slaves in 1865, were electorally oppressed, usually violently, until the Civil Rights Act a full century later.

Other countries with long histories of supposed democracy also failed to extend that beyond their male citizens. Until the twentieth century, women were banned from voting in every country save New Zealand. France introduced universal male suffrage initially, and briefly, in 1792 following the French Revolution, and again for good from the Second Republic of 1848; but France did not give women voting rights until a century later in 1945. Switzerland gave men the right to vote in 1848 but did not extend it to women until 1971, with the canton of Appenzell Innerrhoden holding out until 1990. Full Swiss democracy is as old as a typical millennial.

When we look at the granddaddy of them all, ancient Athenian democracy, we also see a murkier picture than the glossy image passed down through the ages. Democracy in Athens was highly participative, exhausting even. Around one tenth of the electorate met forty times a year in a citizens' assembly, and citizens were also selected by lot to serve on a daily agenda-setting council and on citizens' juries of 200–500 people. Clearly this kind of super-participative system would be hard to scale up – in today's America it would mean an assembly of around twenty-five million people. But it did mean that all citizens were fully engaged in every aspect of civic decision-making, and it has been extolled by people worried about an apathetic citizenry ever since.

However, this participation was possible only for a small subset of Athenian residents – male citizens. Women were entirely excluded. Slaves were also excluded. As were resident foreigners and indeed anyone without Athenian lineage. Athens could afford participative democracy because most of the work and commerce was being done by women and non-citizens. There is a striking parallel in early nineteenth-century America: the hyper-participative democracy lauded by Alexis de Tocqueville was one where only free white men were granted political rights. What's more, unconstrained Athenian democracy was both polarizing – it was Athenian citizens who sentenced Socrates to death for 'corrupting the minds of the youth' – and unstable, collapsing into tyranny and oligarchy over the centuries.

So what we think of as modern democracy is younger than lore suggests. Standing back from individual examples, what does the overall trend of democracy look like? Political scientists often talk about three 'waves' of democracy. The first wave started with the shocks of the American and French Revolutions, continued with the more gradual extension of the franchise in the United Kingdom, and culminated in the widespread creation of democratic republics in Western Europe at the end of the First World War.

But waves, by their nature, crest then crash, In the 1920s and especially 1930s, fascist regimes overturned democracy in Germany, Italy and Spain, and Stalin deepened the authoritarian nature of Soviet Russia.

After this reversal, there was a second democratic wave in the post-Second World War era as Germany, Italy and a number of ex-colonies, notably India, democratized. This was again followed by a second reversal in the 1960s and 1970s as a number of Latin American and African countries tipped into military juntas or personal rule, from Pinochet in Chile to the Argentinian generals to Muammar Gaddafi, Mobutu Sese Soko and Idi Amin.

Finally, a third wave of democratization began with Portugal in 1974, accelerated with transitions in Spain, Greece, Argentina and Brazil through the 1980s, and exploded with the fall of the Soviet Union and the democratization of Eastern Europe in the early 1990s. This was the time of Francis Fukuyama's (oft-misunderstood) book *The End of History*, where he argued that the ideas of liberal democracy had won out over their rivals, possibly for good.

Those ideas are still powerful. But we've already seen that Schumpeter's electoral definition of democracy is not the same thing as 'liberal democracy'. Almost every country in the world now permits all adults to vote – only a few countries in the Middle East (the UAE, Saudi Arabia) restrict voting. But the sticking point is whether their vote matters. Since the turn of the twenty-first century, popular elections have continued to spread almost everywhere but the other institutions that make up democracy are under concerted attack.

Countries from Russia to Turkey to Venezuela have slid back into 'electoral authoritarianism' – elections take place, but they don't really decide anything. Even in countries such as Poland, where democratic elections remain free, fair and contested, other core parts of liberal democracy – the courts, the free press – are under pressure.

Democracy without supporting liberal institutions has often degenerated into aggressive populism. The Hungarian populist Prime Minister, Viktor Orbán, has explicitly argued he is creating an 'illiberal' democracy. One hundred years ago, this distinction would not have made sense – most countries that began granting the right to vote already had substantial legal protections for speech, association and so forth. But the past few decades have seen the rise of many democracies where such rights are not guaranteed and hence where the teeth of the democracy trap are at their sharpest.

We should be careful not to dismiss all electoral democracies – having the right to vote is preferable to no elections at all. But, as we will see, democracy without constraining liberal institutions can be both chaotic and polarized. Majority rule without limits is dangerous. What is to stop a rogue leader from ignoring elections that vote them out? Recall that in politics there is no third party we can call on to enforce our promises – so shouldn't this leader be able to close down any opposition? Such threats, after the 6 January 2021 insurrection in America, have become much realer to even citizens of wealthy democracies. It requires strong institutions to keep democracy alive.

Democracy is both ancient and modern. Some of the ideas about a true rule of the masses date to the classical era. But, around the world, actually existing democracy is not much older than the transistor radio. It has been a struggle of centuries to attain the right to rule ourselves, and the threat of backsliding is ever present. Even then, democracy is an imperfect system. Democracy doesn't guarantee that we actually get good politicians. Nevertheless, imperfect as it is, there are some obvious benefits to democracy too.

We get representation – if we want something, we have the right to vote for it and to stand for office to argue for it. This doesn't guarantee politicians will look like us or think like us. Far from it. But if that genuinely concerns us we can step up and change it ourselves. Almost any voter in a democracy could be the leader of that democracy.

We get accountability – at least in theory. We can throw our politicians out when they do a bad job. We can punish their misdemeanours at the voting booth. And when parties produce manifestos, at the next election we can judge them on how well they lived up to their promises.

And, finally, we get self-government. We own our choices and decisions. Democracy allows us to correct our errors, to avoid bowing obediently to the choices of our ancestors. We are treated with respect by the political system, as citizens, not subjects. Democracy frees us to shape the world as we see fit. There's just one catch. Who are 'we'?

3. The Democracy Trap

If democracy is so desirable, why is it so hard to make democratic decisions? The problems with democracy stem from the fact that countries are not like individual people. They are, instead, groups of self-interested individuals. And the way we make our minds up individually does not translate cleanly into making clear collective decisions. In fact, our individual incentives to get what each of us wants may prevent us from coming to any agreement at all – our politics might fail completely. We get caught in the democracy trap: *there's no such thing as the 'will of the people'*.

A 'will of the people' only exists in the most banal case: when we all already agree. Democratic institutions such as different voting rules cannot conjure up a single, collective vision because they either fall prey to the strategic manipulation of self-interested voters or produce nonsensical answers. Think back to Brexit: MPs couldn't even agree on a voting system to make a decision because what had seemed a simple choice between Leave and Remain turned into a myriad different ways of Brexiting.

Once you have more than two choices, democratic voting can always produce chaos and indecision. But we don't always see chaos. That's because political parties can impose order, though only at the cost of ever-growing polarization. We make decisions but ones that might split the country in half, with festering resentment on both sides. That's where the Brexit debate left British party politics. The Conservative Party became a party of Leave, and Labour a party of Remain (even though both parties had been initially split), with politicians bemoaning bitter 'Remainers' or gloating 'Brexiteers'.

How can we make democratic politics succeed when we don't agree and avoid being bedevilled by chaos and polarization? To answer this question, we need to explore the democracy trap.

The 'will of the people'

The idea that there is a 'will of the people' has a long history. Until the mid twentieth century, most grand debates – the clash of nationalism, liberalism and communism – were around who represented the public will, or what it was. The idea that it didn't exist was barely considered. Hence it's no surprise that people are still attracted to 'strong' or 'moral' leaders who claim to stand for it.

At the heart of this debate was Jean-Jacques Rousseau, and his idea of the *volonté générale*, or 'general will'. Rousseau thought that individual disagreement was an artificial outcome of modern civilization, which produced division and special interest. But there was a solution: a democratic republic. If all people were involved in decision-making, they would, through deliberation, come to understand their common shared goals – the general will. The more participatory and active democracy was, the closer the aggregated will of all individuals would be to that true shared interest.

Following Rousseau, thinkers from very different traditions would argue that if we could just set aside our individual interests, we would see a common interest underneath. For nationalists, the 'will of the people' was simply defined by the nation's borders or by an imagined co-ethnic 'folk'. Socialists had a very different view of the 'will of the people'. Karl Marx argued that common interest was defined by people's relationship to the economy: all workers in the world shared the same interests, as did all capitalists. For Marx, while class divides exist there can be no common interest. But come the revolution and the communal redistribution of all property, then all people will share the same interest. These very different worldviews – Rousseau's republicanism, nationalism and socialism – all started from the assumption that there *is* a single common interest.

For the time being, let's give this idea the benefit of the doubt. Even if there were a single will of the people, there is a problem. Imagine we did all as a society agree on something. If every individual member of society can benefit from achieving a common goal – without putting in effort to help achieve it – then each will want to free-ride on the efforts of others. For example, sustaining democracy itself can be a challenge – we may each want to live in a democratic society but are we willing to pay the individual cost of upholding it? Declining levels of turnout in elections from America to Britain to France over the past decade suggest not. Even if we all agree on an outcome, if we don't all agree on exerting the effort to get there, then the 'will of the people' becomes the beauty show contestant's ambition for 'world peace'.

But most of the time we disagree. If that's the case, how many people do we need to agree to say that democracy produces the 'will of the people'? That depends on how we define it. We can be hyper-inclusive and claim that a will of the people only exists when everyone agrees. Or we can be hyper-exclusive and argue that a wafer-thin majority constitutes the 'will of the people'. History shows the perils of both approaches.

It is possible to design political systems where absolutely everyone has to agree. The easiest way to do this is to give everyone a veto. The word 'veto' comes from Latin and means simply: 'I oppose.' If no one opposes a decision, it is self-evidently the will of the people. Any political system that grants everyone a veto can accordingly make that claim. But you can see the problem here. There are very, very few cases where we do all agree. And so those political systems that have granted individual veto rights tend to fall into paralysis.

The most famous such example is the *Sejm*, the Polish–Lithuanian parliament of the seventeenth and eighteenth centuries. The *Sejm* had a rule called the 'liberum veto', which translates as 'I freely oppose.' During any legislative session, any single member of the parliament could stand up and denounce any ongoing legislation and that would bring it to an end. The entire parliament was dissolved in 1652 because of one single deputy enacting his veto. By the eighteenth century over a third of parliamentary sessions enacted no legislation at all and, as the practice became widely known, foreign powers would bribe Polish parliamentarians to use their veto and derail legislation.

The liberum veto undermined an already fragile Poland, beset by rival powers on every side, and eventually, in 1791, it was removed for good. Unfortunately for Poland, it was too late. Within two years the *Sejm* had, under duress, signed away around half of its land to Russia and Prussia, in the Second Partition of Poland, the very countries who had manipulated Poland's legislators and undermined the parliament through the liberum veto. This very narrow view of the 'will of the people' had terminated an independent people.

What about the other extreme, where countries make decisions based on tiny minorities, claiming the will of the people? Because the stakes are so big in these cases, the election results themselves become the object of contention. The losers attack their legitimacy. The winners go to extremes to compensate for the narrowness of the victory.

The Brexit referendum was notable for causing a series of cries about the 'will of the people'. A *Daily Mail* headline screamed 'Enemies of the People' above photos of three judges who ruled that, despite the referendum vote to leave the European Union, Parliament should have the right to decide whether to actually proceed. In the article, the Eurosceptic MP Iain Duncan Smith was quoted as saying that the judges were 'literally pitting Parliament against the will of the people'. By virtue of winning the referendum in 2016, however narrowly, the 'people' had spoken and the various other institutions of British democracy – Parliament, the judiciary – were subverting their voice. But, of course, the British people and their representatives did not all agree. And that disagreement could not simply be wished away by appeals to a 'will of the people', as became very apparent once Parliament tried and failed to pass a bill finalizing Brexit.

Another vivid example is the US presidential election of 2000, which boiled down to counting a few hundred dubious ballots in the state of Florida. Over the course of the election night of 7 November both George W. Bush and Al Gore had the experience of being declared the winner and loser due to the confusion about how Florida, whose electoral college seats would decide the election, had voted. By the next day, the fate of Florida – and the fate of the US – and perhaps too the fate of distant places such as Afghanistan and Iraq rested on 300 votes. How to count possibly spoiled, poorly designed or incomplete ballots and how long to let the process of recounting play out ended up being decided by the Supreme Court. Here again the decision was made by small margins. In a five to four decision the court ruled to end the recount and anoint Bush as President.

The incredibly narrow Bush win set the scene for a presidency that many Democrats considered illegitimate (not least because Bush had also lost the popular vote). But Bush, as the declared winner, governed as if he had a huge majority, drawing up the largest tax cut in US history and, after 9/11, engaging in massive military interventions in the Middle East. To the winner went the spoils. But to the losers a burning sensation that the election was illegitimate and an unwillingness to accept the outcome. Gore, at least, reluctantly accepted he had lost the election. Donald Trump, by contrast, refused to acknowledge a far larger defeat in 2020, setting the scene for the violent insurrection at the US Capitol on 6 January 2021.

We can think of this as the problem of 'losers' consent'. Will the losers of the election cry foul or will they accept the result? That in part depends on how the winners react, or indeed how the losers think the winners will react. A classic example is the left-wing Spanish Popular Front in 1936, which defeated the conservative opposition in a narrow victory. Before the election both sides declared the inevitability of civil war if the other side won. And once the left-wing coalition had won, disgruntled right-wing politicians conspired to overthrow the government, leading to the Spanish Civil War and the thirty-six-year rule of General Franco.

Majority rule, then, does not guarantee a 'will of the people'. Sometimes the winners of marginal elections over-compensate for the narrowness of their victory by governing as if they had won in a landslide. At other times they are overthrown. But on yet other occasions no one can agree on anything at all.

Chaos

The Marquis de Condorcet was one of the more heroic and important figures of the French Revolution. Naturally, he was sentenced to the guillotine. But before his untimely passing he bequeathed two classic theorems to future social scientists: one optimistic, one pessimistic.

His optimistic contribution was his jury theorem. He argued that there are some outcomes we all agree on – punishing the truly guilty and acquitting the innocent. But we face uncertainty over whether the accused is really guilty or innocent. Condorcet argued that if each of us is more likely to be right than wrong when making our judgement, then once enough people are involved, the probability of us collectively making the right decision – by majority vote – converges to certainty. This is the first modern formulation of the 'wisdom of crowds' – individually, we might not be certain, but collectively we are. This is great news for democracy. And we will return to this positive result later in the chapter.

But what if we don't all agree on the outcome we want? It's here that Condorcet's more pessimistic theory comes into play. Condorcet's paradox, as it has become known, shows that even if each of us can clearly rank some set of outcomes, it may be impossible to come up with a coherent group choice. Instead, we can end up cycling endlessly from outcome to outcome. And this is especially likely when we have more than two options to choose among.

As an example of Condorcet's paradox, let's return to Brexit and the inability of MPs to agree on anything. This was because MPs were split into three groups with very different preferences, and there were (at least) three possible outcomes: Theresa May's deal; leaving the European Union without any deal ('No Deal'); or having a new referendum.

A large group of Conservative MPs and some Labour politicians wanted to pass May's deal. If they had to, they would undertake a No Deal Brexit, but they wouldn't countenance a new referendum.

A different group of Conservative MPs – the self-proclaimed 'Spartans' – believed in the very purest of Brexits: No Deal. They viewed May's deal as a 'sell-out' that would lock in Britain to the EU for ever. They would even prefer a new referendum to that.

Finally, many members of the opposition parties strongly opposed Brexit: they wanted a referendum, and only if they couldn't get that would they accept May's deal. This group viewed No Deal as a catastrophe.

Each individual politician had consistent and rational preferences over the different Brexit policies. But Parliament as a whole was chaotic. Even with the simplest democratic voting rule – majority voting between two options at a time – Parliament might never be able to come to an agreement.

Let's start with May's deal versus No Deal. Her supporters wanted the deal and the opposition parties also preferred a deal to No Deal. So the deal would win in a majority vote.

But then it gets complicated. The opposition parties could say, let's put your deal up against a new referendum, which was their first preference. The Spartans would also rather take their chances in a referendum than accept May's deal, which they didn't view as a proper Brexit. So with this newly assembled coalition a referendum would now prevail in a majority vote.

At which point, May's allies could say, 'The "people" voted for Brexit, however done. So let's put No Deal against a referendum.' Both they and the Spartans would support No Deal in this vote.

But now we return to the beginning, since we initially started with May's deal beating No Deal. We start the cycle of vote after vote all over again. Parliament keeps on spinning, unable to make a final decision.

One reason it was so hard to solve Brexit is that many people have 'multi-peaked preferences'. They prefer either extreme to a compromise in the middle. In our example, the Spartans preferred both No Deal and a referendum to May's compromise deal. Preferences for extremes often also occur in wartime, as some people prefer full withdrawal or total war to more-limited interventions – in the US, the Vietnam conflict has often been characterized in this way. It's these types of preferences for extremes that lend themselves to cycling. One way of ending chaos would be to persuade people to have more-moderate preferences – but that in turn means violating their freedom of choice. Which is not exactly democratic.

You might think that the Condorcet paradox is just an intriguing but rare bug in democracy – a parlour game but not a real threat to collective decision-making. Unfortunately, you'd be wrong. In the 1950s Kenneth Arrow developed a mathematical proof that all forms of democratic voting lead to either chaos or dictatorship.

Arrow examined what happens when each individual ranks different options and then we combine them into a collective ranking for the group as a whole, through some kind of voting mechanism. Can we say that this group has a coherent 'will'? No. Arrow's impossibility theorem states there is no voting rule that satisfies all the following conditions, all of which seem like things we would want any democracy to have:

- First, *collective rationality*: we cannot cycle endlessly, there must be a single collective choice.
- Second, *non-dictatorial*: it can't be the case that one person's preferences always win out.
- Third, *universal domain*: all sets of individual preferences should be allowed – we can't ban people from having a particular ranking.
- Fourth, *unanimity*: if everyone prefers thing A to thing B, then we can't ignore them and choose thing B.
- Finally, and most clunkily, *independence of irrelevant alternatives*: the choice society makes between any two options can't depend on people's preferences about some unrelated third option.

With Brexit, for example, simple majority voting violated collective rationality. Since many people preferred extremes to compromise, we ended up cycling from choice to choice for ever. Other voting rules fall down on different criteria. The crucial point is that all five of Arrow's conditions cannot be met simultaneously. If a voting system is going to produce some kind of fixed outcome, you have to violate one of the criteria, or alternatively sit back and enjoy the chaos.

Returning to our Brexit example, couldn't we just stop after two votes? Wouldn't that satisfy Arrow? After all, each of the three options has been considered at least once. The problem is that in our example above we would have decided a new referendum was better than both May's deal and No Deal, even though only one group – the pro-Remain opposition parties – thought that was true. By insisting on stopping after two rounds of voting they would have become the dictator of Parliament's decision. That violates the second condition – it's dictatorial. But unless somebody takes charge, we are stuck in a loop. In our third vote No Deal beats a referendum; in our fourth the deal beats No Deal, and so on *ad infinitum*. Despite a simple decision to make, and a fair and democratic process to make it, this debate will go around and around indefinitely.

Is there something special about three groups of voters and three choices? Not really. Adding more choices or more voters only raises the chances that somebody has preferences that begin this kind of chaotic cycling. What if we tried to convince the Spartans or the opposition that their preferences were wrong and solve the problem that way? Well, that might work. Except now we have abandoned another core principle of democracy: letting everybody choose their preferred rankings and not just deciding for people what's best for them. We've violated the third condition.

You might think, OK, sure, there are problems in principle, but politics is pretty stable, so this is all very interesting but ultimately unimportant. And that's right much of the time, because our political institutions are in fact constructed to violate some of these principles in day-to-day politics.

Our institutions can make our political promises credible and stable by reducing the likelihood of chaos. Control of the political agenda – through the order paper in the British Parliament or through congressional committees in the US Senate – deliberately reduces the number of options under vote or restricts the number of votes we can have. Had we either reduced Brexit choices to two on the first pass, or said we can only have majority votes twice, then we could have made a decision. But in that case whoever set the agenda would then be favouring the outcome that was ultimately chosen – dictatorial, not democratic. We make democracy by violating it.

Chaos breaks out when governments can't choose a single policy. But sometimes it can be hard to even form a government at all. Towards the end of 2011, Belgium managed to take this to a new extreme. For 589 days the country lacked an elected government at all.

This does seem rather odd – and it's hard to see how it could happen easily in a country with an elected president or where political parties regularly win majorities. But Belgium has both a proportional representation electoral system, in which parties rarely get more than 20 per cent of the vote, and a huge regional divide between Dutch-speaking Flanders and French-speaking Wallonia.

In the 2010 Belgian election, the largest party – the conservative New Flemish Alliance – got just 17.4 per cent of the vote. The runners-up – the Socialist Party of Wallonia – had diametrically opposite politics, language and regional support but around the same number of seats (twenty-six versus twenty-seven). Added to this were five other parties with over a dozen seats in a parliament with just 150 in total. No one was anywhere close to a majority, though that was usual in Belgian politics. You need compromise to make a government. But in June 2010 that compromise was impossible to find.

Belgium, like many small European countries, still has a monarchy. And the job of the king – rather less exciting than leading an army into battle – is to pick an 'informateur' – a politician charged with putting together a coalition that commands a parliamentary majority. The king picked the leader of the New Flemish Alliance to negotiate a coalition. This failed. So the king called on the leader of the Socialists to take a turn. No luck either. Three months passed. The king then moved to 'mediators' from each party. No dice. He went back to the leader of the New Flemish Alliance, appointing him as a 'clarificator'. The name change didn't help. He moved to a mediator from the Flemish Socialists. As 200 days passed, this mediator issued a sixty-page proposal. It was rejected. This was then followed by a new informateur, then a new mediator, and finally a 'formateur'. To no avail.

In the end, in December 2011 – a year and a half after the election – an agreement was made, and a government formed. During this time students had held an underpants-only protest rally and various luminaries, from politicians to actors, recommended that men go on a shaving strike, or that female politicians go on a sex strike. The whole country seemed to be in a fever dream.

What on earth was going on? The reason no one could agree in Belgium was that there were fundamental differences on economics, regional rights, language, even on whether to have an amnesty for Flemish Nazi collaborators. Since all the parties were similarly sized, any of them could be a potential coalition partner, and that meant they all had a veto. Since the parties differed on so many issues, it was always possible to derail a coalition you didn't like by finding a new dimension on which you agreed with some parties but disagreed with others. And just as things settled, some new dividing line could emerge and shatter the whole process.

There is another reason that collective choices prove difficult to resolve. This is the fifth of Arrow's conditions, the 'independence of irrelevant alternatives': the choice between two options should not be affected by the presence of an unrelated third option. In a restaurant, this is like deciding to have steak rather than lobster but, after the waiter announces that there is a sea bass special, then choosing lobster. What seemed a simple binary choice has become muddled by a new option. If people let third options influence their votes, then the whole process can be derailed by new choices suddenly being introduced. Worse, it also means that we will be haunted by the problem of strategic voting.

Any voting system where you have at least three options and no restrictions on people's preferences is either dictatorial or open to strategic voting. Which means that almost all cases of voting that people face, outside up–down referendums, are prey to strategizing. That's not to say that strategies always work. Researchers have found that one third of attempted strategic votes by voters in countries such as Australia and the United Kingdom actually backfire. But regardless of whether people get their strategies right or wrong, it is impossible for voting to elicit people's sincere preferences.

Strategic voting doesn't only affect voters – it also manifests in legislatures. Often politicians will vote for policies they don't really like – let's say subsidies for sugar producers – if they can agree a 'vote trade' with another politician to get something they do want – military bases. This mutual backscratching is called 'logrolling' and it means a myriad of different policies that a majority of legislators would not support in a single up–down vote can nonetheless be voted through in an omnibus bill. The Smoot–Hawley Tariff Bill passed by the US Congress in 1930 is often blamed for worsening the Great Depression. The bill raised tariffs on thousands of unrelated goods as each member of Congress protected his or her own favoured industry by cutting mutual deals with other politicians. The average tariff shot up from 40 to 60 per cent – and trade and employment collapsed in the following years.

Voting system enthusiasts often argue that countries that use plurality voting to elect representatives, such as the United States, Canada or the United Kingdom, end up excluding third parties because would-be third party supporters vote strategically for one of the two large parties who actually stand a chance of winning. They recommend ranked-choice voting systems such as the Single Transferable Vote or the Alternative Vote to give people a wider range of meaningful choices. In recent years these systems have been adopted sub-nationally – for the New York mayoral elections, in Alaska and Maine for US Senate elections, and in the Scottish and Welsh Parliaments. But even these systems fall prey to strategic voting by individuals.

Recall Brexit once more. Iain McLean and I had been asked to Parliament to come up with a voting system that might somehow corral MPs into voting for something. The most promising rule was the Alternative Vote system, AV for short.

In AV, each voter ranks options in their preferred order. If no option is the top choice of a majority, the choice with the fewest first places is eliminated. People who most preferred that unlucky choice aren't ignored: we look at which choice came second on their ballots, transfer their votes to that choice, and keep going until one choice wins a majority.

The problem with AV occurs when voters have polarized preferences. In the case of Brexit, almost everyone had polarized preferences – a No Deal Brexit on one side, a new referendum on the other. Very few MPs held compromise positions. Because AV gets rid of options that have the fewest first-place votes, compromise options might get turfed out in the first round, even if everyone could have lived with them. Despite its purpose – to seek a consensus on a decision – using AV might lead to an extreme option.

We had a backup plan: the Coombs rule flavour of AV, which works by removing options that are most hated – the ones ranked last by most people – first. In other words, the compromise solutions might survive, even thrive. But the Coombs rule was not viable either. MPs might misrepresent the option they disliked the most. Nothing was to stop MPs pretending that they hated the compromise options and trying to win their most preferred choice by manipulating the voting system.

In the end MPs settled on 'approval voting'. Here each option was put up on its own with MPs simply voting on whether it should continue to be considered. But even this failed because of strategic voting. Some opposition parties would not approve remaining in the EU's single market, concerned this might doom a referendum. The Spartans refused to back May's deal in the hope that a harder option would prevail. MPs misrepresented their preferences about what deals they could live with, in the hope that something more to their taste would turn up. Because of strategic voting, not a single Brexit option survived even approval voting.

Strategic voting leads to chaos as self-interest undermines the best-laid plans. Everyone has an incentive to lie to get the outcome they want. If everyone is trying to manipulate the system, not everyone can be right, and we end up with endless cycles of strategizing.

This problem spills over into how we decide to decide. If people already vote strategically *in* any given voting system, then they might also vote strategically *about* the voting system. So the chaos spreads from the choices we make over policies to how we choose to choose. Collectively, we can't decide how to decide. We are stuck in the democracy trap: *there's no such thing as the 'will of the people'.*

Democracy can't solve this problem. It *is* the problem. There's no quick fix. Arrow's theorem means there's no technological solution that can conjure up a collective democratic preference. Nor are the appeals of a strongman leader to a 'will of the people' convincing. If we want to let people choose different options – to disagree – we need democracy. But to make democracy work – to make politics work – we need some way to stabilize it.

Polarization

If chaos lurks behind every voting system, why do most seem stable? Stable politics is always possible, but only when we limit the range of choices people have, or the types of votes that can occur. We have to place restrictions and structure onto politics. We have to keep democracy in chains. That way, we end the chaos of cycling.

Most politics in wealthy countries operates along a single dimension of competition, where one issue drives all political competition. We still use the terms 'left' and 'right', dating back to the French Revolution, to signify this single dimension. Typically, the single dimension of politics is competition over money. With money people have clear preferences. Richer people usually prefer lower taxes and public spending, and poorer people prefer higher levels. For the country as a whole, we can line people up from those who want the highest spending (the very poorest) to those who want the lowest spending (the most wealthy).

If we asked people to rank their preferred levels of public spending, they should have coherent views. If your 'favourite' level of spending on, say, public education is 5 per cent of national income (about the average for rich countries), then we would expect you to prefer a level of 4 per cent to one of 2 per cent, and to prefer a level of 6 per cent to one of 10 per cent. The further we get from your favourite spending level, the less happy you are.

These 'single-peaked preferences' mean that you don't have odd rankings where your favourite level of spending is low, but your second favourite is extremely high. If we have single-peaked preferences, then I have good news for you – the chaos of democratic politics goes away. But I also have bad news for you – it's replaced by polarization.

To get single-peaked preferences we need politics to be about fights on a single dimension, such as taxes. It is multi-dimensional politics that creates chaos and cycling. If we are somehow able to reduce things to a single dimension of politics, we can get stability. In theory, we might even reach a middle-of-the road consensus. But, in reality, if you reduce things to a single dimension, you often see permanent conflict. We have replaced the dilemma of chaos with a new problem – political polarization. Polarization creates conflict and mutual distaste among our fellow citizens. It produces gridlock when parties have to agree with their opponents and scorched-earth policies when they can rule unchecked. And this venom can sometimes spill over into the end of democracy itself.

Anthony Downs had a rather unusual career. In the first half, he wrote seminal works on the economic theory of democracy. In the second half, he became the chair of a real estate investment consultancy. The two are closer than they might first appear because Downs's theory of democracy was all about location.

He argued that if voters were spread out across a single dimension, then politicians should locate themselves at the centre. He borrowed the idea from Harold Hotelling, who had made the same claim about shops – along the high street, it would make sense to locate your shop right in the middle. That way the furthest shoppers would need to walk would be half the street. If you sited your store at the north end and the other shopkeeper put her store in the middle, then she would get every customer from the south end up to halfway between the middle and the north end. You'd lose business unless you too open your shop in the middle. That's why shops tend to cluster.

Downs thought parties would cluster in the centre too. A party that positioned itself on the far-right end of the political spectrum, while its rival stayed in the centre, would lose not only everyone left of the centre – it would lose a bunch of right-of-centre voters too. This is what happened to Barry Goldwater in the 1964 US presidential election, which he lost in a landslide to the incumbent, Lyndon Baines Johnson. Goldwater had proposed using nuclear weapons as a regular tool of armed warfare and making Social Security voluntary – not obvious vote-winners. He was also famous for saying 'extremism in the defence of liberty is no vice'. Perhaps. But it's not an ideal electoral strategy.

The Downsian view of the world is called the 'median-voter theorem': parties will converge on the political preferences of the voter right in the middle of the political spectrum. This median voter's preferred policies should win out in every party's manifesto and in the types of policies that parties enact once in power.

It's an intuitive argument, and it sometimes holds. In the late 1990s and early 2000s, voters in Britain, Canada and the United States sometimes complained that politicians were 'all the same'. If Downs is right, that's the point of electorally successful politicians! Politicians also spend a good deal of time targeting swing voters, presumably in the middle of the political spectrum. In the US, these are 'Reagan Democrats' and 'Soccer Moms'. In the UK, they have names like recently found Palaeolithic corpses: 'Mondeo Man', 'Worcester Woman', 'Workington Man'.

But perhaps the turn of the century was the aberration. Today most middle-aged people came of age during the becalmed 1990s and early 2000s. But the 1980s were marked by the 'politics of conviction' – code for a sharp turn to the right in politics and policy under Ronald Reagan and Margaret Thatcher. Since the Iraq War of 2003 and the Great Recession of 2008, parties in North America and Europe have been more polarized than they have in decades. What happened to the calming influence of the median voter?

The problem is that single-dimensional politics can be very easily shunted 'off-centre'. Politics is more complicated than where to place a shop on a busy street. Politicians aren't only concerned about voters in a general election – they also need to keep their members and donors sweet. And the more important the single dimension becomes in politics – and money is pretty important – the more polarized and influential these members and donors are likely to be.

Let's start with party members. Political participation is costly unless people derive some ancillary benefit. The kinds of people who are most likely to enjoy participating in politics are those who either see major financial benefits from their party winning, or who deeply believe in the party's ideology. This means party members are more likely to be at the extreme end than in the centre.

Financially, the very poorest might benefit most from a left-wing government providing a guaranteed income. Similarly, the very richest should benefit most from a right-wing government slashing taxes. So both groups will have a greater incentive to join their party than someone in the middle, who, if the median-voter theory is right, ought to feel fairly indifferent about both parties. It's even easier to tell a story about ideology – if you truly believe in a party's mission, if you believe that the welfare state has a moral function as well as an economic one, you're unlikely to be a swing voter in the middle, and more likely to be a party member.

Why do people actually join a party? In many countries the party's candidates or leaders are first elected by members through some kind of primary election. In some cases, the actual policy platform of the party is even decided by the members. Party members can drive the leadership, candidates and policy positions towards their preferences. And with single-dimensional politics that's towards the extremes.

The rise of figures as different as the Republican President Donald Trump and the socialist UK Labour leader Jeremy Corbyn is a product of the same phenomenon: party members pushing to the extremes of the left–right dimension. Legislators and parliamentarians have also been affected by primary-induced polarization. There has been a sharp trend towards polarization in the US Congress since the 1970s, driven particularly, but not exclusively, by Republican politicians moving to the right. This has resulted in tax policies becoming ever more distinct – Trump's 2017 tax bill slashed corporate tax rates to unprecedentedly low levels; by contrast both Elizabeth Warren and Bernie Sanders ran for the 2020 Democratic presidential candidacy on wealth tax policies directly targeting well-known billionaires.

These growing divides cannot simply be blamed on party members. Campaigns cost money. And political donors, like members, will be attracted to extremes. The return on investment for a hedge fund manager keeping favourable tax treatment is far larger than any benefit a middle-class voter could ever feasibly achieve. And hedge fund managers can, of course, give much larger campaign donations.

Campaign contributions largely support the policy preferences of the very wealthy, and candidates, especially on the right, have pivoted to court them. Political scientists have argued this has driven US politics 'off-centre'. They point to an earlier era – between the 1940s and early 1960s – when American politics seemed more consensual, more centrist, and when bankers paid much higher rates of tax.

Superficially, the 1940s and 1950s might seem a halcyon era of consensus politics. But American politics was only less polarized because it was multi-dimensional. Civil rights for African Americans cut across the standard economic left–right dimension. The Democratic Party was split between Southern Democrats who wanted to maintain the racist status quo of Jim Crow laws and Northern Democrats who supported civil rights reform. The Democrats became increasingly split over these policies through the 1960s, and while the Republican Party largely supported civil rights in the 1960s, as it picked up ex-Democratic seats in the South, it too became fragmented in the Nixon years. On the surface, the post-war era looks consensual: both parties agreed on relatively high taxation and a similar Cold War strategy. But this cross-party consensus was largely because of an intra-party split over maintaining racial repression. Even though polarization may be undesirable, that doesn't mean its absence is necessarily an improvement. Be careful about calls for civility and consensus – sometimes it hides dark currents of racial animosity.

The contemporary era of polarization has different costs – by reinforcing partisanship, it makes politics an endless tug of war. Party identities come to define people's own self-image and a winner-takes-all spirit dominates. According to a Pew poll in 2016, just under half of Democrats and Republicans saw the other party as a threat to the nation's well-being. Michael Anton, the Trump security advisor, tastelessly called the 2016 presidential election a 'Flight 93 election' – life or death for Republicans unless they 'rushed the cockpit'. Rather less threateningly, but still depressingly, 38 per cent of Republicans would be 'very' or 'somewhat' upset if their child married a Democrat and exactly the same number of Democratic parents feel similarly about their child marrying a Republican. In the UK a third of

Labour-voting parents feel the same about their child marrying a Conservative.

Polarization can also produce gridlock. In 2011 the United States was in a political maelstrom, with blood-curdling cries of impending economic doom and market panic followed by Wall Street rallies. All because of a bizarre rule that Congress set itself many decades earlier, which it didn't really want to follow, but that was a powder keg for political polarization – the 'debt ceiling'.

When it reluctantly allowed President Woodrow Wilson to bring the US into the First World War, Congress created a debt ceiling to permit flexible spending on the war effort, rather than directly approving the Treasury Department's borrowing requests each time. Over the years, what was intended to provide flexibility to the government ended up hamstringing it. US national debt has a tendency to go up, and that meant Congress would regularly have to vote to lift the debt ceiling so that the government could implement its spending plans and keep running. Each time, Congress would theatrically bemoan the increased spending and then, without fail, raise the limit.

Well, almost without fail. Although the debt ceiling had been raised for both Democratic and Republican presidents – by Democratic and Republican Congresses alike – in 2011 American politics was unusually tense and polarized. President Obama faced a Republican Congress fired up by the anti-spending Tea Party movement. They were in no mood to abide by traditional niceties. Congress demanded that if Obama wanted the debt ceiling raised, he would have to agree to spending cuts. If the debt ceiling wasn't raised, ultimately the US would have to default on its national debt, something it has never done.

Both Obama and the Republicans stood firm. Markets panicked, with the Dow Jones stock average losing around 20 per cent over the summer. A series of wacky ideas were concocted for how to avoid default if Congress remained stubborn. This culminated in an astonishing plan for the Treasury to mint two platinum trillion-dollar coins to deposit at the Federal Reserve and thereby reduce the national debt. While this would have produced the greatest heist movie plot in history, it did not need to come to pass because, two days before a potential default, Congress and Obama signed a deal to raise the debt ceiling. Credit markets were unimpressed and issued the first downgrade ever of US sovereign debt. But at least the grid-lock of polarization had finally ended . . . for two years at least, because exactly the same brinkmanship and chaos occurred again in 2013.

Polarization, just like chaos, can produce gridlock, with added bad blood for good measure. But when parties are unconstrained and polarization happens from election to election, we trade gridlock for volatility. The history of Argentina since democratization in 1983 is a prime example, characterized by swings back and forth between economic populism – Peronism – and centre-right liberalism. Typic-ally, the story has been one of Peronist victories followed by surges in public spending and nationalization, and conservative victories followed by fierce squeezes on spending and currency crises.

Such volatility can lead to radical policy proposals that make the partisan back and forth of America and Western Europe look peace-ful by comparison. To give a few examples from the past decade – the Peronist government of Cristina Fernández de Kirchner fully nation-alized all private pensions, restricted foreign exchange and defaulted on Argentina's debt. Her successor, Mauricio Macri, then removed all controls on foreign currency, producing a 30 per cent collapse in the peso, and promised, though ultimately failed, to remove all income tax.

Not all of Argentina's economic problems can be blamed on demo-cratic volatility – the military junta that ruled between 1976 and 1983 was also an economic disaster – but Argentina's endemic economic volatility is largely a function of its political dysfunction. Simon Kuznets claimed there are only four types of economy in the world: developed countries, developing countries, Japan and Argentina. This was not a compliment.

Finally, polarization produces even worse outcomes than gridlock or volatility if you always end up on the losing side. Brian Barry argued that democracy only worked well with 'shifting majorities', where even though on today's issue you were on the losing side, tomorrow you may win on a different topic. But if politics only has one dimension, there is only one issue. If you're not on the winning side, you lose for ever. And that in turn might threaten democracy itself. Losers' consent might be impossible if losers think they can never be winners. So, instead, they might act like the Spanish Fascists of the 1930s, or Augusto Pinochet in Chile in 1973, and end democratic elections in a military coup.

To save democracy, to make it work effectively and stop our politics from failing, we need to figure out how to end chaos and polarization. We need to find out how to escape the democracy trap.

4. Escaping the Democracy Trap

Democracy has not had a glorious twenty-first century. What was once a seemingly unstoppable wave of democratization cresting across the world has dried up. If anything, democracy has gone into reverse, with backsliding in countries as dissimilar as Turkey, Myanmar and Hungary. Xi Jinping and Vladimir Putin have advocated a 'new world order', where American-led democracy promotion is replaced by spheres of influence dominated by authoritarian China and Russia.

Democracy has also come under rhetorical attack. The rise of Western populists, disdainful of the compromises of liberal democracy and applauding the clarity of 'strong leadership', has been the defining political event of the past decade. Best-selling books have argued that our voters are too irrational for democracy, that democracy cannot keep up with technology or our demands as consumers, or that democracy is simply captured by elites. The chaos and polarization produced by the democracy trap have made it harder for the defenders of democracy to bat away these critiques.

Can we save democracy? Are we doomed to veer drunkenly between chaos and polarization? Is democratic politics doomed to fail? We shouldn't give up. Not least because, as Churchill famously argued, all the other options are even worse. But we need to be aware of what democracy can't do. Democracy can't make us agree. And democracy can't always help us decide what to do. There are times when our preferences can't be easily packaged into a simple answer by a voting rule. And even when they can be, we're all self-interested enough to try and manipulate the process to get what we really want. We need to be realistic about the demands we place on democracy.

There are things we can do. We can try to manufacture a more coherent will of the people. We can redesign our political institutions, or strengthen our social norms, so as to shield us against the blows of chaos and polarization. But what we cannot do is escape politics altogether. The sceptics of democracy – be they illiberal populists, techno-libertarians or simply outright autocrats – ultimately offer doomed alternatives because they wish away political differences and the challenges of keeping our political promises to one another.

Why can't we save democracy by cutting out the bits we don't like – conflict, contention, sometimes chaos – and replacing them with a simpler or more efficient way of making decisions? The problem is you can't cleanly excise the messy business of politics. We get rid of it in one place and it pops up somewhere else.

Modern-day populists – of both right and left – talk about politics as if decisions could get made if only we removed the politicians. If we drained the swamp. The problem is that politicians bicker because we bicker. There usually isn't nationwide agreement on most issues and certainly not a perfect consensus. We already saw with the doomed seventeenth-century Polish parliament what happens if you give everyone a veto – nothing gets done at all.

Of course, populists don't actually believe that we do all agree – they pit 'the people' against a shadowy group of elites. But once we ask who comprises that elite, it turns out to be a rather large and disparate group who all want different things. As indeed do the mythical people. So a 'strong leader who gets things done' leads in one of two directions. Either a (possibly thin) majority of people backing the leader get what they want – losers be damned – until the next election. Or, more worryingly, the leader begins to dismantle the institutions of liberal democracy itself that stand in her way. Neither outcome is a genuine solution to the problems of democracy, though they might mark its end.

One apparent alternative to populism is to make more 'efficient' decisions by applying technology, expertise or markets – a technocratic form of government. Liberal democracies already have a host of independent and politically neutral agencies and institutions that use expertise or judgement rather than tallying up votes to make decisions: courts, central banks, scientific agencies. There is an important role for non-democratic institutions in democracies. Courts and ombudsmen can protect the rights of minorities against the tyranny of the majority. Scientific advisors and central banks can help us – politicians, in particular – avoid the temptations of short-term policies that harm us in the long run. But in both cases there is a dilution of democracy – our right to govern ourselves.

Protecting losers from democratic votes sounds moral and reasonable when we think about minorities suffering from segregation imposed by the majority. But it takes on a different tenor when those losers are billionaires seeking to avoid higher taxes or onerous regulations imposed by a democratically elected government. And sometimes questions of expertise cannot be divorced from broader political questions. Should scientists have the indefinite right to introduce COVID lockdowns? Why shouldn't democratically elected governments be able to directly change interest rates that affect the well-being of the voting public?

Besides, technocracy as a form of governing has come under increasing political attack. Experts cannot be hermetically sealed off from the people their decisions affect. A democracy cannot simply say to its voters: 'Be quiet and listen to experts.' If voters disagree with that rejoinder, in a democracy they can act on it. Eventually a newly elected politician will arrive and defenestrate those experts. To escape the democracy trap, we may need institutions that counter the brute force of majority voting, but they cannot *replace* democracy.

If expertise from on high can't resolve politics, can we reshape politics from the bottom up? We could borrow the logic of markets and let voters bid for policies, cutting out politicians. But a 'market in democracy' suffers from the problem that, whereas in consumer markets we can choose just how much to spend on things, in politics we have only one vote.

Eric Posner and Glen Weyl have developed an innovative solution to this problem by letting people vote multiple times to indicate how much they like various policies. Instead of providing everyone with a single vote, we give people a 'budget' of voting tokens that they can use to cast votes across multiple policies or candidates. When people vote over an issue, they use a mobile app to allocate a certain number of tokens to buying votes.

But here's the catch. Each vote costs you an ever-higher number of tokens. Your first vote might cost you one token but your second – for that choice – costs you four (two squared) and your third vote costs nine tokens (three squared). Because the cost of each vote is squared, they call this 'quadratic voting'. The more you want something, the more and more you have to pay.

What's the advantage of quadratic voting? It allows people to demonstrate how much they care about each policy. But they have to make hard choices: the more they care, the more tokens they will lose. Political influence becomes increasingly costly the more you want it. Contrast this to campaign financing, where every dollar has the same impact and so the very richest can simply bung in more dollars. Quadratic voting potentially prevents one problem with democracy – that minorities can never get anything they want – by allowing them to use more votes to make up for their lack of numbers.

But quadratic voting can't take the politics out of democracy. If there are multiple options under consideration, we may still end up with chaos, because ranking choices still produces strategic voting. Worse, quadratic voting could even increase polarization. The kinds of people who are willing to pay the highest cost for policies will likely be those with most extreme preferences, who can use the weight of multiple votes to make up for their small numbers.

Technological advances may make ideas such as quadratic voting feasible, but they can't entirely dismantle the democracy trap. They may even worsen it. Machine-learning algorithms have advanced so much in the past decade that we can increasingly predict and model people's political preferences with great accuracy. Facebook's business model (perhaps inadvertently) has accentuated this trend by giving people more of the information and opinions they find interesting. The problem is that people are attracted to information that reinforces their existing beliefs and prejudices. Inevitably this has pushed people into 'information silos', where they only hear voices they agree with, producing ever-greater online political polarization.

Nor can technology resolve the problem of chaos. We can use algorithms to structure our political preferences and find out what we might like on new issues – the internet is full of apps that help you figure out how to vote in elections from local to national. These apps might help us make rational individual decisions. But collectively they can still add up to chaos – technology cannot overthrow Arrow's impossibility theorem. Just because I now know exactly what I want doesn't mean that we can easily combine my views with yours. Collective decisions are hard to make *because* we all have different preferences. If we empowered these apps to vote for us, we might still end up with chaotic cycling but at the speed of microprocessors.

Since we can't avoid politics, how can we shape it so democracy works? We need to design political institutions and develop social norms that help us avoid chaos and constrain polarization.

Let's start with the easiest case: where we already agree. The democracy trap arises because we are rarely in agreement. But are there ways of helping people come to a common set of views? If we agree, then we don't need to worry about the vagaries of voting rules – they would all produce the same outcome: the thing we agree on.

It sounds a little naïve. A bit 'Why can't we all just get along?' But the group can be more than the sum of its parts. Sometimes it can help everyone get to the right answer. And perhaps it can change people's minds.

We have already encountered one such argument with Condorcet's jury, an early version of the 'wisdom of crowds'. Often, we all want to know if something is true. We might each have a hunch but be pretty far from certainty. Condorcet argued that the guess of the group as a whole was much more likely to be right than each of our individual guesses. Let's say we just had a 55 per cent chance of being right – not much but slightly better than a coin flip. Condorcet's theorem shows that using majority rule to decide, with 10,000 of us, each with that same vague 55 per cent probability, we would get collectively the right answer 95 per cent of the time. There is a power in numbers. And democratic politics, at root, is the process of amassing the views of large numbers of people.

This is called the *epistemic* theory of democracy – that is, democracy brings us greater knowledge. We need democracy because it can get the big questions right. Dictatorships and aristocracies count the views of fewer people, so they are more likely to get big questions wrong. Even worse, in autocracies people have an incentive *not* to provide accurate but disappointing information. If your position, your life perhaps, depends on telling higher-ups what they want to hear, it may simply be easier to mislead.

Recall the argument that democracies don't suffer from famines because information about food shortages percolates upwards. By contrast, tens of millions of Chinese villagers died of malnutrition during Chairman Mao's Great Leap Forward, in part because cowed bureaucrats misrepresented grain production, creating an 'illusion of superabundance'. This misinformation accelerated the famine as the Chinese leadership replaced grain with cash crops and increased grain exports to earn foreign currency. Even as the grain ran out, Maoist China lacked the ability to self-correct, because misrepresentation drowned out information.

Democracy will be good for us when we all agree we need answers to a problem, and we would all also agree to follow that answer, if we knew what it was. Lots of problems look like this. They occur when we face common foes – disease, military enemies – or when we are trying to forecast events – weather, sports scores, elections. The wisdom of crowds is often better than the forecasts of experts, who may be guided by their theory of how the world works rather than facts on the ground. If we can use our democratic tools to canvass people's opinions, we might find that people feel more engaged and listened to *and* that we produce better results.

Ironically, the wisdom of crowds is also good at predicting how the crowd itself will behave. The political polling business is now a multimillion-dollar industry in the US, UK and Europe. But its accuracy has come under attack, after a recent series of shock elections. Pollsters rely on the voting intentions of their respondents, but either those respondents had misstated their intentions or important groups of people – particularly those with lower education in rural areas – were being missed entirely.

However, when people are asked in surveys not how they would vote but how they think other people would vote, they can often be more accurate. People use their own communities and networks to forecast how their friends and neighbours will vote – giving us information survey firms don't have. We get the most accurate results by looking at groups of people in different electoral districts, asking them how they think their district will vote and letting Condorcet's magic do the rest. In the British general election of 2015, which pollsters got completely wrong, and in US presidential elections from 1988 to 2012, citizen forecasts were significantly more accurate than the polls. The epistemic theory of democracy is even good at figuring out democracy! But just like the polls, citizen forecasts completely missed both Brexit and the victory of Donald Trump. Perhaps we are all struggling to understand our contemporary era of polarization. Our consensus can sometimes be plain wrong.

Most things in political life are not consensual, and then we return to our old enemies: chaos and polarization. To avoid chaos we can, ironically, learn something from polarization, which occurs when people's preferences fit along a single dimension. Sometimes we are more worried about chaotic, unstable cycling of politics, and less about polarized views. In that case we should try to compact politics into a single dimension.

One way of doing this is to put people in the same room. By asking them to deliberate over complex, multi-dimensional issues, we can induce some structure into their differences. That doesn't mean taking differences away, but instead clarifying what the really important dimension of difference actually is.

We can scale this up by using citizens' assemblies. Ireland used such assemblies before its recent referendum on changing abortion law and on other major societal issues from the ageing of the population through to climate change. Part of the merit of these assemblies was in helping people clarify what the real differences and opinions of their opponents were. Each time, people were asked to debate and discuss multiple issues in each area – for ageing, this included pensions rates, retirement ages and care of the elderly.

By considering all these issues at once and deliberating over them, the assemblies helped structure debate on a simpler level. Chaos could be held at bay by conversation. Citizens were forced to identify trade-offs – it's not possible in politics to have everything we want – and to understand, if not agree with, the arguments of their opponents.

This helped them create a new norm of listening and responding constructively to those with whom they disagreed. And so it became apparent when there was actually consensus, and if there wasn't, whether there might be an option at least a majority could abide.

The time devoted to discussion also meant that the assemblies could discuss a wide variety of considerations. With abortion, a highly polarizing topic, the assemblies were asked to consider various situations prompting an abortion (from the real physical danger to the mother's life, to the mental health risk, to socio-economic reasons to unrestricted abortion), along with different time limits for abortion (from no limit to twelve weeks, twenty-two weeks and never). Rather than becoming polarized to the more extreme options, assembly members tended to cluster in the middle, willing to consider legalizing abortion under a wide but not unlimited set of conditions. The official legalization of abortion in Ireland in 2019 ended up following this moderated model – legalizing abortion for any reason up to twelve weeks but only under certain strong conditions thereafter. Abortion will never be a consensual topic, but by following the assembly's recommendations, the Irish government had conformed closely to the way average citizens had made sense of these stark trade-offs.

Thanks to information technology we don't need people to even be physically in the same room to deliberate. The internet and social media are regularly blamed for political chaos and polarization because of the propensity of people to stick in online echo chambers where they only hear views they agree with, no matter how niche. But, like any technology, whether the internet helps us or hurts us depends on how we use it and the political choices we make.

An encouraging example is Taiwan's experiments with e-government. Led by the hacking prodigy – and, at the age of thirty-five, the youngest ever Taiwanese cabinet member – Audrey Tang, the country has developed a model for locating consensus. Tang has created a number of apps – vTaiwan, Join – that work off a common model. In each case, a contentious issue is debated by people placing comments online. Others can then vote these up or down. But what makes this different from commenting on YouTube or

Reddit is that Tang's apps don't allow people to reply. Tang argues that the absence of replies prevents the apps from devolving into incessant trolling and insults.

Instead, if you disagree, you have to write a new comment that can also be up- or down-voted. This minimalist set-up allows the app developers to examine the networks of agreement and disagreement with particular comments among different groups of users. As users figure out their position is not shared by others, their response may be to write a new comment that tries to bridge differences. A new norm develops among users to find solutions that more people can abide. And as these more consensual comments gain popularity across different user networks, slowly the app can figure out what positions are commonly shared across users who might initially have disagreed vehemently.

Thanks to Tang's position in the Taiwanese cabinet this model has been used by the government to develop consensual positions, albeit only on internet-related policies such as regulating Uber or allowing online alcohol sales. The resulting policies have usually been gradualist – permitting Uber but with strong regulations; allowing online alcohol sales but forcing people to collect at stores to prevent children obtaining booze. Even though an infinity of comments and hence policy proposals are permitted, chaos doesn't end up ruling, as the back and forth among users allows them to understand where their views are and aren't shared more broadly. The internet can bring us order, as well as chaos.

What can we do if our concerns are about polarization? Putting people in a room to deliberate may end up with metaphorical, perhaps literal, blood on the floor. There are two key problems with polarization: one is the conflict and mutual distaste it creates among fellow citizens, and the other is the problem of losers – nobody likes being a loser, and how losers react can determine the course of a nation. The unwillingness of Donald Trump to accept he lost the 2020 US presidential election, culminating in the 6 January 2021 insurrection, demonstrates this problem can beset even the largest, richest and oldest democracies.

We can try and resolve conflict either by changing people's minds or by changing the political system they are in. Encouraging greater feelings of empathy among people can help reduce conflict. In other words, we try to change the political norms people follow. Psychologists have found that encouraging higher levels of empathy can make people less likely to stigmatize disadvantaged groups. Barack Obama has bemoaned America's 'empathy deficit' and argued empathy could solve the country's political polarization.

Trying to understand other people's points of view and concerns is certainly praiseworthy. But we should be cautious. Political scientists have found that more-empathetic people are most likely to show concern for others in their own 'in-group', and this could, ironically, produce greater polarization. This can even happen among people who denounce the very idea of in-groups. The cosmopolitan supporters of the British Labour Party leader Jeremy Corbyn were often avowed believers in universal rights and a society free of prejudice. Yet some of them also indulged in stereotypes of the older, white, working-class supporters of Brexit, even though many of this group had been long-time losers in Britain's economy. Empathy does not always stretch as far as we hope.

If we can't always change people's minds, can we change the incentives they face? Political primaries and campaign finance both heighten polarization by encouraging political parties to swing to extremes. Clamping down on money in politics would be likely to reduce polarization. But in America, at least, the ability to do that is constrained by the Supreme Court, which has equated campaign contributions with free speech.

Getting rid of primaries has fewer obvious legal obstacles, but it would be much more controversial because we are essentially saying that democratic participation is harmful *within* parties, but good between them. And that feels contradictory. But democracy among party members drives politicians to the extremes, pushing them further away from what citizens as a whole want. In purely democratic terms, pooling the views of the greatest number of people, we might be better off without primaries.

A possible solution is to have open primaries where people who are not members of a particular party can still vote for candidates. Ideally, this would push candidates towards the middle of the voting public as they would need to cater to the interests of independents and persuadable members of other parties. But remember this is democracy – nothing is simple. Partisans from the other party might take advantage of an open primary to strategically vote for a candidate who they think would do worse electorally. Here we have chaos messing with polarization. In 2008 some Republican voters strategically voted for Hillary Clinton in open Democratic primaries, concerned that Barack Obama might be a more effective candidate. But these 'fake' Democrats were just as likely to vote for the Republican candidate, John McCain, in the general election as those less conniving Republicans who had simply sincerely voted McCain in the Republican primary.

Could we instead tame polarization by expanding who gets involved in politics during general elections? The US has fierce primaries and heightened political polarization. But it also has very low turnout in presidential and congressional elections compared to other countries. Not least because polarization may put off apolitical people from voting. If voting were made compulsory and turnout thereby increased, would that solve the problem?

Just over twenty countries, including Australia and Argentina, have some form of compulsory voting. Typically, non-voters must pay a fine for failing to cast a ballot. People are not forced to vote for a party – they are allowed to spoil their ballots – but they do have to take part in the election. Fines are not huge – for example, most Australian provinces charge somewhere around $20, though this can increase tenfold if they are not paid. Although the cost of abstaining is low, the effect on turnout is huge. Well over 90 per cent of Australians have voted in each election since compulsory voting was introduced in the 1920s.

Does compulsory voting reduce polarization? Until 1992 Austria had compulsory voting in many of its states. On average, the main effect was bringing in non-partisan voters who had little interest in politics, dampening polarization. But that's not always the case. In Australia, after the law was introduced, the chief beneficiary was the

Australian Labor Party, whose vote share increased by up to 10 percentage points. Ironically, its rivals, the Liberal Party, had thought they would be the winners from the law change. Poorer voters become more likely to vote, both because in most countries they are less likely to turn out if given the option to abstain and because the fines hurt them proportionally more. But this does create quite a moral dilemma for left-wing parties. Compulsory voting might help them win elections but also means proportionally harder financial punishments for their base if they don't show.

Finally, what can we do about the perpetual losers of polarization? Recall the argument that democracy works best with shifting majorities. One way to achieve this is by reintroducing new dimensions of political debate – ones where losers can become winners. William Riker referred to this as *heresthetics*, the talent of reframing political debates.

Riker's favourite example was Abraham Lincoln, who reframed American politics over the question of slavery. From 1800 to the start of the Civil War, the Federalist, then Whig, then Republican parties held the presidency for just nine years, while their rivals – the Democratic-Republicans, then Democrats – governed for fifty-two years. The battle lines were drawn over whether land (the Democrats) or commerce (the Federalists–Whigs–Republicans) should control American policymaking. Most people worked the land and hence the Democrats won.

As a Republican running for the Senate in Illinois in 1858, Abraham Lincoln faced the harsh likelihood of being on the perpetually losing side. Republicans had cast around for some new way to frame political debate so that they could finally win politically. Lincoln realized that anti-slavery would work as a new dividing line – a way of winning over Northern Democratic voters, who opposed slavery but otherwise remained part of the Democratic coalition. By heightening their discontent over slavery, Lincoln could peel them away and bring them to the Republican side.

In the famous debates between Lincoln and the incumbent, Democratic Senator Stephen Douglas, Lincoln was able to carve Douglas's base in half by simply asking whether Douglas could ever accept that a new US territory could ban slavery within its borders. This eventually created a no-win situation for Douglas. By answering yes, Douglas was able to keep the votes of anti-slavery Northern Democrats in Illinois and defeat Lincoln. But two years later Douglas's run for the presidential nomination split the Democratic Party as angry pro-slavery Southern Democrats, recalling Douglas's answer, chose their own candidate. This time, of course, Lincoln was the winner.

Reframing creates new axes for politics. It can reinvigorate politics and allow people who have felt voiceless to feel heard once again. Which is not to say that everyone will now get along – after all, Lincoln's victory precipitated the US Civil War. But it does provide a way to change what we are polarized about and permits long-time losers to feel the glow of political victory. Witness the reaction many British voters had when a new dimension – Brexit – allowed them to express their views and finally win an election. But Brexit also reminds us that with the opening of political space chaos can creep in.

Is there a way of making sure that losers can always have their voices heard not just when political entrepreneurs reframe the debate? We know that no democratic system can entirely avoid the problems of chaos or polarization. But some electoral systems do seem to temper both – and help us escape the democracy trap.

The most obvious is proportional representation, or PR. Under PR, the proportion of seats a party wins in a legislature is proportional to the number of votes cast for it. There are uncountable flavours of PR – different vote thresholds, district sizes, vote-ranking systems – but let's keep it simple, along the lines of the Dutch electoral system. In the Netherlands, the parliament has 150 seats and they are allocated to parties proportional to their nationwide vote. As long as you get more than 1/150th of the total vote, you're in. Other countries, from Israel to Sweden to Denmark, have very similar models, though usually with a higher threshold for getting in, which slightly advantages larger parties. In PR systems it is extremely rare for any party to have a majority in parliament. And that means they need a coalition.

Coalition-making can go wrong – witness Belgium's struggles to

form a government in 2010. But on the whole the post-election negotiations are smooth. And they can make sure losers' voices are heard.
In PR the party with the most seats is usually asked first to form a
coalition and so it needs to make deals with, and listen to offers from,
the smaller parties. And here is where a little chaos can help with
polarization. The small parties represent different interests and identities in society, and they can clearly protect their constituencies by
joining the governing coalition. But if they are in opposition, they
also have some power. If they don't like the policies of one of the
parties in the governing coalition, they can try to break it by suggest-
ing a side deal with the other coalition parties.

Of course, this does create instability – PR systems are known for
regular prime ministerial changes and shifting coalitions in government. But it also means that most parties in a legislature get a regular
turn in office. Witness, for example, the recent governments led by
the Dutch Prime Minister, Mark Rutte, of the right-wing VVD
party. His first cabinet was with the Christian Democrats and tacitly
supported by the far-right PVV. His second was with just the Dutch
Social Democrats (PvdA), and his third and fourth were with the
Christian Democrats, the liberal D66 and the religious Christian
Union. Five other parties were part of government over a decade.

This inclusiveness of proportional representation may explain
why PR systems generally have higher public spending – either
because more parties mean more interests in different types of spending or because PR systems tend to have left-wing parties in
government more often than majoritarian systems such as in the UK
or USA. Countries with PR seem also to have lower inequality and
more policy stability. They may have weaker or less decisive government than their majoritarian rivals but perhaps they make up for this
with a comfy consensus.

How do we escape the democracy trap? Unconstrained democracy
produces chaos or polarization. Each of us has an incentive to strategize and upset collective decisions; or to push for our side of the
debate no matter the cost to others. So we need to bind democracy –
to keep its energy, its ability to course-correct and its capacity to

provide meaningful self-government, but lose its instability and volatility.

The solutions we've examined provide a structure to democratic decision-making, whether formally through political institutions, or informally through norms of behaviour. Some of these are counter-majoritarian institutions – the 'liberal' parts of 'liberal democracy': courts to protect rights, independent agencies, and the press to monitor and hold governments accountable.

But we don't have to rely on anti-democratic institutions to constrain democracy. We can improve democracy through more democracy. We can do so at a very local level through citizens' assemblies, helping people with disagreements to discover where they do have a consensus and build up from that first block of agreement. Or we could move to the national level and consider changes that might engage more people in the voting process, including those with more-moderate views, to prevent politics being dominated by the loudest, most polarized voices from each side of the divide. That could mean compulsory voting, but it could also mean reforms that make voting easier – from same-day registration to early voting. Or it could mean electoral-system reform such as PR. The crucial thing in both cases is to keep these institutions stable, not just using citizens' assemblies for the occasional controversy; not changing voting laws election to election.

We can also escape the democracy trap by encouraging norms of listening and deliberating. Chaos comes from our individual strategizing, polarization from our distaste for others' opinions. We are human – we can't eradicate these impulses. But we can try to suppress or counter them. Developing new forums for political discussion that discourage trolling and flame-wars, as in the vTaiwan experiment, is one path; citizens' assemblies another; and still a further, open to charismatic politicians, is to try to change the axis of popular debate away from antagonistic issues. Democracy is ultimately about opinions. Learning how to express our own effectively and to tolerate those of other people is the only way we'll ever reach consensus. We will always disagree in general. But we will need to agree, in the end, on something.

PART II

Equality

Equal rights and equal outcomes undermine each other

5. Jeff Bezos Goes to Space

In July 2021, after he had landed from his brief private space flight, run by his personal space company, Jeff Bezos, then the richest man in the world, had something to say. 'I want to thank every Amazon employee and every Amazon customer because you guys paid for all of this,' Bezos remarked during a post-flight press conference. 'Seriously, for every Amazon customer out there and every Amazon employee, thank you from the bottom of my heart very much. It's very appreciated.'

Amazon's employees work on a rather less galactic scale than Jeff Bezos. According to the BBC, Bezos 'earns the median US Amazon employee annual salary every ten seconds'. Put another way, he earns just over three million times as much as that typical employee. As well as the pay inequality, Amazon's work conditions have also come under scrutiny. The investigative journalist James Bloodworth worked in an Amazon warehouse in Staffordshire, England, recounting the long hours, rigid enforcement of timing, and near impossibility of taking toilet breaks. It's not obvious that Bezos's thanks to his employees would have been received entirely graciously.

Jeff Bezos's flight took place just over fifty years after America first landed a man on the moon. At the time of the moon landing in 1969, when the only people permitted in space were highly trained, publicly paid astronauts, American inequality was at a historical low. The astronauts' family life when back on earth was an epitome of the nuclear family, male earner, stay-at-home mom, picket-fenced households of American sitcoms of that era.

Shortly after the moon landings, the fortunes of rich and poor in America began to diverge. In the 1970s America's richest 1 per cent of earners brought in 11 per cent of national income. The poorest 50 per cent of adults collectively earned just over 20 per cent of national income. By 2014 the top 1 per cent took in 20 per cent of total income and the bottom 50 per cent just 12 per cent. The positions of the two groups had completely flipped.

It's no surprise that the slogan 'We are the 99 Percent' emerged as the motto of the Occupy anti-inequality movement. But perhaps the slogan should have been the '99.9 Percent'. In 2018 the top 0.1 per cent – that's the top one thousandth – of Americans held almost 20 per cent of total wealth: $70 million each. Jeff Bezos had plenty of multimillionaires and billionaires for company.

How did America get this way? Why wasn't there a successful political backlash to skyrocketing inequality? No matter how wealthy the 1 per cent are, it should be impossible for them to defeat the bottom 50 per cent in a democratic election. And yet politics in America seems to have failed: it has underpinned, rather than undercut, inequality. Inequality has kept on rising, benefiting only a tiny majority, with politicians seemingly helpless, or perhaps unwilling, to do anything about it.

Why has American politics failed to respond to inequality? America has become caught in the equality trap – *equal rights and equal outcomes undermine each other*. The equal economic freedoms Americans cherish have made it hard to clamp down on unequal outcomes. And the individual incentives for each of us – from the general public to politicians to billionaires – have made it hard to escape this trap.

Which brings us back to Jeff Bezos. Since the 2008 financial crisis, some politicians had been frustrated by the perceived reliance of big American corporations, from Amazon to Walmart, on state and federal welfare subsidies to make up for what we might call, to alter Walmart's famous slogan, 'always low wages'. The socialist senator from Vermont, Bernie Sanders, had even introduced an Act to Congress in 2018 called 'Stop Bad Employers by Zeroing Out Subsidies', or for short 'Stop BEZOS'. And over the course of 2019 these politicians began to aim even higher – at Jeff Bezos himself and those in his elite class.

2019 was the year that the Democratic primaries for the presidential election of 2020 really got going. The front runners included Bernie Sanders and the progressive Massachusetts senator and law professor Elizabeth Warren. That summer both politicians developed proposals to directly tax the wealth of America's elite. To give an example, Bernie Sanders planned to tax wealth over $10 billion at 8 per cent annually, with his wealth tax kicking in at the more modest threshold of $32 million. For Jeff Bezos, had it been in place since 1982, this plan would have reduced his wealth in 2018 from $160 billion to a pitiful $43 billion. The wealth tax seemed to offer an escape from the equality trap.

But neither Warren nor Sanders became President. The promise of a wealth tax was not enough to push them through the primaries. Nor did the eventual winner, Joe Biden, implement a wealth tax. Republicans remained entirely opposed to a wealth tax, as did much of the Democratic Party. 158 million American voters who would benefit from such a tax seemed stymied by the 75,000 households who would be hurt and by a political system that didn't seem interested.

This raises a rather obvious question. Why don't most democracies, including the USA, actually have a wealth tax? Very few people would pay it and lots of people would benefit from it. Shouldn't the political equality of democracy lead to the curtailing of economic inequality? Why does our politics fail us here?

Taxing billionaires runs up against the equality trap. We each want equal rights to spend how we want, work where we want, vote how we want. But these equal rights make it impossible to guarantee that the distribution of incomes, of resources and of opportunities is equal. More than that, they often worsen them. Our individual incentives drive against equal collective outcomes.

Billionaires, like the rest of us, have equal economic rights to choose how to spend their money, where to live and how to behave. And this makes it challenging to tax them effectively if we want to equalize outcomes. Facing a tax on their wealth, billionaires could choose to spend down that wealth, madly frittering their money away on mansions, rocketships and hair transplants. Or even by funding political campaigns against a wealth tax.

The economic inequalities produced by granting equal economic rights fundamentally alter our political system, making it much harder to legislate for more-equal outcomes. Indeed, the ability of billionaires to push politics 'off-centre' is a function of the equal rights they have under democracy to lobby and cajole. Since the Citizens United court case of 2010, American billionaires such as Bezos have had the right, along with the means, to fund political advertising with minimal restrictions. Our politics fails to curtail billionaires in part because it has been captured by them.

In fact, worldwide, rich people are often the biggest beneficiaries of democracy because democracies are so much better at protecting their property rights and their rights to free speech than authoritarian countries. Being a billionaire in China or Russia is dangerous territory. You can find yourself expropriated, arrested or, well, not alive any more. The political power of the masses in democracies doesn't translate into despoiling the rich. Quite the opposite: democracies protect, as well as tax, wealth. Equal political rights can also undermine equal economic outcomes. This leaves us in a quandary – we cherish our equal rights, but they often go hand in hand with soaring inequality.

And so, through the COVID-19 pandemic, the election of a Democratic President and a war breaking out in Europe, the wealthiest American billionaires have remained untouched. Not everyone in America had given up – Bernie Sanders took to tweeting 'we must demand that the extremely wealthy pay their fair share'. Elon Musk, who took over from Jeff Bezos as the richest person in the world in 2022, responded: 'I keep forgetting you're still alive.' The idea of paying a 'fair share' of taxes was apparently still inflammatory.

As for Jeff Bezos, a week after he had touched back down on the planet he currently calls home, Senator Elizabeth Warren, whose wealth tax plan had not made her President, but who was still a powerful player in a Democratic-controlled Senate, continued to argue for a wealth tax. She appeared on CNBC with a warning: 'I want to see us tax wealth, however your wealth is tied up. It shouldn't make a difference whether you have real estate, or whether you have cash or whether you have a bazillion shares of Amazon. Yes, Jeff Bezos, I'm looking at you.'

6. What is Equality?

For centuries, people have imagined what it would be like to live in an equal Utopia. The word itself originated in Thomas More's *Utopia*, written in 1516. More envisaged a society in which possessions were held in common, everyone worked as a farmer, and even houses would be rotated among citizens every decade. That each household in More's Utopia would also have two slaves rather undermines this picturesque tableau of equality. Nonetheless, philosophers have long been attracted to the idea of an equal society, free from the stultifying hierarchy of traditional life. From Jean-Jacques Rousseau to Karl Marx to John Rawls, thinkers who sought to redesign society have made equality the core principle of their imagined communities.

Let's imagine we too were taken by the whim of designing a new society. How would we make it equal? We could start as More (without the slaves) or Marx did and insist that everyone has the same possessions. We could do that by having no property rights at all – in More's Utopia there were no locks on the doors – with everything held 'in common'. In John Lennon's famous words, 'imagine no possessions'. Or, noting that food at least can't be consumed by everyone, we could give people private possessions but in exactly the same quantity. Either way, we have ensured everyone gets *equal outcomes* in terms of their possessions.

So is our society equal? On one level, absolutely. But immediately we face the question of who produces these possessions. Are we hoping our citizens will just work equally hard for us because we'd like them to? Will we have to put them in a chain gang instead? If we care about giving people *equal rights* to work where, when and as hard as they would like to, then it's not obvious we will produce enough to survive if we only offer equal outcomes in return.

A society of completely equal outcomes might also offend our sense of fairness. Are people receiving rewards equal to their efforts, or to what they deserve? If someone works harder, or is better at their job, or produces more benefit for society, shouldn't they be rewarded more? We might think that what matters is the equal opportunity to work, not that the outcomes of work are themselves equal.

But now if individuals work where, when and how they want, it will be impossible for us to attain a collective goal of equal outcomes. Different people will work more or less hard, or have particular skills, and ultimately they will earn different incomes. Indeed, we could end up with skyrocketing economic inequalities and the emergence of a billionaire oligarchy at the top.

We are left with two extremes, neither of which is entirely palatable, but both of which are equal in different ways. At one end, we have a society of completely equal possessions where we may have to compel our citizens to work – in other words, to accept unequal rights and freedoms. At the other, we give people equal economic rights and let the market rip but potentially end up with massive inequalities in outcomes and the danger of a self-perpetuating elite. Either way, politics has failed.

In both cases we face the equality trap – *equal rights and equal outcomes undermine each other.* If we grant equal rights, we won't be able to obtain equal outcomes. And if we force equal outcomes on people, we will have to restrict equal rights in terms of their freedom to live the life they want. We can't just split the difference and say that we are fans of *all* kinds of equality – there's an inherent trade-off at work here. If we value one type of equality, we have to sacrifice another. And, ideally, find some trade-off in the middle where we can keep most of our cherished freedoms without unleashing a winner-takes-all dystopia.

These equality trade-offs emerge whenever we think about equalizing some domain of human life – it might be political rights, educational rights or civil rights; it might be economic outcomes, or happiness. But equalizing one of these creates inequalities elsewhere. Across history, the expansion of equal economic, political and social rights has coincided with massive inequalities in outcomes. And collapses in economic inequality have often occurred during periods of collapsing freedom, from wartime to communism. This is not entirely coincidental.

Just as with politics in general we find ourselves facing a tooth-paste problem – if we squeeze down an inequality in one part of the tube it will build up in another. Our politics will fail if we pretend this trade-off doesn't exist and try to promise everything to everyone.

The core question that underpins all debates about equality is 'equality of what?' Diverse thinkers – socialists, libertarians, utilitarians – clash endlessly over particular inequalities, be they of outcomes or rights. But they have a basic similarity: all of them believe in the fundamental importance of some form of equality. We all live on what Ronald Dworkin called the 'egalitarian plateau'. Vanishingly few respectable political arguments view people as essentially unequal and hence deserving of different treatment. Equality is an almost universally held good. But what people mean by equality differs. And therein lies the rub.

Free marketers and libertarians from Milton Friedman to Friedrich von Hayek to Robert Nozick don't believe that people should receive equal resources or even that people should be rewarded equally by reason of effort, need or desert. But they do believe that everyone should have equal rights to own property, and to trade and exchange in the market. They do not mark out people who belong to some ethnicity, religion or gender as being unworthy of equal treatment.

Similarly, socialist thinkers in the Marxist tradition believe all people should have an equal relationship to 'the means of production' – everyone should have an equal share in society's ability to produce things. Again, this is a universalist claim. Come the revolution, we are all equal; there are no differences according to colour, creed or characteristics. But Marxists certainly don't think people should have equal rights to buy, use or sell their private property. They don't believe in private property at all! And they favour equal outcomes over equal opportunities: as the line goes, 'From each according to their abilities, to each according to their needs.'

What is in common in the rarefied air of the egalitarian plateau is that people are *treated as equals* in some domains, if not in others. Will Kymlicka puts it like this: 'egalitarian theories require that the government treat its citizens with equal consideration; each citizen is entitled to equal concern and respect'. Amartya Sen uses the term 'impartiality' to mean roughly the same thing. Either way, this core concern is common to very divergent philosophies from left to right. But the problem with the egalitarian plateau is that treating people equally in one dimension may mean treating them unequally in another.

It's easy to forget that we have not always been egalitarians. Philosophers of the past often treated people as fundamentally unequal. Plato envisaged a republic where highly trained 'philosopher-kings' would decide matters for the rest of us. Aristotle argued that slaves and women did not deserve equal treatment to male citizens. In the seventeenth century, the proponents of absolutist rule and the divine rule of monarchs argued that rulers should have unlimited rights over the ruled. And religious claims that adherents of a religion should necessarily be treated differently to non-believers also fall off the egalitarian plateau.

Indeed, until the Enlightenment, most theories of how society should be organized were inegalitarian. Since then, inegalitarian beliefs have been marginalized, but they did not vanish. Herbert Spencer, one of the most famous philosophers of the late nineteenth century, was a biological determinist – in his view inequality was the result of evolutionary differences, ones Spencer blithely connected to jaw and head size. Friedrich Nietzsche was explicitly anti-egalitarian. Witness this quote denouncing egalitarians: 'what they sing – "equal rights", "free society", "no more masters and no more servants" – has no allure for us. We hold it absolutely undesirable that a realm of justice and concord should be established on earth . . . we consider ourselves conquerors.' The explicitly racist fascist movements of the mid twentieth century were building on generations of intellectual prejudice.

Over the past few decades such ideas have lost first academic and then public respectability. But we still see their shadows, from Charlottesville to Budapest, in the dark tones of the contemporary radical right. Quasi-scientific chest-beating about essential inequalities still has its fans – and fanatics. But they live now on the fringe, even in our populist age. The norm of egalitarianism, for good reason, still rules our debate.

We may live in an egalitarian age, but paradoxically it is also one of high and rising economic inequality. Since the financial crisis of 2008 there has been a great deal of media interest and political concern about inequality in wealthy democracies, not only the United States but across Europe and beyond. Our contemporary democracies give people nominally equal political power and equal rights to live the life they choose. But they seem, nonetheless, to tolerate high levels of inequality in how much people earn and own.

That inequality does not come without costs. There is substantial evidence that countries with more-equal incomes end up with a whole host of other goodies: from higher life expectancy and literacy to lower drug use, school dropout rates, prison rates and homicides.

Some nations seem to have been better able to move towards more-equal outcomes than others, even while retaining the equal political and economic rights we associate with capitalist democracies. In particular, some countries have found it easier to tax their highest earners and redistribute to poorer citizens, narrowing the day-to-day inequality people experience.

To compare inequality across countries we use a measure called the Gini index. The Gini varies between zero – everyone receives exactly the same – and one – one person gets everything, everyone else gets nothing. Higher numbers mean more inequality, lower ones mean more equality.

If we look just at people's earnings, most wealthy countries have quite high inequality. Some have a Gini of just over 0.50 – not only the usual suspects such as the USA and UK but also Italy, France and Greece. Others have somewhat more-equal earnings: Sweden, Norway, Korea and Switzerland all have Ginis below 0.45. But, really, these are pretty small differences. The political equality of citizens in democracies is very far from guaranteeing equal earnings.

But that is not the end of the story. What people earn is not the same as what goes into their bank account. The government takes (in taxes), and gives (in benefits); so it can reduce the Gini index by redistributing income from rich to poor. And this is where the action is. Some countries, such as Finland, France and Belgium, have very activist governments, reducing their inequality by over 40 per cent. France's Gini drops from over 0.50 to 0.30 once the government gets involved. Not so much in the USA, South Korea, Israel or Switzerland. Here the government still matters, but it only reduces inequality by about 20 per cent. The USA, similarly unequal to France in earnings alone, only reduces its Gini to 0.40 through redistribution.

Where does this difference come from? Politics. The government can get us closer to equality – perhaps help us to escape the equality trap. But, as we'll see, that may not come without cost. Higher taxes arguably reflect greater limits on equal economic freedoms and in excess they might even constrain growth. Navigating the equality trap will require us to take these trade-offs seriously.

Most inequality statistics focus on people's incomes. After all, that's what we see month to month in our bank accounts and that's how governments get most of their tax revenues. But they are not the only important form of inequality. Inequality in wealth is far higher than inequality in incomes. The US has an income inequality Gini of just over 0.50. Its Gini for wealth is a staggering 0.90. The 5 per cent of Americans with highest incomes make about a third of overall income. The 5 per cent of wealthiest Americans have more than 70 per cent of overall wealth.

Even in places that seem to have been able to escape the equality trap when we look at incomes, things are not quite so rosy with wealth. Sweden and Norway, both among the most equal countries in earnings, have wealth Ginis of over 0.80. Places that seem otherwise egalitarian often turn out to have a small group of stupendously wealthy families, whose fortunes remain untouched.

And that raises a paradox: how have we been able to maintain such fundamentally unequal societies even as we have granted universal political, civil and social rights? In fact, the history of inequality shows that this unlikely relationship between equal rights and unequal outcomes – and on occasion between unequal rights and equal outcomes – has been with us for centuries.

The origins of equality

The history of the world's wealthiest countries has been a clash between equal rights and equal outcomes. Today we have more freedoms – of speech, of profession, of movement – than our ancestors of even a generation or two ago. And yet we live in countries with vast gaps between rich and poor. Where the richest citizen's wealth is a million times larger than an average citizen's income. Equal civil, economic and political rights coexist, quite happily it seems, with extraordinarily unequal outcomes. Were we doomed to end up this way?

There must have been near equality in the very beginning of our modern life as *Homo sapiens*. Our first material possessions, be they stone tools, bone necklaces or fur clothing, had to be hand-crafted and portable. The sheer amount of possessions that individual hunter-gatherers could have owned was limited. There was a fixed limit on inequality – even if one tribesman owned almost all the tribe's possessions, almost all wasn't all that much, and others still had enough food and clothing to survive. So the Gini index for the wealth of hunter-gatherers was around just 0.25 (compared to typical modern-day Gini indices for wealth of over 0.70).

There was a sharp upward shift in inequality just over 10,000 years ago at the end of the last Ice Age. Why did a warming planet produce inequality? Higher temperatures and wetter weather meant wild grasses producing energy-rich cereal seeds could grow more widely. Humans learned how to select those plants that produced more-nutritious seeds, permitting the emergence of settled cultivation. More-abundant plant life also made it easier to feed large herbivores that humans learned to domesticate. Warmth gave us farming. But farming gave us inequality.

Walter Scheidel refers to this period of our collective history as the *great disequalization*. Farming both freed and tied down humans. It freed us from the vagaries of happenstance that hunter-gatherers faced with wild food, and it freed us from the material limits imposed by constant nomadic foraging. But it tied us down to fixed locations, ones that also faced uncertainty, but now of weather or of theft and attack. Agriculture created not only unprecedented wealth but also highly hierarchical societies to govern and protect that wealth. With freedom came inequality.

The crucial thing provided by agriculture was a food surplus. Which meant there was enough to feed people performing crafts and trades of various types, producing new manufactured goods. And these new resources could be distributed among people more or less equally. Sedentary agriculture was also a potentially attractive target to both local nomadic tribes and other settled societies. To protect resources early agricultural societies needed guardsmen and soldiers, who in turn needed to be organized and commanded.

Most agricultural societies consequently developed hierarchical political structures led by a small cadre of soldiers, administrators and priests. Claims to ownership were codified in early legal systems, which in turn reinforced existing inequalities. Nearby tribes were raided and their citizens taken as slaves, adding a further layer of inequality.

Since the political dynamic in such systems was like a pyramid with a massive base and tiny tip, what was to stop economic inequality from mirroring it? What prevented ever-rising inequality was the fact that people had to have enough to live. Bluntly, if you are not alive you can't be counted in the inequality statistics. Once we account for subsistence, in poor societies the amount of remaining surplus to go around might be quite limited. That placed a cap on how high inequality could actually be. That also means the richer places got, the more surplus they had to be unequally distributed and the higher their inequality could be.

For instance, take the Roman Empire at the death of Emperor Augustus in AD 14. The Gini measure for disposable income in classical Rome is estimated at around 0.39. That's not so bad – similar to the USA in 2000. But average income in classical Rome was only twice subsistence levels. So half of all income *had* to be distributed equally or people would die – meaning that the highest the Gini could possibly have been in classical Rome was 0.53. Let's compare that to the USA in 1999, where average income was 77.7 times subsistence. That's the power of industrialization. Theoretically, the Gini for the USA could have been 0.99 – a very, very high Gini – while still keeping the population alive. With the wealth of our modern world, we have made it possible for inequality to surge.

From the medieval era onwards inequality rose as overall living standards improved. An era of rising civil and political freedoms was also one of growing inequality. This was not accidental. As peasants had their feudal ties to the countryside removed, they migrated to the growing urban areas. Restrictions set by monarchs and guilds on what could be produced and by who were gradually loosened, meaning merchants could access wider markets and produce new goods.

As the cities grew in economic importance, inequality rose simultaneously. More goods being produced in the cities meant there was more surplus to distribute unequally. Those who owned the newly built factories or the better-cultivated fields took the spoils of this new growth. Equalizing the right to live wherever, and the right to produce whatever, ultimately produced more-unequal outcomes. Today, we still see similar patterns. When developing countries urbanize and industrialize, inequality often initially grows – it's a feature not a bug.

Still, the historical rise of inequality has not been unbroken since the Ice Age melted away. There have always been peaks and troughs. The Black Death dramatically lowered inequality throughout Western Europe in the fourteenth century because the labour scarcity caused by people dying horribly from the plague pushed up the wages of those who survived. More recently, from the First World War until the mid 1970s inequality declined dramatically across the industrialized world, a phenomenon called the Great Compression. The era of *Happy Days*, suburbanization, picket fences, etc. really was more equal than our own today. So, what happened?

There's a nice story and a not so nice story. The nice story is that in densely packed urban areas workers were better able to organize for higher wages and politically were able to tax and regulate the rich. In particular, the expansion of mass primary and secondary education helped reduce income gaps by chipping away the premium that old elites had when only they were literate or numerate. In other words, development helped the poor to claim their just deserts.

Education and worker power did expand during the Great Compression. But the timing of the collapse in inequality – coinciding with both World Wars – points to the not so nice story: violence and its consequences. The wars reduced inequality partly through the actual destruction of capital but also through the massive demand for labour they produced – witness for example the entry of women into the workforce in munitions factories.

Post-tax inequality was also reduced because of huge increases in taxation on the wealthy and the expansion of public spending. The US federal income tax was created during the US Civil War; its top rate increased from 15 to 67 per cent the year that the US entered the First World War; and the bottom rate quadrupled when the US entered the Second World War. At the end of both wars, governments often promised new social programmes, creating what the British Prime Minister, David Lloyd George, called 'a fit country for heroes' in 1918. The British created their National Health Service, pensions and sickness insurance programmes, and mass public housing in the first few years following the Second World War. The times when freedoms were most restricted in modern memory – wartime – have also been those that most restrained inequality. Unequal rights, more-equal outcomes.

Since 1980 the story has reversed, as income and wealth inequality have risen dramatically across advanced industrial countries. Overall, the pattern is striking – in most countries, the richest 1 per cent of earners had around 20 per cent of income before the First World War. After that war, and particularly after the Second World War, this share collapsed, to under 10 per cent by 1970. But then a reversal began.

Take America. By the mid 2000s, the richest 1 per cent had a similar share of national income to 1900: 20 per cent. Canada, the UK and Germany had risen back to 15 per cent. Even in Sweden and Australia, where the rich are relatively less rich, their share of income doubled from 1970.

Inequality in most places has risen so dramatically because many of the freedoms – the equal rights – we have come to enjoy in the past few decades have also galvanized inequality. Globalization is a striking case. As we have granted citizens from other countries the equal right to trade, invest or move to richer countries, there is evidence that this has pushed down the wages of workers in Western Europe and North America. On the flipside, freer global markets have created lucrative new opportunities for those in the West who are highly educated or have money to invest.

Another culprit is technology. Computing and mobile phones have both helped skilled workers such as consultants, bankers and engineers make more money, but have also replaced less skilled workers on both the assembly line and in the back office. At the same time, the ever-growing importance of university education for access to high-paying jobs means skilled workers pulling ever further away from the unskilled. Meritocracy is a double-edged sword. Education provides more-equal opportunities for advancement than old hierarchies based on birth. But the new winners have created their own new 'educational aristocracy' that hoards opportunities.

Finally, the deregulation of labour and product markets may have widened inequality further. Countries such as Denmark, with widespread unionization and strong employment protections, have had more-limited increases in inequality. Where people have had greater market freedoms, the market has rewarded those at the very top – a 'winner takes all' form of economy. Inequalities are most pronounced when we compare not simply the top 10 or 1 per cent of citizens to everyone else but when we look at ever-smaller groups of rich mega-elites – the 0.1 or the 0.01 per cent and so forth.

The political tumult of the last decade in wealthy countries reflects in part a reaction to these inequality-increasing forces. In particular, populist politicians of both left and right have blamed globalization and 'globalists' for declining average incomes and rising inequality. Higher education too has become targeted as a cartel of well-to-do liberal elites, and increasingly tech companies have come under suspicion from the new populists, especially of the right. The liberal defenders of the freedoms to trade, immigrate, innovate and educate have been too quick, perhaps, to assume that these freedoms would come without economic, or political, cost.

Across the decades we see a similar story: a tension between equal rights and equal outcomes. Inequality has only declined substantially in eras when rights were restricted – during wars, plagues, famines. As the world has opened up, as people have had more-equal rights to choose the work they want, who to trade with, where to live, inequality has bounced back. And so we remain caught in the equality trap. Equal rights for the rich to secure their property rights and invest in what they want, when they want, appear to fundamentally threaten equal outcomes across the wealthy world. Is that inevitable?

7. The Equality Trap

We'd all like to be treated the same. But is that in terms of means or ends? We cherish our equal freedoms: our rights to work where we want, vote how we want, say what we want, marry who we want. But we also care about equal outcomes. Soaring inequalities – slums sitting at the foot of gleaming penthouses – make us uncomfortable.

We have a collective goal of equality – to close the chasm between rich and poor. But we have individual desires to use our equal rights to live our own best life as freely as possible, which push against this common ambition of equal outcomes. And if we really did have completely equal outcomes, would we have to sacrifice our equal freedoms? Our politics gets caught in the equality trap: *equal rights and equal outcomes undermine each other.*

Each of the equal rights we have acquired over centuries of political struggle has an uneasy relationship with the goal of equal outcomes. This is most obvious with equal *economic rights* – our economic freedoms to acquire, hold and dispose of property. Capitalism. To fully equalize economic outcomes when our economic system pushes so hard against them may mean forcibly repressing our economic rights, perhaps our civil and political ones too. But to go 'all-in' on economic freedom may mean a society politically dominated by the wealthy with the possibility of economic redistribution foreclosed for good. For politics not to fail we need to balance carefully between equal economic rights and outcomes.

The equal *political rights* that come with democracy are also not always happy bedfellows with equal outcomes. In fact, democracy often emerges because of inequality, as newly enriched groups of people seek to protect their wealth from greedy authoritarians. People in equal authoritarian countries often remain equally repressed with no rival sources of power left to challenge the leader. For politics not to keep failing in dictatorships we may need more inequality, not less.

Finally, even equal *social rights* don't always mean more-equal economic outcomes. Think back to the 1950s. While families of that era had more-equal incomes, they also limited women to lives largely out of the workforce. We have seen both great strides in equal rights granted to women and rising household inequality in the decades since. Our desire to make sure people are treated equally doesn't always show up in the inequality statistics. If we want our political systems to create more equality in both how people are treated and how they are paid, we have much further to go.

Equal freedoms vs equal outcomes

The wealthy countries of the world embody a paradox. They are by and large democracies, where the final decision is made by popular vote. They are also capitalist – economic outcomes reflect billions of voluntary decisions made by firms and consumers, secure in the knowledge that their assets cannot be arbitrarily seized, thanks to equal rights to own property.

Why is this a paradox? Democracy diffuses political power – it's the rule of the people: one person, one vote. Capitalism concentrates economic power – those who already own the lion's share accumulate ever-greater wealth.

But political power can overrule economic power. The democratic state has sovereignty – it can rule through the writ of its laws or the threat of force. If political power is vested with the masses and economic power with a small elite, what's to stop the former from seizing the wealth of the latter and equalizing incomes? Possibly at the point of a gun. And facing this threat, what's to stop economic elites from trying to subvert democracy to avoid that outcome?

We see here the core of the equality trap. Capitalism (theoretically) grants people equal economic freedoms – everyone has the same equal right to own and dispose of property – but this undermines equal outcomes. And to get equal economic outcomes, we have to compel the beneficiaries of capitalism to give up their gains, potentially overriding their equal economic rights.

At the heart of democratic capitalism lies this unavoidable dilemma. And, unchecked, that tension could threaten democracy itself. In one direction we swing towards completely equal outcomes, compelling, potentially forcibly, everyone to accept the same. This most likely means the quashing not only of equal economic rights but also equal civil and political rights, as has happened in countless examples of the outright levelling of incomes from the Jacobins to the Communists. We end up with Bolshevism.

In the other direction, where we insist on the sanctity of equal economic rights and let capitalism rip, we risk a winner-takes-all economy, with a few oligarchs accumulating ever more spoils of the system. This too presents a clear and present risk to democracy as the tiny economic elite distort democratic decision-making through lobbying, control of the media and corruption. We end up with oligarchy.

The wealthy capitalist democracies of Europe and North America have avoided these twin perils for the past half-century. They have balanced between equal economic rights and equal economic outcomes. But that balance is not inevitable, as our predecessors one hundred years ago discovered. To stop our politics from failing, we have to learn how this tension can be harnessed to keep economic inequality low without abandoning our cherished freedoms.

Initially, as political rights expanded, the dilemma between capitalism and democracy was resolved by taxing the rich. The long march of democracy in the wealthy world, though incomplete and frustrating, means that the average citizen of these countries has far more political power than even a century ago. And over the last century tax levels rose, at first precipitously, to levels that would have given Victorian aristocrats a nosebleed.

But then taxes largely stopped rising. By the late 1970s, a limit to the growth of the state had been reached. A political backlash led to the scything tax cuts of the 1980s under leaders such as Margaret Thatcher and Ronald Reagan. Since the 1970s, income and wealth inequality have risen dramatically. But the response to this new gilded age has not been draconian taxes – if anything it has been a growing demand for *more* tax cuts. This presents us with a puzzle. Why didn't democracies push for ever more equal incomes?

Scholars who look at the interplay of inequality, democracy and taxation rely heavily on an arcane economic theory called the Meltzer–Richard model after Allan Meltzer and Scott Richard. Allan Meltzer taught for decades at Carnegie Mellon University, where he received my very favourite professorial title – he was the Allan Meltzer Professor of Political Economy. A professorship named after yourself is quite the thing to aspire to.

Meltzer and Richard imagined the simplest model of taxation, in which everybody pays the same rate of tax on their income. In their model, the amount you pay in taxes depends on your income, but everyone gets exactly the same benefits. If you are a high earner, 20 per cent of your income in taxes could be a lot of money, and if you're a low earner, not so much, but either way you receive the same amount of money back in benefits. Accordingly, anyone with above-average income should want no taxation, and poor people should want a tax rate as high as possible. The message of the model is simple: the lower your income, the more you like taxes; the higher it is, the more you hate them.

What are the implications for democracy and inequality? Democratic governments mean rule by the masses or, more explicitly, the 'median voter' that we met in the democracy trap. For Meltzer and Richard, they will be the person with median income – exactly half-way along the distribution of income from poor to rich. Since they will be the swing voter in a two-party election, what they want should drive policy.

Inequality should change what the median voter wants. Inequality rises when the rich get richer but the median voter's income stagnates. This presents a political temptation for them. Their income is the same but there's more money in the pockets of the rich. Which makes taxing that money ever more attractive. So Meltzer and Richard argued that when inequality rises in democracies, so too should taxes, maybe dramatically. Democracy should act as a check on capitalism. Equal economic freedoms should be replaced by equal economic outcomes. This would be a path towards socialism by democratic means.

Democracies ought to 'steal from the rich to give to the poor'. However, as we saw with rising inequality since the 1970s and massive tax cuts over the same period, they generally don't. Political economists call this the 'Robin Hood paradox'. Why don't democratic governments take from the rich to give to the poor like the feather-capped English bandit of yore?

The simplest answer is that we can't tax people at draconian rates and expect that they won't change their behaviour. Since people enjoy their leisure time, when taxes get too high they work less hard and party more, or simply up and move somewhere sunny where the tax rates are lower. This means less income to be taxed and hence lower tax revenues.

Here we see the equality trap. If we want equal outcomes, we need to stop people from individually deciding to slack off when taxes rise. But that means removing the equal right to decide how much each of us wants to work.

To see, *in extremis*, how enforcing completely equal outcomes plays out, think about the 1930s in the Soviet Union. Since there were minimal rewards to effort, people did as little as they could get away with. That led the Soviets during Stalin's rule to resort to exhorting people or enslaving them. Citizens were encouraged to follow the model of Aleksei Stakhanov, a miner who exceeded his daily quota fourteen-fold in 1935. Working for the good of the nation rather than oneself was the moral lesson to follow.

Anyone who has read *Animal Farm* will recall Boxer, the workhorse who exhausts himself in service to the porcine revolution, only to be sold to the knacker's yard. Stakhanov, by contrast, was able to retire with honours, a rare case where George Orwell's allegory is more horrific than reality. But since not all citizens were natural Stakhanovites, Stalin compelled them to work in collectivized farms, soviets or the Gulag. Equal outcomes were enforced by removing equal economic, civil and indeed political rights.

Can fully equal outcomes work in a liberal democracy, as opposed to a totalitarian regime? G. A. Cohen argued that this reconciliation was only possible in the presence of an 'egalitarian ethos'. If we give people equal rights to work where or as much as they want, the only way to achieve equal outcomes is if those who could earn more (by dint of effort or 'talent') are willing to accept equal rewards to everyone else. If not, then they would withdraw their labour or skills. Cohen argued equal outcomes are possible, but everyone must want and accept them, including those who materially lose out from not earning as much as they could. We would need a social norm about the importance of equality that was self-reinforcing.

This would be an idyllic situation – if people are happy to willingly give up being richer than others, then we get equal outcomes without restricting freedoms. But it seems some distance away from the world we live in. Not least because for many people what matters is not equal outcomes but equal opportunities to succeed, while accepting outcomes will always be unequal.

Indeed, we might actually need unequal outcomes to get people to work hard. Put simply, why expend extra effort if you can't personally benefit? In other words, there might be a trade-off between equality and 'efficiency'. In the 1970s, Arthur Okun developed the memorable concept of the 'leaky bucket' to portray this trade-off. In his analogy, we redistribute money from the rich to the poor in a bucket. But the bucket has a small hole in the bottom from which money leaks out. When we haul our bucket over to the poor, we discover that not all the proceeds of taxing the rich remain. We can't equalize incomes without losing something. Perhaps the wealthy work less hard so there's less money to spread around. Perhaps the government wastes resources because of bureaucracy or corruption. Perhaps people hide money from the government, finding taxation unfair. Either way, trying to equalize outcomes is wasteful.

Does the bucket really leak? At the extreme, if there was a 100 per cent tax then perhaps no one would work unless they were forced to. But the taxes we encounter are much less rapacious. Economists have found that the inefficiency effects of taxation only kick in at highly punitive rates of taxation, over 60 or 70 per cent. People in the recent past have paid these kinds of taxes – George Harrison wrote the famous Beatles song 'Taxman' as a wry complaint about Britain's 'supertax' of 95 per cent during the 1960s. But since the 1980s governments have abandoned extreme taxes because the rich either avoid them through loopholes or emigrate. In the battle between equal outcomes and equal freedoms, governments have shifted towards the latter.

This shift to equal freedoms has its own political traps. Just as political power can be converted into economic power, the reverse is true. Democracies may work on a one-person, one-vote basis, but much of our politics is less egalitarian. Campaign finance, lobbying and other forms of political influence rely much more on a one-dollar, one-vote logic.

Inequality and political polarization have a particularly insidious relationship. When inequality rises, the rich and poor become increasingly different in their political preferences, with the rich becoming ever less supportive of redistribution and the poor ever more so. It also heightens the value of lobbying and campaign advertising for richer citizens, who have even more money to protect.

That means that when political parties which are backed by the rich – typically right-wing parties – enter office, their incentive is to cut taxes further and faster. But it's true that if the left enter office we should see the reverse – so polarization should cause volatility but leave things the same on average. But in countries where minority parties can block legislation – those with many checks and balances, such as the USA – then right-wing parties can block tax and spending increases when in opposition. We get a ratchet effect whereby taxes fall but never rise for long. And so inequality becomes self-reinforcing as richer citizens are able to push politics 'off-centre'.

We can tell a similar story for wealthy liberals in America and abroad. The rising importance of education for people's jobs and income prospects means that the premium to attending prestigious universities or receiving graduate degrees has risen over the past few decades. Wealthy educated parents know this especially well and can use their higher incomes to afford the private tuition or schooling that helps their kids over the entry threshold. This produces the phenomenon of 'opportunity-hoarding' where the already well-off monopolize the resources needed to make it into the upper-middle class. Many of the beneficiaries of opportunity-hoarding are well-educated liberals who valorize the collective goal of equality. But their individual incentive is always to make sure their kid makes the cut. And collectively the barriers to entering the elite are pushed higher and higher.

In both cases rising inequality produces a 'lock-in' effect. The politics of inequality is self-reinforcing, and what began as equal economic rights to enterprise and education – to opportunity – becomes a defence against equalizing outcomes. Our politics fails as we get further and further away from being able to substantively lower inequality, even if many of us claim we want it.

But perhaps these twin outcomes – of a draconic enforced equality and a hyper-capitalist inequality – are too extreme. Maybe there are ways in which we can both have equality and keep our economic freedoms.

We might ask if there really is a trade-off between equality and efficiency in the real world. When we compare countries' levels of inequality to their levels of income per person, there is basically no relationship at all. There are wealthy, unequal countries – the United States, Australia – and wealthy equal countries – Denmark, Norway, Sweden – and wealthy countries somewhere in the middle – Switzerland. Similarly, there are less wealthy, unequal countries – Greece – and less wealthy, equal countries – the Czech Republic. Some countries seem to be able to escape the equality trap; others to have the worst of both worlds – inequality *and* inefficiency.

That the Scandinavian countries are both wealthy and equal suggests that countries really can have it all. The Swedish model, in particular, has been attractive to left-wing parties around the world as it promises a true 'economic democracy', where socialists could reform the market economy from within. The socialist US senator Bernie Sanders, whose wealth tax we saw earlier, has argued the US should 'look to countries like Denmark, Sweden, and Norway'. Enthusiastic 'new left' political movements have seen Sweden as a model for 'democratic socialism'.

But that doesn't mean countries such as Sweden have completely avoided the equality trap. Things haven't been quite as smooth in actually existing Sweden as they appear in the utopian Sweden of campaign speeches.

From the 1950s to the 1970s it looked superficially as if Sweden had managed to sidestep the equality trap – it combined a liberal democracy and relatively free markets with a narrow gap in earnings (a Gini of just 0.22 in disposable incomes). Behind this 'sweet spot' was the so-called Rehn–Meidner model, named after two Swedish economists who worked for the country's main labour union. It worked like this – unions would insist on national wage-bargaining across most firms and keep the gap between the best- and worst-paid workers narrow. Since all firms had to pay similar wages, the least efficient ones would be squeezed out, keeping Sweden's economy productive. The most efficient firms in return got a great deal: they only had to pay their most highly skilled workers the national rate, making them more profitable. All good things went together – wages were compressed across firms and so inequality was low, and the most productive firms thrived.

But there were tensions in this system. Centralized wage-setting limited the freedom of the most productive workers, who earned much less than they otherwise would. Indeed, it meant their employers were making huge profits off their hard work. And so the next plan was to return these profits to the workers. The Meidner Plan was developed in 1971: each company was to invest 20 per cent of its profits by issuing shares to its workers, the so-called 'wage-earner funds'. The plan was to gradually provide workers with an important stake in the running of their companies. Democratic socialism was on its way.

Except it wasn't. The wage-earner funds proved remarkably politically unpopular. In the name of greater equality of outcomes, the plan had been to restrict the equal rights of firms to make investments as they thought best. The Social Democratic Party, which felt compelled to promote this policy designed by the unions, was highly reluctant to proceed. Its opponents argued the wage-earner funds would lead to firms fleeing Sweden or refusing to invest. The equal freedoms of firms to leave the country or to decide on their investment plans had run straight up against equal outcomes.

Eventually, the Social Democrats implemented a highly watered-down version of wage-earner funds in 1982. Though that didn't prevent tens of thousands of people protesting against them in central Stockholm. Their electoral unpopularity meant that the wage-earner funds were discontinued when the Social Democrats lost power in 1990, and, for decades after, the word 'fund' was unofficially banned in the party. Since that high point for democratic socialism, Sweden has largely drifted rightwards, with inequality rising and taxes declining. Bernie Sanders, though, was not dissuaded – in 2019 he advocated a 2 per cent tax on US corporate profits to buy shares for workers until they hit 20 per cent of company stock.

That some attempts to increase the equality of outcomes backfire does not of course imply that economic inequality naturally produces better outcomes. In fact, we can often end up with the worst of both worlds. Economists talk of a 'Great Gatsby' curve, where higher inequality leads to reduced social mobility, ultimately cutting out potentially productive but currently poorer people, with a consequent hit taken to economic growth. Here we need some equality to get efficiency.

Many industrialized countries have high inequality but without high personal incomes. Countries such as Spain and Greece have highly regulated, protectionist product and labour markets. Where a few politically connected firms can dominate major industries, or where becoming a professional requires family connections, we can end up harming both equality and the economy. Bad things can often go together.

The case of Italy is instructive. Since the turn of the millennium Italy has barely had any growth in average incomes. Yet its inequality in earnings remains high – similar to the USA and UK. Part of the blame lies in heavily regulated labour markets at both the bottom and top end of the income ladder. Italy has a large number of poorly paid informal workers, excluded from the well-protected formal labour market. But there is also a myriad of protections among professionals, which create highly lucrative opportunities for the lucky few.

Perhaps the biggest beneficiaries of these kinds of protections are Italy's public notaries: 'notaios'. Over a decade ago, I lived in Florence for a year. On my walk to the bus each day, I would pass through the wealthiest part of Florence, where the Four Seasons hotel is in a Renaissance palace. On street after street were shiny gold signs saying 'notaio', affixed to grand palazzos. These were the notary offices – a far cry from the dowdy notary publics you might see in a strip mall in the US. But the job was largely the same – to certify the legal validity of everyday documents, from house sales to contracts, and before 2006 even the sale of a used car. Italian notaries have been able to protect their industry from interlopers such as lawyers and title companies. And the ensuing bottleneck is highly lucrative – with the average notaio making several hundred thousand euros per annum. In return, the cost to homeowners of paying notaios for the legal recognition of a housing sale is around 2 per cent of the price.

As the example of notaries suggests, there isn't always an equality/efficiency trade-off. Inefficiency can beget inequality and inequality can contribute to inefficiency. And this extends beyond economic inequality to unequal rights more generally. A particularly stark example is the negative effect of racial prejudice on economic growth in the United States. The systematic political suppression of African Americans through lynching and Jim Crow laws also suppressed black Americans' ability to innovate. The rate of patents acquired by black Americans collapsed at the start of the twentieth century as lynching reached its peak. Here we have the worst of all worlds – unequal political and civil rights which produced lower growth, racial inequality and endemic, state-sponsored violence. A tragedy of both lost individual opportunity and lost collective wealth.

That we cannot easily have both equal rights and equal outcomes does not, sadly, mean that it isn't possible to have unequal rights and unequal outcomes. For oppressed groups the world over, that has been an unhappy but not unusual experience.

Equal votes vs equal outcomes

Capitalist democracies face powerful centrifugal forces – they are pulled towards coercive equality and oligarchic inequality. But what of non-democracies? How do more-equal outcomes affect the chances of getting equal political rights in the first place? Are unequal dictatorships more likely to survive or be overthrown?

You might think equal political systems emerge in places that
already have more-equal economic outcomes. But that's not generally the case. Instead, we have the other side of the equality trap – when
we have more-equal outcomes, we don't get more-equal political
rights. And that means we might need quite a bit of inequality to get
democracy.

The rise of democracy was a glacial and uneven process over the
centuries. Popular rule was rarely long-lasting before the nineteenth
century – when the masses overstepped the mark, elites would react
with force. Athenian democracy gave way to the distinctively
undemocratic sounding Thirty Tyrants. Two millennia later, the
popularly elected French National Assembly soon found itself curtailed when Robespierre and his Jacobin populists met the guillotine
and were replaced first in the Thermidorian reaction and later by
Napoleon.

Why were elites so often unwilling to countenance direct rule by
the people? One popular – but I think incorrect – theory goes like
this: the elites feared Robin Hood. Where elites were rich and the
people very poor, they had a lot to worry about. Popular rule might
mean having their landholdings split up and handed out to the peas-
antry, or having their lavish incomes taxed to meagreness. With the
French Revolution, long-standing fears of popular rule were realized
as the land of nobles and the church alike was redistributed to com-
moners, and the tax privileges of the aristocracy were removed. To
adapt Karl Marx's famous opening line, a spectre haunted the elites,
the spectre of redistribution.

My colleague David Samuels and I call this the 'redistributivist'
theory of democracy. (An ungainly term, I acknowledge.) The idea
is that inequality makes democracy less likely. Put yourself in the
(expensive Italian) shoes of a ruling elite in a highly unequal dictatorship, where you control not only political power but also the
country's wealth – the fields, the mines, the oil. Imagine you are
being asked to consider the merits of extending political power to
the people. Once you do so you lose all ability to stop taxation or
nationalization or any other nasty '-ation' that will take away your
wealth.

The people could say to you: 'Don't worry, we promise not to tax you heavily, you can trust us.' But the moment you relinquish political power, what's to stop the people from deciding that, after all, they would like a piece of your castle/mansion/penthouse apartment? The people have a 'commitment' problem – their promises aren't credible. Similarly, a dictatorship can't credibly promise to raise taxes on themselves and transfer money to the people. The promises of an unconstrained elite are even less trustworthy. There is no third party outside politics that can force either elite or people to stick to their promises.

What the people can do is to threaten a dictatorial elite with ongoing tumult if they don't hand over power. The elite will have to balance the costs of repressing the people against the costs of putting up with democracy. How much are you willing to pay to crush the people beneath your dictatorial heel? How bad would it be for you to let them govern?

This quandary leads us back to equality. Democracy is more or less tolerable depending on the level of equality. Where economic inequality is low, then the elite and the people don't look that different. If the people seize power in this scenario, they probably won't enact punishing taxes – they'd have to pay them themselves and the elite aren't rich enough to be worth taxing heavily. But in a highly unequal dictatorship – a much more common reality – the threat to the current elite from giving up power is huge. They might own wide swathes of land, productive mines and oilfields, and countless factories, banks and townhouses. All this is threatened by the huddled poor seizing power. So democratization only happens in equal countries. Unequal countries remain controlled by authoritarian elites.

The 'redistributivist' view of the world is one where equal economic outcomes and equal political rights do go together. Superficially, this looks like an escape from the equality trap . . .

It all sounds quite plausible. It would be nice if it were true. But I have some questions. If I ask you to think of a country with highly unequal wealth in the world today, many of you would picture the United States. Perhaps you might say Brazil or Mexico or South

Africa. All democracies. Think of the great chroniclers of poverty amidst riches in the industrial era – Charles Dickens, F. Scott Fitzgerald, John Steinbeck – all writing about the travails of rich and poor alike in democracies.

Let's look instead at some of the most equal countries of the last century. Yes, we see Sweden and Norway, though even here wealth is much more unequally spread than incomes. But we also find China under Mao, Khrushchev's Soviet Union or contemporary Belarus. These were (or are in Belarus's case) highly equal dictatorships. Why didn't the 'elite' in these countries simply hand control over to the people? Your first answer is probably that they were Communist dictatorships and so 'equality' was part of the package. But that invites the question of whether imposing equal outcomes really does go along with the equal rights we associate with democracy.

It's not solely the case that economically equal dictatorships are the preserve of Communism. Imperial China in the late nineteenth century was also very equal in an economic sense, with a Gini estimated to be just 0.24. Most people in China at the time were equally poor. And while there was a small elite who ruled, there was simply not enough 'stuff' being produced in China to be distributed unequally to them for that to show up in the inequality statistics. Imperial China was deeply politically inegalitarian, but it was not economically that unequal.

Now we have a situation with the reverse pattern to the redistributivist argument: unequal democracies and equal autocracies. It is often inequality that produces democracy.

I find this line of argument more convincing. My reasoning goes like this. There are two ways we can get more inequality. The first is to take the stuff you already have and divide it unequally, so a small group get a bigger share of the same pie. The second is to make new stuff and give it out unequally, so a small group gets disproportionately more of the extra pie.

Now let's take our metaphor of the pie and replace it with the economy. If the economy is stagnant, any rise in inequality must come from the rich seizing assets from the poor. But if the economy is growing, a rise in inequality could occur because some group is claiming more of this new growth. That group would have to be better off than the rest of the population for inequality to rise. But – and this is important – it doesn't have to be the governing elite.

Let's add more flesh to our story. Think of the Industrial Revolution. In 1600 or so, most wealth in England was agricultural. Inequality rose when aristocratic landlords threw peasants off their land so that they could graze more sheep and sell valuable wool. It declined if – as rarely happened – large landholdings were split up or lots of poor peasants died from the plague, meaning the average peasant had more land.

As the Industrial Revolution took hold, unimaginable amounts of new wealth were created. Wealth that didn't depend on the land. More stuff to go around means more stuff to spread unequally. And the profits went to a new group of people – urban factory-owners and merchants who were enriched by industrial growth. The life of the poor did not change materially for a good century or two – they were poor in the fields and they were poor in the factories. But a new economic elite had emerged. The problem was that the political system didn't recognize them.

The story of Britain's gradual democratization over the nineteenth century was one of adjusting to this new elite's political demands for representation. That meant the enfranchisement of the industrious 'well to do', the representation of the new industrial cities in Parliament and a series of pitched battles over the long-standing privileges of the agricultural elite. Economic growth meant rising inequality. Rising inequality meant the emergence of a new economic elite who were not, yet, the political elite.

Once you start looking for them, you can see these kinds of battles between new and old elites everywhere. They occur at times of growing, not declining, inequality. Inequality means a new player on the scene. And that can be good for democracy. Equality means stagnation and that often means continued dictatorship. Here we have the other side of the equality trap – sometimes equal outcomes can undermine equal rights. Inequality, by contrast, can be good for democracy if it shakes up traditional elites.

Why would new elites care about democracy? Wouldn't they just want to control the state themselves and lord it over everyone else? They might. But more commonly new elites try to expand protections from the state, and popular, constitutional rule usually allows them to do that. When new wealthy groups come on the scene, they have usually made their money from commerce or industry, rather than owning land and the agriculture on it or minerals beneath it. Industrial and commercial industries are much more complex than simply extracting value from the soil. They require reams of contracts, highly differentiated products, networks of trade around the world and an active base of consumers.

Dictatorships struggle to provide and protect these social and economic links. Because there are few constraints on dictators they cannot credibly commit not to renege on contracts, block trade or expropriate wealth. The political promises of a dictator can be withdrawn at the barrel of a gun. And so rising elites constantly face the risk of being expropriated or held to ransom in dictatorships.

The uneasy relationship between Russian oligarchs and Vladimir Putin's government in Russia is an apt example. The oligarchs are largely a group of men – and it is almost always men – who made their fortunes by getting privileged access to previously state-owned enterprises and concessions after the fall of Communism.

As Putin deepened Russia's authoritarianism, those oligarchs who opposed the regime found themselves in serious legal issues – or worse.

The arrest in 2003 of Mikhail Khodorkovsky, then head of the gas giant Yukos and the richest man in Russia, was a pivotal moment. Khodorkovsky had begun supporting opposition parties and think-tanks, including Open Russia. As he boarded a private plane in Novosibirsk, Siberia, he was arrested and charged with fraud and tax evasion. Yukos was removed from his control entirely and he was jailed for a decade. Other oligarchs weren't so lucky. Many met unexplained deaths in exile, including the media mogul and Putin opponent Boris Berezovsky, found dead in his bathroom in his mansion near London. Following the Russian invasion of Ukraine, at least seven other oligarchs died mysteriously. For these wealthy businessmen, higher democratic taxes might have been preferable to the arbitrariness of fate in an autocracy.

Democracy might mean higher taxation but it also means law courts and constraints on rulers. At least there is taxation *with* representation. That's why inequality is not always an enemy of democracy. The American War of Independence was motivated by the increasingly wealthy colonists' abhorrence of taxation without representation and it was led by the great and good of the rising commercial cities of Boston, New York and Philadelphia. When independence had been won they were not keen to impose an American monarch of their own. They sought – as George Washington put it – a 'democracy if you can keep it'. The American political model was based around a separation of powers to prevent any single institution from dominating and to protect property rights. For the new winners of commerce, democracy was a good thing.

But we should be careful before assuming that economic inequality is always more likely to summon equal political rights. American democracy was only equalizing from the view of white male citizens. It was they who had demanded equal rights to protect their property from the state and taxation. The vast plantations of the South, toiled on by slaves, remained *in situ* through the nineteenth century. That kind of inequality – rural, violently enforced, and backward – could only be kept in place by depriving African Americans of their liberty, due process and any political rights at all. That kind of inequality was deeply authoritarian.

Equal treatment vs equal outcomes

The fights for equal economic freedoms and equal political rights had largely been won in today's Western democracies by the end of the Second World War. The great battles of the past half-century in these countries have instead been about equal social rights for those groups who had been traditionally, and often legally, treated as unequal to white men. The civil rights, women's rights, and gay rights movements still encounter an uneven playing field, even today. But discrimination in the labour market and in politics more generally is far less common than even a few decades ago.

Despite this epochal improvement in the equal treatment of people, economic outcomes have become increasingly unequal since the 1950s. However we measure them, the gaps between the most and least highly paid workers have widened substantially over the past several decades. This feels paradoxical but it represents yet another snare of the equality trap.

One of the reasons for growing economic inequality is that the composition of the workforce has changed dramatically. In particular, the entry of women into the workforce – the result of more-equitable hiring processes – has coincided with rising inequality among workers in terms of their pay. If women are more likely to take part-time jobs and this isn't accounted for in annual pay comparisons, this can widen inequality as they work fewer hours. Of course, if women also end up in worse-paid jobs than men this could also widen inequality.

This suggests that hiring and remuneration processes are not in fact equitable across genders, even if there is greater equality in the chance of having a job at all since the 1950s. This imperfect path towards fully equitable treatment means a series of new economic inequalities that still remain while women are systematically paid less than men, as is true even in the ostensibly gender-neutral Scandinavian countries, where women are still paid around 20 per cent less than men.

To see how the emergence of equal treatment can produce more-unequal outcomes, we can look at how women's entry into the workforce plays out across countries at different stages of economic development. Countries with average annual incomes around $5,000 have strikingly low female labour force participation – around 50 percentage points lower than for men. The pay gap in these countries is even larger, with female pay 65 per cent lower than male earnings. Among rich countries, with average incomes around $45,000, the labour force participation gap is less than 10 per cent and the gender pay gap is also lower, but still sizeable at just under 40 per cent.

There are two implications for inequality. First, because gender gaps in pay are larger where fewer women are in the labour market, in the initial stages of women's entry into the workforce they end up in poorly paid jobs, relative to men, and this pushes up inequality. This is not simply a function of women working much fewer hours in poorer countries – in fact, the gender gap in hours worked varies little across countries by wealth. Second, even in the wealthiest countries women are systematically disadvantaged in the labour market, creating ongoing and stubborn inequalities. Since the 1980s, the gender gap has been persistent in rich countries, declining by only a little over 10 percentage points.

Why is the gender gap so persistent? It is particularly striking, given that in most wealthy countries more women attend college than men, which ought to have reversed the gender gap. One of the key ways in which the labour market is inequitable is in how women are punished professionally for giving birth. Economists have found that while men's earnings are stable after the birth of their first child, women's earnings drop to almost half their pre-birth level up to a decade after the birth.

Initially this comes from differences in participation in the workforce – men's participation doesn't change after childbirth but women's drops sharply with maternity leave. Those women who continue working the same hours straight away after childbirth don't see an immediate shock to their hourly pay. But after a few years a large gap opens with men who had children at the same time. This reflects two things – a gap in advancement prospects even for those women who remained at work after their first child; and lower wages for those who took time out when they re-enter the workforce. Economists have found that the wage penalty for having children comes almost entirely from the loss of on-job experience and the different types of – more flexible – occupations women take on once they have children. And this penalty is even larger for more-educated women who have higher potential earnings.

The question is why in allegedly equal labour markets, without explicit employment discrimination, these gaps still hold. The answer is that, beneath formal legal equality, profound inequalities still exist within the household. In every wealthy country, women do far more unpaid household work than men: ranging from just under an hour in Sweden to over three hours in Portugal and Japan. Some of this relates to different employment patterns. But in a study of household behaviour in England during the COVID lockdown, even in families where the mother earned more than the father, women ended up doing more housework and childcare and less uninterrupted paid work than men.

Even in those countries with gender-neutral parental-leave policies, such as Sweden, the division of household work remains stubbornly gender-biased. Sweden grants 240 days of paid leave to each parent, with 150 of those days transferable to the other parent. That means ninety days of the father's leave are not transferable: these 'use it or lose it' days are called 'daddy quotas'. However, men only take 25 per cent of total days of leave and only 13 per cent of households have a roughly equitable split of days. Moreover, fathers who received the 'daddy quotas' after they were introduced were no more likely to look after their sick children than those men who had not received the leave. What appears superficially an equitable policy can mask pre-existing inequalities in the household about who gets to continue their career at full steam and who must make sacrifices.

For equitable parental-leave policies to actually produce equality within the household, broader norms in society may need to change. The use of such leave policies by fathers snowballs – according to Norwegian data, men are much more likely to take parental leave if their brothers or co-workers do. Workplace norms also have strong effects in discouraging men from taking their leave. Japan has some of the most generous paternity leave policies in the world – up to twelve months at around 60 per cent pay – yet only 6 per cent of Japanese fathers take it. Researchers have found that their reluctance is explained by an overestimation of the negative reaction of other men. At the same time, some Japanese firms have been accused of sidelining men who do take their leave. These unequal norms for parents mean an ostensibly equitable policy ends up reinforcing inequalities.

Comparing inequality across households also shows the complexity of how more equal treatment can hide other inequalities. In the 1950s most households would have a single male earner, so if we were comparing household incomes, we were essentially comparing the incomes of men. Women entering the workforce means that households now usually have two earners. And if marriage or cohabitation follows a particular pattern, this can radically change how inequality across households plays out.

The idea of 'assortative mating' is that like marries like. So high-skill, high-income professional women marry high-skill, high-income professional men. Similarly, lower-paid women marry lower-paid men. If that's the case, it amplifies existing differences in household income – crudely it doubles the income gap between rich and poor households.

Let's see a simple example. We begin with our *Happy Days* 1950s households – one with a single male earner in a working-class job, bringing in $40,000 a year, and another with a single male earner in management making $80,000 a year. The gap between the households is $40,000. Now imagine two *Friends*-era 1990s households, where both men and women work. If opposites attract, a working-class man might marry a female manager and a male manager might marry a working-class woman and then each family would earn $120,000 and household inequality would vanish.

But that's not what has happened. Instead like marries like and we have a working-class household making $80,000 and a managerial household making $160,000 and we now have a gap of $80,000. In relative terms the managers' household is still twice as rich as the working-class one but the *absolute* gap has doubled in size. What's more, divorce rates tend to be lower among wealthier couples so there's a good chance that the wealthy family with the $160,000 income stays intact, whereas we end up with two working-class single-earner households of $40,000 each.

What does the data about household inequality and assortative mating look like? There's mixed evidence but, overall, it appears that assortative mating is responsible for a sizeable share of the rising income inequality experienced by wealthy countries over the past half-century. Scholars estimate that the increase in American income inequality between 1967 and 2005 would have been around 25–30 per cent lower if assortative mating stayed at its lower 1960s level. Sociologists also estimate that up to half of the correlation between parents' income and children's long-term income is due to assortative mating – meaning it also reduces intergenerational mobility.

Similar effects have been found in countries from Denmark to the United Kingdom, Germany and Norway. But there are differences. Assortative mating seems to be weakest in places with stronger labour market regulation – the Scandinavian countries – and strongest in the less regulated labour markets of the English-speaking world and Eastern Europe. Where labour markets are more strongly regulated and there is greater gender equality in earnings, as in Scandinavia, higher wages are compressed and a lawyer and teacher, for example, become a more likely couple, not least because the earnings gap between them is lower.

Assortative mating can hurt equal outcomes across households. But the phenomenon of assortative mating was initially driven by concerns about equity – that women be treated equally in the workforce. Greater access to professional jobs in law, finance and medicine means plenty of dual-lawyer, dual-banker, dual-doctor households. Equal treatment in the workforce along with the equal right to marry who you want produces inequality on a different dimension – household incomes. As Christine Schwartz puts it, 'Husbands and wives have become more equal over the past several decades . . . increases in the resemblance of spouses, however, may have unanticipated consequences, namely, increasing inequality across families.'

It's our old dilemma of the equality trap once more. If you give people equal rights to behave as they wish – and even if you treat them impartially and equitably – their decisions can end up producing highly unequal outcomes. Our politics will fail if we simply assume that equal treatment will necessarily lower economic inequality. Instead, we need to make sure that policies such as parental leave take seriously existing gender inequalities in how employers react to returning workers and how long-standing household inequities can undermine the best-laid plans.

8. Escaping the Equality Trap

How can we curb the excesses of capitalism while retaining our democratic freedoms? Although, as forcing complete equality might mean restricting our rights, few of us want to go that far. Instead, we would like to start closing the ever-growing gaps between rich and poor in wealthy countries – to push back against inequality and prevent it from subverting our democracies. We can escape the equality trap – some countries, such as those in Scandinavia, combine much more equal incomes with a vibrant and liberal democratic culture. But we can't get there without politics.

It would be foolhardy to think we can reduce inequality through the magic of the market or technology. Free markets, in the absence of government intervention or organized labour, will almost always push towards the accumulation of wealth, especially if the already wealthy can safeguard their own children's entry into the affluent classes through elite education. It's true that market shocks sometimes do reduce inequality, but historically that has been through famine, plague, war and recession. Which doesn't seem much of an escape.

Could technology make us equal? That depends on the technology. Cheap communications technology could bring new opportunities to those traditionally locked out of national and global markets. But most recent technologies have not favoured the already poor. Instead, information technology has disproportionately benefited skilled workers, heightening the importance of education, and enriching professionals and managers rather than workers.

Ultimately, we can't rely on outside forces to lower inequality. We will have to do it ourselves through political decisions – to educate our workers differently, to regulate our industries and labour relations more effectively, but, first of all, to find ways of taxing the enormous spoils of wealth created by our unequal economy. If both death and taxes are the only inevitabilities we face, we might as well do the latter effectively.

Larry Summers shuffled his papers and walked up to the microphone. One-time Treasury Secretary, President of Harvard, Chief Economic Advisor to Barack Obama, Summers had spent his whole professional career at the intersection of the economic profession and the Democratic Party. He was about to torch the pretenders to the throne.

He had been preceded on stage by Emmanuel Saez, part of a highly influential group of French economists including Gabriel Zucman and Thomas Piketty. Saez and Zucman had developed a proposal for a wealth tax that had America's billionaires in its sights. The aim was to target the very richest people – like the Fortune 400 wealthiest people in America whose share of national wealth had nearly quadrupled from 0.9 per cent in 1982 to 3.3 per cent in 2018.

Saez set out his proposed plan: an annual 10 per cent tax on wealth over one billion dollars. His scheme had inspired similar wealth tax proposals by then front runners in the Democratic presidential primary for the 2020 election: Elizabeth Warren and Bernie Sanders.

Warren's recommendation was a 2 per cent tax on wealth over $50 million and a further 4 per cent surcharge on wealth over a billion dollars. Just 75,000 households would contribute almost $4 trillion extra in tax over a decade. Bernie Sanders claimed his wealth tax would raise even more revenue, starting at a 1 per cent tax of wealth above $32 million and rising incrementally to 8 per cent on wealth over $10 billion. The top fifteen richest people in America had almost a trillion dollars in wealth in 2018. After Warren that would be $434 billion. After Sanders, $196 billion. That's a real comedown in terms of the private islands you can buy.

Whichever wealth tax you chose, both the politics and economics seemed clear. Politically, this was a face-off between fewer than 100,000 of the wealthiest Americans and, well, everyone else. Surely, if democracy were to mean anything, it would be the ability of the vast majority to curtail the riches of the few? Had the Sanders tax plan been in place since the 1980s, the share of America's wealth owned by the 400 richest people in America would have barely grown. In reality, it had more than tripled.

Larry Summers was not convinced. He denounced Saez's data and calculations. And he argued that a wealth tax would not even succeed on its own terms. First, he didn't think that cutting the wealth of billionaires would have any effect on political power. In his view, both political parties and special interests were funded by affluent people far lower down the wealth spectrum, who would be untouched. In fact, a wealth tax might lead people affected by it to spend *more* of their wealth on lobbying in order to avoid the tax.

Second, the rise in wealth inequality tracked the rise in income inequality because it largely comes from diverging incomes. So that was the problem, not wealth per se. Third, Summers noted something that has puzzled many scholars of wealth inequality. In countries with a large safety net, or publicly provided pensions, people hold less wealth because they are publicly insured. Consequently, we see very high levels of wealth inequality in countries like Sweden *because* middle-class people don't need private pension funds as they have guaranteed future state or occupational pensions.

Finally, according to Summers, taxing wealth means potentially taxing investment, because if rich people save their wealth it gets taxed. But if they spend their wealth on luxury trips around the world or on campaign contributions, it doesn't get taxed. In a free country, rich people can adjust their own behaviour to minimize what they'd pay in a wealth tax. So what do you think rich people would do? For Summers, the equality trap snares us: unless we curtail some other form of equality – equal rights to contribute to political campaigns, to spend money as we please, to move country or change citizenship – we can't be confident that we can secure more-equal outcomes.

Are there ways of using a wealth tax that can help us escape the equality trap? The solution that Thomas Piketty, of *Capital in the Twenty-First Century* fame, has developed is a global wealth tax. As things stand, there is a plethora of micro-states – or, rather, tax havens – that offer low tax rates for foreign investors moving there. While collectively we might all be better off making sure billionaires pay their fair share, if they can exercise their freedom to move where they want, then these small countries may take individual advantage, figuring that a tiny tax rate on a billionaire might still provide valuable revenue. A global wealth tax including all countries would stifle this. Moving country wouldn't help billionaires avoid taxation. Finally, this builds on existing success with international agreements over corporation tax. In 2021, 136 countries agreed on a minimum corporation tax of 15 per cent. But are billionaires harder to tax than companies?

The problem with the global wealth tax is its disregard for politics, a problem Piketty himself acknowledges. As a technocratic solution to tax-dodging billionaires it's unimpeachable. But it runs right into the equality trap. On the face of it we resolve this by saying billionaires still have an equal right to live where they please, while imposing a wealth tax that we can use to equalize outcomes. But we have removed another equal right: that of people in democracies to choose their preferred tax rates. And not simply micro-states who can easily be pushed around by the big players. A global wealth tax also sets up a fierce fight between America and Europe, China and India about what its rate should be, who benefits and whether it can vary across borders. In other words, we run into the buzzsaw of international politics – we don't just have to convince one government to implement a tax but perhaps all of them.

The politics of wealth taxes is also complicated when we look at public opinion. You might think wealth taxes would be a sure thing for public support, given so few people would be affected. And yet, while people often support taking from the rich in the abstract, when it comes to the specifics, they become suddenly more reticent. Relying on a 'moral leader' who can persuade the public to understand that wealth taxation is the 'right thing to do' runs up against the inconvenient problem that the public don't agree.

A classic example is the Bush tax cuts of 2001. These essentially ended inheritance taxation in America by 2010. Bush's tax bill was so slanted towards wealthier taxpayers that, by 2010, 51.8 per cent of its benefits went to the richest 1 per cent of households. Yet, despite

Americans thinking rich people didn't pay enough in taxes, it was extremely popular.

In 2005 Larry Bartels published an article called 'Homer Gets a Tax Cut', featuring a cartoon of Homer Simpson clutching a couple of dollar bills in glee, while Mr Burns, standing in front of bags of money, cackled 'Sucker'. While the cartoon doesn't win any points for subtlety, it does point at an apparent disconnect in American attitudes. Bartels found that while 52 per cent of Americans thought the rich currently paid too little in taxes, fewer than 20 per cent said that they opposed the Bush tax cuts which would have the rich pay even less.

Why do people support both taxing the rich more in general and cutting specific taxes that mostly rich people pay? Bartels argued that people have 'unenlightened self-interest'. People think they – more precisely, their estate on death – will have to pay taxes that, in reality, only affect people much richer than them. People think they are acting in their own self-interest but are acting in the rich's instead: attitudes towards the Bush tax cuts were shaped by whether people thought *they* were taxed too much, rather than whether they thought the rich were taxed too much.

There are other reasons why people don't like wealth taxes. Because housing is the largest component of most households' wealth, inheritance taxes largely fall on the family home. People have sentimental reasons for not wanting the family home, farm or business to be claimed by the grey suits of the IRS. Even if most people won't lose this heirloom, anti-tax politicians can find sympathetic examples of families who have. People also have moral reasons for opposing wealth taxation. Wealth often comes in the form of savings, and many people object to the idea of being taxed 'twice' on their hard-earned labour. Others fear that paying taxes on wealth is logistically difficult – incomes and transactions can be taxed at source, but wealth must be sold, or borrowed against, to pay taxes.

When the general public are asked about wealth taxation, they tend to be sceptical. A 2015 poll asked whether the various taxes imposed by the British government were fair or not. Large majorities found taxing alcohol and cigarettes fair. Just over half thought income tax was fair. But only around 20 per cent thought inheritance tax was fair, with almost 60 per cent finding it unfair. Stamp duty – a tax on housing transactions – was similarly unpopular. The British public were most averse to precisely those taxes that hammer the wealthy hardest, and most positive towards those that fall on the poor. The question is: why?

In a survey I conducted in England and Wales in 2021, I found taxing wealth such as inheritances was still very unpopular – fewer than 20 per cent of those I asked thought inheritance taxes were too low; over 60 per cent thought they were too high. Yet in 2019 fewer than 4 per cent of deaths even incurred any inheritance tax. People don't pay it, but they hate it anyway. We asked them to provide a sentence explaining their attitudes on wealth taxes – the most common phrases they used were 'already taxed', 'pay tax', 'work hard' and 'people save'. In other words, people find wealth taxation unfair – even if they won't pay it – because they view it as double taxation.

On the other hand, perhaps if they can be convinced that wealth comes from luck, rather than merit or effort, they might find taxing it fairer. In 2020 my colleagues and I ran an online laboratory experiment with several groups of participants, each two dozen in size. We were interested in how these groups would feel about income and wealth if we let them tax each other.

A few days before the experiment began, we emailed the participants to let them know they would receive a chunk of money without having to do anything – this was their 'wealth'. Then, in the experiment itself they had to perform a very boring task to earn some income, where they would be paid based on performance. We experimentally varied both the value of the wealth and how much people would get paid in the task.

At the end of the experiment, we told everyone how much they had earned in total – wealth plus income – compared to others. They then picked separate tax rates for wealth and income and the proceeds were distributed evenly. The first thing we found was that people are, unsurprisingly, self-interested. People who had higher incomes or higher wealth wanted lower taxes.

But what was more surprising was what happened with one group of people who we provided with extra information. This group were told how they stood relative to others not only in total but also separately in income and in wealth. So they knew if their earnings had come because they had worked hard or because they had just got lucky.

This group reacted to the extra information they had about the distribution of income by doubling down on their self-interest – if they had earned a lot, they became even more opposed to income tax. Because performing the task involved effort, people cared greatly about how they did relative to others. They had worked hard: they deserved their money; others had clearly slacked off. But how people compared to others in terms of wealth had no similar effect. With wealth, people knew that it was completely random who got what and so this extra information didn't seem to matter.

What we learned was that if people believe wealth comes about via luck rather than effort, taxing wealth might prove less polarizing than taxing income. People can recognize when they have received an arbitrary windfall. They know they didn't 'deserve' it. So perhaps they may be persuaded to forgo some share of it. And the people who didn't receive the windfall also know those who did were just lucky – making them more supportive of taxing it.

This suggests that taxing some types of wealth might be easier than others. People emphatically do not like having their savings taxed, because that feels like being taxed on your past hard work (and hence double taxation). Inheritances are a little more complex – from the perspective of the beneficiary it is a windfall, but the money usually comes from parents' savings – so hard work, one generation removed. And, except for the very rich, inheritances rarely contribute massively to lifetime inflows of money (under 5 per cent a year for most people), so they will not be that effective at reducing inequality. More plausible is taxing gains people make from speculative assets, where prices have risen with less (or zero) relation to the effort people make – cryptocurrencies, shares, second homes.

How can we design an effective wealth tax? We need to follow the political grain – since most people are sceptical of wealth taxes, even if it's very unlikely they would ever have to pay them, we need them to be transparent and clearly targeted. The most politically viable form of wealth to target is unearned, 'windfall' type wealth, which people attribute to luck rather than hard work. Existing inheritance taxes fulfil this in part but they also hit two sentimental hotspots – family and housing. If our concerns are mostly about intergenerational wealth transfer among the very rich it might make more sense to limit inheritance tax to very large fortunes but to enforce it vigorously.

Instead, it might be better if we focused on equalizing taxes on gains to wealth with income taxes. In many countries, capital gains are taxed at much lower rates than personal earned income. By highlighting this discrepancy between gains from luck and those from effort, we could build on the social norm about the merits of work over windfalls that we saw in the experiment above. Ultimately any tax is only politically effective and long-lasting if it meshes with our underlying sense of fairness.

If people are hard to tax, what about shifting our target to things that can't fight back (at least, one hopes not): robots? The 'robot tax' has been debated in the pages of *The New York Times* and the *Wall Street Journal* and has been championed by Bill Gates. The automation by robots of tasks once completed by humans has arguably hollowed out the middle of the labour market, removing millions of decently paid jobs and raising inequality. The idea of the tax is to stop companies from replacing workers with robots (or, perhaps, artificial intelligence) by disincentivizing this through the tax system. This could be a literal fee per robot, or be tied to lost workers, for example by insisting that companies continue to pay the employer share of Social Security, even after a worker is replaced. Gates advocates treating the robot as if it were a human – a robot (or their owner) ought to pay the same income tax and so forth as the worker it replaces.

Can a robot tax help us escape the equality trap? The benefits of a robot tax are twofold: first, it replaces revenue streams lost to governments when workers are let go; second, it encourages employers to think twice about replacing workers and to consider how to make existing workers more productive. If each individual firm has an incentive to introduce robots in order to cut costs, it will be hard to prevail on them to train workers for the collective good. The robot tax could give the upper hand to human workers over our silicon rivals. It might, in the long run, also help embed norms among companies about training workers first.

Robot taxes barely exist currently. South Korea has a policy sometimes called a 'robot tax' but that's not quite the case – instead the Koreans removed an existing 'robot subsidy' that had given tax breaks for investment in robotics. Presumably the absence of such taxes is not because governments are fearful of upsetting legions of robot voters. The big problem with robot taxes is in defining a 'robot'. For example, robotic arms in manufacturing are included in the US Census Bureau's survey of manufacturers but not driverless forklifts. Once we move into the realm of software, this task becomes even harder. Is each algorithm a robot, or the full set of connected algorithms in a piece of software? How do we measure how many people have lost their jobs – or never been hired in the first place – because of a company's investment in artificial intelligence?

But the broader problem with the robot tax is the idea that it is a tax that avoids politics. Taxing robots is popular because it seems like we are taxing a group of unfeeling entities, who won't complain. But, of course, a tax on robots ultimately falls on a human. Somebody who owns the robot, or uses it, has to pay. And that means all our political debates about whether we should reduce inequality and who should pay for that come back into play. If our concerns are about the inequality produced by a technological explosion, focusing on the inputs to the production of technology – robots – rather than the outputs – rich owners of technology companies – it seems like we might be missing the point. If we want to effectively solve the equality trap, we can't ignore the very richest in society. And that might mean heading back to their wealth . . .

Whatever the pros and cons of wealth or robot taxes, they are ultimately just a way of tidying up inequality 'after the fact'. Tax policies get their redistributive effect by taking whatever inequality is produced by the market and then taking money from citizens with more resources and giving to those with less. But this doesn't get us to the heart of the problem. Such policies presuppose there will always be one group of people richer – perhaps vastly so – than another. They do little about underlying inequality.

Is there a way that policies can reduce inequality before we come to taxes and transfers? This idea about making market incomes more equal has the slightly ungainly moniker of 'predistribution'. It's a long word for a simple idea – the state should focus on reducing inequalities at their source. This means regulating and investing rather than taxing. Regulation by the state allows it to push up the wages of lower earners, either directly through minimum wages or more indirectly by facilitating wage-bargaining by trade unions. The collapse of trade union membership in the US and Western Europe has arguably been one of the key forces behind rising inequality.

Another way of reshaping and equalizing earnings is to look at the economy as a whole. The central bank could keep interest rates low and access to credit loose to encourage employers to hire more workers. High employment rates typically increase workers' bargaining power as employers compete to hire them in a tight labour market. However, as the experience of the post-COVID economy has shown, it can also encourage inflation.

Finally, and this does involve some spending, the government can invest in its citizens' productivity through education, upskilling, and research and development. Presuming the market rewards these skills – and that they are targeted at poorer citizens who might not otherwise receive them – this should push up wages and lower inequality, while improving the nation's productivity.

This last strategy sounds attractive. A silver-bullet solution for equality perhaps. This idea is often promoted as 'social investment', contrasted to 'social consumption' policies, which are about transferring money to the old, ill, poor or unemployed. Social investment looks like it could release us from the equality trap. It boosts the wages of poorer workers by improving their skills and productivity, while avoiding the 'bad incentives' of simply transferring money. And it appears to infringe less on people's equal freedoms within the market to take the jobs they want. But is there really this kind of simple, technocratic solution to the equality trap?

Maybe. Education spending certainly can be equalizing. When countries democratize and grant poorer citizens the vote, they expand spending on education. Similarly, left-wing parties, who typically represent poorer citizens, behave similarly. But spending on education does not always translate simply into more-equal societies. The idea of 'meritocracy' is superficially attractive – why shouldn't people with more skills and talents be paid better? – but how people acquire those skills and talents is usually not especially equal.

This is particularly apparent when we look at where the money for education comes from. Money spent on education is rarely spread evenly and quite often benefits relatively wealthier students. Higher-education spending may be good for national productivity (it's certainly in my interest as an academic to make that case!). But entry into higher education correlates strongly with income. That means richer citizens prefer to spend money – both their own and the government's – on higher education than primary education. Whereas democracies spend more on primary education, more-authoritarian countries tend to tilt spending towards universities and away from primary education.

With political parties in wealthy countries there's an intriguing pattern. When university enrolments are low, right-wing parties are more likely to increase higher-education spending. But as enrolments rise this pattern flips and instead left-wing governments become the bigger spenders. More students in universities means the average student is coming from a poorer background and so the political incentives shift. That means we can't extract politics from education policy like a painful, rotten tooth. Spending on universities is attractive to different people, and hence to different political parties, at different times.

More skills and mass university enrolment may look attractive from the perspective of equality-promoting left-wing parties, but there is, as ever, a catch. While modern labour markets demand ever-greater numbers of skilled workers, there are limits to the ability of the economy to absorb university graduates. Sometimes degree-holders end up in jobs that make little use of their (perhaps expensively acquired) skills.

These mismatched graduates are less satisfied with democracy, the economy and life in general; less trusting of politicians; and more likely to vote for radical-right parties than their fellow graduates who found graduate-level jobs. A centre-left party hoping to use social investment as a way to bind together a voting coalition, spur on the economy and create a more equal society might find itself instead with a set of radicalized and possibly unemployed 'mismatched' graduates.

Meritocracy has its limits as a solution to the equality trap. Higher education is an integral part of our high-tech, complex economies – it is unrealistic to expect students to finish education at eighteen and move straight into industries from data science to pharmaceuticals to finance. But it is also implausible currently to believe the economy can find graduate-level jobs for the entire population. And that means either we have a large class of non-graduates or large numbers of mismatched and embittered graduates.

The meritocratic argument that your job status reflects your skills and effort quickly slips into self-justification and back-patting by the system's hyper-educated winners, most of whom just so happen to hail from well-to-do backgrounds. At the turn of the millennium, politicians from Tony Blair to Bill Clinton saw education as an apolitical way of getting higher growth and equality. But education has winners and losers. The past decade has seen education emerge as the key political divide in modern elections. If we are to see education as a solution to the equality trap, we can't simply push half the population to university and declare the job done. The half who don't go can see right through that. So what, instead, can we do for them?

University education is not the only way to upskill an economy. Many politicians are attracted to vocational education – apprenticeships, on-the-job training, etc. – which is easier to target at lower-income students and promises to directly improve productivity. For generations, politicians from across Europe have been obsessed with Germany's 'dual-track' apprenticeship system.

From the age of fifteen, German students can opt into a three-year programme, where they mix time spent learning skills with an employer with classroom training. Around 40 per cent of German students opt for the dual track and they each spend 70 per cent of their week 'at work' with the remainder in school. The dual-track system has long been thought of as the bedrock of Germany's traditions of high-end manufacturing and craftsmanship, as well as boosting skills and wages among people at the bottom or middle of the income spectrum. Is this a solution to the equality trap that improves equality but through a vibrant private sector?

The dual-track system builds on centuries of apprenticeships, initially developed by Germany's medieval crafts guilds. It's not a social investment policy that can simply be cut out and glued into the education systems of other countries. But this doesn't stop politicians from trying.

Political institutions are complicated but necessary ways for us to make promises to one another about how we'll behave in the future. Training institutions are similar. The skills that students learn on apprenticeships are highly specific to a particular company or task. Should that company go bankrupt, or machinery become obsolete, the investment in those skills might be for naught. Firms also worry about paying the costs of training apprentices, only for them to quit for higher wages at a rival company. So, to make a system like this work, firms and apprentices need to make and trust a whole bunch of promises.

For workers that means the government or companies need to find ways either to subsidize their investment in firm-specific skills or to bail them out if those skills become redundant. For firms, this means agreement not to poach newly trained workers. Given how long it takes to train these workers, those firms may have to convince banks to give them long-term loans. Workers will want to jointly organize in trade unions to make sure that firms don't exploit workers whose training is only valuable at that particular firm. And the school system needs to deal with students coming in for only 30 per cent of the week for highly technical training.

The German model produces economic equality by placing limits on firms poaching workers, on the most productive workers making higher wages, on financiers withdrawing money. In other words, to get equal outcomes we need to restrict some equality of choice or opportunity.

Having relatively high but uniform wages for workers is a double-edged sword for firms. Expensive workers mean it is crucial that factories are highly productive to get the most out of each employee – arguably this has pushed German firms high up the 'value chain' to produce top-range cars, domestic goods and machinery. But uniform wages mean that German firms benefit from not having to pay their most productive workers 'what they are worth'. So the 'German miracle' relies on this balance, with both workers and firms accepting limits on how they can behave.

The German model isn't just dual-track apprenticeships that other countries can simply copy over. To make this kind of training work you need coordinated business groups, trade unions, patient banks and generous unemployment insurance. In other words, you need a particular 'variety of capitalism', a term invented by Peter Hall and David Soskice.

The experience of introducing apprenticeships in countries without all these supporting institutions, such as the UK, is not promising. British crafts unions in the early twentieth century had an antagonistic rather than cooperative relationship with employers, leading the latter to avoid apprenticeships. British banks were reluctant to lend to manufacturers, preferring foreign investment. And unemployment insurance was substantially less generous than in Germany.

When British governments sought to improve vocational education as a way to reduce inequality in the 1960s, again in the 1990s and in the early 2000s, each time they ran up against a lack of interest from employers, suspicion from students and a school system that was not able to deliver training valued in the workplace. And so, over the years, rather than being the path to equality, British vocational training became viewed as a dead end. And that means reform requires much more than simply introducing apprenticeships.

But such changes would have to be epochal. When the UK Labour politician Ed Miliband sought to push Britain towards the German model in his 2015 election campaign, the very creator of 'varieties of capitalism', David Soskice, suggested a wholesale shift like this wasn't feasible and that the UK had to accept it was 'much more like the US' and head in that direction instead.

How can we escape the equality trap? Solutions to the equality trap can't be piecemeal. If the natural tendency of capitalism is to ever-greater accumulation, then our politics has to push steadily back, without tipping into expropriation. We will need to build stable institutions that can withstand the flows of the electoral cycle.

The 'predistribution' agenda advocates both the regulatory powers of competition and financial protection agencies to push down profit margins and support for organized labour to push up wages. This means giving up some of our equal economic rights – regulation prevents companies from charging whatever is profitable, unions prevent workers from cutting individual deals. But this is operating within the spirit of the free market to compress the gap between rich and poor. And institutions such as trade unions can help support the kinds of vocational-education systems that thrive in Continental Europe. The notably lower levels of earnings inequality in countries such as Sweden and Denmark, with their strong regulatory bodies and trade unions, suggests one route out of the equality trap.

But we have also seen that the real differences in inequality across countries come *after* the tax system has intervened. To lower inequality in people's living standards, we need robust and transparent tax systems. We are unlikely to return to the days of 90 per cent income tax rates of the 1960s – nor is that obviously wise. So to deal with rising inequality, we would do better to turn our focus to wealth, where disparities remain perniciously high. This means designing wealth taxes that don't spook average voters who are unlikely to pay them. And it may mean international cooperation to prevent billionaires simply shifting jurisdictions.

Escaping the equality trap also requires us to take seriously the norms held by most citizens of capitalist democracies. Taxation is rarely popular, and in particular people resent the idea of double taxation and effort going unrewarded, so focusing wealth taxes on windfalls will be most effective. Norms about gender roles will shape the effectiveness of well-meaning parental-leave policies. Shifting employers' expectations about men taking their full parental leave could be as effective as legislating for it.

Finally, norms about education also matter. If the beneficiaries of elite education view their status as entirely meritocratic, ignoring the advantages that helped them acquire it, we may end up with educational divides replacing previous class divides. If we want equality and efficiency, we need to develop education systems that don't simply send half of school-leavers to university and abandon the rest.

PART III
Solidarity

We only care about solidarity when we need it ourselves

9. Obamacare: Saturday, 20 March 2010, Washington DC

Congressman and civil rights hero John Lewis walked towards the US Capitol in the final days of debate over the Affordable Care Act, soon to become known as Obamacare. To the horror of Lewis, and fellow African American congressmen André Carson and Emanuel Cleaver, crowds gathered nearby began throwing racial slurs at them. Cleaver was spat at. Representative James Clyburn, the third-ranking member of the House, noted that 'I heard people saying things today that I have not heard since March 15, 1960, when I was marching to try to get off the back of a bus.' It was fifty years later. The crowds of protestors weren't castigating a civil rights bill. They were racially abusing politicians voting for a modest healthcare bill.

From the perspective of most citizens of other wealthy countries, the vicious politics around healthcare in America seems, to put it bluntly, insane. At the start of 2010, the United States had by far the most minimal public provision of healthcare of any rich country. I say 'provision' because American public spending on healthcare was not particularly low. The United States government spent on average $3,857 per person per year on healthcare, a little more than Canada, France, Germany, Sweden and the United Kingdom. But all those countries covered 100 per cent of their residents. By contrast, in America in 2010 over 18 per cent of people were uninsured: forty-eight million citizens.

What's more, the $3,857 per person was just public money. The total amount spent per person in the American healthcare system was just under $8,000. In other words, the public spending that failed to cover a fifth of Americans was still less than one in two dollars spent on health in America.

At the start of 2010, the American healthcare system had two main problems: it was incredibly expensive and it didn't cover everyone.

American healthcare was a byzantine patchwork of different systems. Unlike most other rich countries, in the early post-war era
America never developed a universal public healthcare policy. There
was neither direct public provision, as in the British National Health
Service, nor public insurance of private medicine, as in Canada.

Instead, most Americans paid their healthcare costs privately. Or,
rather, their employers did. Americans are unusually dependent on
employer-provided health insurance. In the 1930s most people had
paid doctors directly. Health insurance was usually 'sickness insurance' to cover lost earnings, not to cover hospital and doctors' fees.
But by the 1940s commercial health insurance providers had emerged
and were allowed to choose who to insure – which meant they preferred to insure the least-sick people. This foreshadowed the perverse
structure of today's American healthcare system, where sick people
often find it hardest to get treatment.

A crucial 'founding moment' in American healthcare came in 1954
when the federal government made employer-provided health insurance tax-exempt. Employers piled into the 'group health insurance'
market, where insurers pooled together risks across large groups of
people, making it cheaper than individual insurance. Employer-
provided insurance was a much better deal than buying it on your
own. So most Americans became reliant on their employer for their
healthcare, and it became part of their overall compensation package.
If you weren't employed or were self-employed you were thrown
into a fierce, expensive private-insurance market. In that case, you
might just forgo insurance, since it cost so much.

Government had got into the healthcare game through the back
door: it was giving up tax revenue by exempting health insurance
costs. As healthcare costs rose over the decades in everything from
medical technology to doctors' salaries, it created a black hole for the
US Treasury. Since the users of healthcare – everyday employees –
were shielded from the rising costs because employers provided health
insurance, there were few constraints on demand. America became an
ever-greater healthcare consumer, with 'concierge healthcare' and
'Cadillac medical plans'. Overall spending on healthcare rose from
around 5 per cent of national income in 1960 to 18 per cent today.

What about people who no longer had employers – the retired and the unemployed? Lyndon Johnson had their backs in 1965 with the creation of Medicare, for the elderly, and Medicaid, for the poor. These programmes still worked with private doctors and hospitals but provided public subsidies. Medicare became very politically popular and expanded from hospital care to outpatient care to prescription drugs over the decades. Medicaid, on the other hand, as a programme for the poor, became politically stigmatized, and was implemented in partnership with US states, many of whom provided it very meagrely, particularly to ethnic minorities.

So this was the system that President Barack Obama and congressional Democrats were trying to reform in 2010. They weren't the first. Senator Teddy Kennedy tried to pass universal national health insurance in the 1970s. President Nixon promoted a more restricted but still generous plan. To no avail. The Clinton administration had a new attempt two decades later, led by the First Lady, Hillary Clinton, only to have the plan pilloried as 'Hillarycare'. And that last failure had left Democrats uneasy about future attempts.

Why was it so hard to reform US healthcare? The proposals of the Affordable Care Act were hardly revolutionary. The main additions were a mass expansion of Medicaid subsidized by the federal government; the regulation of the individual health insurance market to guarantee coverage of pre-existing conditions and limit expenses; and the creation of an individual mandate requiring all Americans to buy health insurance or pay a tax penalty. Even so, a decade after the Act passed in 2010, 8.6 per cent of the US population didn't have health insurance at any point in 2020.

Contrast this with healthcare in other comparable countries. The British have the National Health Service, where doctors are employed by, and hospitals run by, the state, with universal coverage and no co-payments, and costing just over 8 per cent of national income – half of what Americans spend in total on health. Or Canada, where all citizens are entitled to publicly provided insurance and doctors and hospitals are a mix of private, non-profit and public bodies. Or France, where citizens must pay health insurance premiums to non-profit insurers, doctors are private and the government reimburses most of the costs. There are many ways to get to universal health insurance – some, like France, not enormously different from the US. So how was the response to the baby steps of the Affordable Care Act?

The reaction of much of the public was not encouraging. The newly formed Tea Party movement was dead against it. Recent vice-presidential candidate Governor Sarah Palin claimed the act would introduce 'death panels' that would decide on citizens' access to life-saving healthcare like some kangaroo court. Confusingly, many citizens appeared to think the ACA was an attack on Medicare – President Obama bemusedly noted. 'I got a letter the other day from a woman. She said, "I don't want government-run health care. I don't want socialized medicine. And don't touch my Medicare." ' But Medicare is, of course, publicly funded.

The reason even a moderate reform like Obamacare was so contro-versial was because it set off the solidarity trap: *we only care about solidarity when we need it ourselves.* US politics was failing to bring together those who needed health today and those who might need it tomorrow.

Obamacare tried to resolve the solidarity trap by compelling people to buy health insurance – the so-called individual mandate. But the mandate was unpopular. People who were currently well thought, I'm healthy. I won't get sick. Why should I be forced to buy this insurance I don't need? In good times, people didn't want to pay for people currently in bad times. And they weren't going to worry about what would happen to them in bad times, not even if they had to pay a tax penalty for failing to buy insurance.

The mandate to buy health insurance had been in the bill as a solu-tion to a classic problem in healthcare – adverse selection: people who most want to buy insurance are those with the worst risks. But if insurers are only selling to people with bad risks, then insurance can't work. You need good risks to compensate. Obamacare forced insurance companies to accept the bad risks through 'guaranteed issue' of insurance. Hence a mandate was needed to compel the good risks to join to prevent bankrupting the insurance industry. You can see the tension here between the individual self-interest of low-risk people – don't bother paying for insurance – and the collective logic of trying to provide universal coverage.

People were also confused by American healthcare. They thought of new public spending on healthcare as going to 'those people' – the lazy, indigent and feckless – while convinced that similar public spending on Medicare was somehow meritorious. The fact that so much government healthcare spending was channelled through the employer health insurance tax deduction made it even harder for people to connect what they wanted with what the government actually did. My company pays for this, they thought, why does the government need to get involved? But, of course, the government was subsidizing employer-provided health, just through the opaque tax system.

And, to take us back to the start of our story, there were some particularly ignoble motivations connected to racial politics. Political scientists have long known that creating solidarity across ethnic groups is challenging since many members of the ethnic majority either prefer to spend on themselves or actively oppose spending public money on ethnic minorities. Many American social programmes have become associated with racial minorities and stigmatized as a result – from food stamps to welfare payments.

The Medicaid expansion in 2010 followed similar lines. Although the ACA had expanded access to Medicaid, the Supreme Court ruled this should not be compulsory. The pattern of states who chose to refuse the federal subsidy was telling. By the summer of 2021, only twelve states remained opted out; eight of them were old members of the Confederacy in the Deep South. Whereas around 75 per cent of African Americans supported Medicare expansion in almost every state of the union, white opinion varied dramatically, being particularly low in Deep South states such as Alabama, Louisiana and Mississippi. America's racial politics still poisoned the possibility of universal healthcare. Solidarity from one American to another was hard to find.

10. What is Solidarity?

Life is unfair. Some people get sick and lose their health and liveli-hood. When factories shut, some people lose their jobs. Some people are born into poverty and attend failing schools. We recognize that the luck of the draw – in health, where you work and who your fam-ily is – shapes your life. We crave some kind of security, some protection against the vicissitudes of fortune. But how? And who from?

One hundred years ago, for most of us, that answer was family, and failing that you were on your own. Today, we rely on the state. The state insures us, protects us, educates us, heals us – but it's only able to do that because we all pitch in for each other by paying taxes. And yet, what the state should do for us is the topic of endless polit-ical debate. We want to be there for each other. Until we don't. We desire solidarity but we don't adequately fund it. Our politics fails us when we can't bridge this gap. We fall into the solidarity trap – *we only care about solidarity when we need it ourselves.*

What is solidarity? The term comes from Emile Durkheim, who sought to explain how communities were bound together both in the past and in his rapidly industrializing nineteenth-century France. Solidarity is 'common feeling' – a sense of shared fortunes among a community. We see it when the fortunate help the unfortunate, poor, ill and elderly in society. Durkheim's challenge, and ours, was how to transfer the social ties and mutual aid that developed over centuries in small rural villages to our anonymous, urban modern world.

Solidarity is a form of charity, or insurance, among people in the same community. Most people agree today that communities have responsibilities for their less fortunate members. But people will dif-fer on whether they think the state or society at large should be responsible for putting solidarity into practice. And, if the state does get involved, what kinds of policies best promote solidarity.

Let's be more concrete. What kinds of policies or aid are we talk-ing about? The most basic and historically long-lived is aid to the poor. In most religions this is the charitable act of 'almsgiving'. In modern states, this is often called 'welfare'. While this is where soli-darity began, most money transferred to people today now goes not to the poor, but to people who have left their time in employment either permanently – through retirement – or temporarily – through unemployment or sickness. This leads to old-age pensions, unemploy-ment insurance and sickness/disability benefits. Finally, we have the kind of solidarity that is provided 'in kind' as opposed to 'in cash'. The most obvious examples are healthcare and education, but we also have modern services such as job training or day care. Altogether, these different forms of solidarity make up what we know as the 'welfare state'.

This list moves from types of solidarity where the recipient is granted something they otherwise could never afford – long-term poverty relief – to systems where people could theoretically save pri-vately in advance – pensions or unemployment insurance – to services where people could theoretically, and often do, pay entirely privately – health, education, childcare.

Politics differs sharply across these kinds of solidarity. People might not want to pay for poverty relief because they think they'll never need it, whereas they might not want to pay for other people's healthcare or childcare because they are already paying for their own or they don't currently need it. But at each step we trigger the soli-darity trap: people only care about solidarity when they need it themselves.

The solidarity trap is pervasive because solidarity costs money. This could come from completely private charity or full public insurance. In both cases, the fortunate are asked to provide resources to the less well-off. But the degree of compulsion and the amount demanded are rather different. Our contemporary discussions about solidarity see us agreeing that helping the unfortunate is a good idea in principle. But then debating vigorously how or if the state should do so.

At one extreme we have the view that the state should 'stay out of the solidarity business'. Solidarity is an individual responsibility, motivated by religious or moral principles, and is found in voluntary charitable donations and almsgiving. This might be organized through churches or charities, or *in extremis* purely through individual acts of altruism.

At the other extreme we have the position that almost all individual differences in fortune – be they economic, social or health-based – are essentially arbitrary and should be compensated for by the state. The state becomes a giant insurance agency, collecting premiums and disbursing payouts.

Superficially, we might expect that social insurance like this is disliked by the rich and supported by the poor because taxes fall on the former. And certainly in surveys poorer citizens tend to be more supportive of pensions and unemployment insurance, and so forth. But it's complex. The richer you are the further you have to fall, so you might want to buy more insurance. That's how life insurance works. If state-provided pensions or unemployment benefits are tied to income, then wealthier people get more back when they retire or lose their job. That means, in sharp contrast to the equality trap, the rich might actually be fans of public spending on social insurance, if they have risky jobs.

Beyond charity for the poor, or social insurance against risk, there is an argument commonly made for something called 'decommodification'. It's an ugly word but it's useful. It means detaching people's welfare from their experience in the labour market, where they are treated by companies as a commodity, with a wage that depends on how valuable firms think they are. A large public welfare state can narrow the gap between the lives people would experience if they were left to the whims of the market and what would happen if everyone had the same salaries. Hence policies that promote solidarity can also promote equality. But that also means we can't detach the solidarity trap from the troubles described earlier with the equality trap: very high taxes might discourage work or even lead to emigration.

Solidarity in most wealthy countries today is provided through a mix of institutions that correspond to both ends of this debate. Catholic hospitals, Anglican schools and Islamic *waqfs* all coexist with their publicly run counterparts. That said, in most wealthy countries in the modern world public money provides the lion's share of spending on solidarity.

Let's get a clearer view of how much countries spend. Social spending as a percentage of national income is generally lower in poorer countries – the Mexican government spends just 7.5 per cent of national income on social spending. But among the world's wealthiest countries there's ample variation – France spends almost a third of national income on social spending, while Ireland spends less than half that. Countries also seem to cluster in groups – the English-speaking countries have lower government spending on social services (between 15 and 20 per cent of GDP), whereas the Scandinavians are big spenders (25 per cent of GDP or over).

What explains these differences? We've already seen national income matters. But among the wealthiest countries some are also more reliant on private spending on solidarity. Realistically, though, charity can only make up a small share of national spending – the United States is number one by spending just under 1.5 per cent of national income on charity. The real differences come from how welfare states are structured.

First off, we have differences in *who* gets solidarity. Some welfare state programmes are universal. Everyone who's a citizen can access the policy. Others are means-tested and targeted at the poor or needy. The latter sound like effectively targeted charity. But policies only the poor receive are often poor policies – they lack political support and are easy to weaken. Since most people don't receive means-tested benefits, this creates general disgruntlement with paying taxes but not receiving benefits. What's more, the people who do receive the benefits are often viewed as undeserving, lazy or worse. Such programmes can be stigmatizing. There's a trade-off between wanting solidarity with those most in need and the political reality that such schemes can prove very unpopular.

Second, we have differences in the overall generosity of a welfare policy – this is the question of *how much*. Most countries have a universal public pension scheme. But they vary greatly in how generous – and hence how expensive – they are. The UK state pension only replaces just over 28 per cent of an average earner's income at retirement, whereas even in Canada and the USA they would receive around 50 per cent, and in Austria almost 90 per cent. I should have moved to Austria . . . People in the UK typically have occupational or private pensions that make up this gap. But that is in response to the low generosity of the British state.

Generosity also varies widely in how long people can claim unemployment benefits. In Belgium, people can claim unemployment insurance indefinitely in principle (initially at 65 per cent of income). In Sweden, unemployment benefits are a generous percentage of income (80 per cent) but limited to 300 days. And in the UK the unemployed receive a low flat payment for just 182 days.

Finally, welfare state policies differ in *how variable* they are. In some countries, everyone who receives a policy gets exactly the same thing. We call these programmes 'uniform'. A good example is the British National Health Service (NHS). Every British citizen has the same entitlement to the same publicly provided healthcare at the same upfront cost of . . . nothing. No matter their wealth, everyone queues up – which British people love doing, of course – in the same order. When the former Prime Minister Boris Johnson almost died after contracting COVID-19 in 2020, he was not treated by a private surgeon, though he almost certainly could have afforded one. Instead, he was treated at the NHS-run St Thomas' Hospital by NHS-employed staff.

By contrast, many other policies provide benefits that are proportional to the amount you pay in. The US pensions system, Social Security, works in this fashion. The size of the pension you receive in the end depends on the amount of your contributions: not simply the number of years but the amount of money you contributed. So people with higher incomes get better pensions. That's the way that pensions systems and unemployment insurance generally work in Continental Europe. What you get back depends on what you put in. Although such countries often have superficially very large amounts of public social spending, this doesn't mean the chief beneficiaries are the poor. A lot of social spending is going to replace the higher incomes of middle-class people when they become unemployed or retire.

The final thing we need to think about with any policy, be it targeted or universal, meagre or generous, proportional or uniform, is the borders we draw around who deserves our solidarity – and who doesn't. Every policy we have spoken about so far is a national one. The recipients are citizens or permanent residents. Sometimes immigrants are permitted to access services (usually education, often pensions they have paid into), sometimes not (unemployment insurance and aid to the poor). Sometimes residents who have moved abroad can receive benefits from their home country (pensions), but typically not. Solidarity is hard to achieve across diverse groups in the same country. Extending it beyond our borders is harder still.

The history of solidarity

Today we live in a world where the state cares for us from birth to death, often quite literally. We are born in publicly run (or subsidized) hospitals, shepherded into this world by publicly trained midwives and doctors. Most of us attend publicly funded schools and perhaps universities. When we get sick, we're back in those publicly supported hospitals, or at home receiving publicly mandated sickness pay. When we lose our jobs, we claim public unemployment cheques or disability payments. And when we retire, we draw on our publicly provided pensions.

Solidarity doesn't come from nowhere – we also contribute to each of these services. Throughout our lives we pay general income taxes and sales taxes that keep the state flush with the cash it needs to pay for these transfers. We squirrel away funds into national insurance schemes, tied to our social security numbers, building up a pot of money tied to us. We are all both givers and receivers of solidarity through the state. We might want to pay for more or less of it. But no one in a modern society is truly independent of it. We are all engaged in the securing of solidarity.

But this is a recent phenomenon. Picture yourself as a peasant in seventeenth-century Europe. Growing up, you would have been set to work as soon as you could scare birds, feed the pigs or gather wheat. You would have entered adulthood, and died, illiterate. If you had become sick, you would have recovered naturally, or died. If the harvest failed and you became destitute, you might have received alms from the church, perhaps enough to keep you alive. Or you could have chanced your arm, broken your feudal obligations, and left your village for opportunities elsewhere, or perhaps a life of banditry. Had you lived in the growing towns you might have had better luck, become apprenticed to a local craftsman, perhaps lived in an almshouse if destitute and unable to work. But you too would have been reliant on the erratic charity of friends, family and the church.

Our world of all-pervading public solidarity is a remarkably new one, just a few generations old. Birth, childhood, sickness, death – these destined staging points of life – were traditionally matters for the family or the church. Of course, in many ways they still are – just with the gaze of the government hovering eagerly over their shoulder. But until the late nineteenth century, at the very earliest, the state was not in the business of securing its citizens' welfare. How did we then get to today's solidaristic state? And what does this journey tell us about why it's often so hard to sustain?

The solidarity trap emerges because people only demand solidarity when they need it; when they think they will be the core beneficiary. In the premodern world that was difficult to achieve. Solidarity is hard to provide when societies are split between antagonistic ethnic or religious groups. Or when people live predictable lives, staying in the same place or same job for their whole lives. Or when few people grow old enough to think they'll ever need support in their dotage. And, of course, people need enough money to be able to save for bad times to offer solidarity at all. Before the nineteenth century there was little demand for national public programmes of solidarity and even less ability to pay for them.

As each of these conditions changed, solidarity could expand: nation states replacing disconnected localities, creating a much larger, national 'us' that demanded solidarity. Urbanization and industrialization led to complex economies with high-risk jobs, whose workers demanded social insurance. The gradual growth of life expectancy meant a demand for old-age pensions. And the growth in economic development caused by these earlier factors created the surplus revenues to pay for these schemes.

We can think of the development of public solidarity as the culmination of the growth of the modern state. There were three key stages in this development: outward conquest, inward conquest and the solidaristic state.

Outward conquest was the capacity of a nation state to both defend itself from other states and attack them, if need be. One of the most famous aphorisms in political science is Charles Tilly's 'war made the state and the state made war'. The process of war-making required the state to develop a set of new extractive capacities – to extract military service from its population through conscription and to extract the taxes to pay for it. This was a state that protected its population but through coercion. From the Middle Ages to the Napoleonic Wars, when the state expanded bureaucracy and taxation it was to fight, and win, wars. From the very beginning solidarity was about the nation state defining an 'us' against 'them'.

Inward conquest was the period when the state began to get involved in the everyday lives of its citizens, beyond its purely military needs. From the early nineteenth century onwards, the state turned from protector to provider. It took responsibility for order (prisons and policing), knowledge (schooling and libraries) and 'health' (asylums, vaccines).

The states of this era were not building schools, asylums, prisons and so forth for entirely disinterested reasons. This was not charity. It was the state getting involved in the daily rhythms of social life – creating an ordered society. This was particularly urgent as the Industrial Revolution drew poor peasants into the chaotic cities. New risks – of crime, of disease, of workplace injury – hastened the need for solidarity.

It also meant a usurpation of the church's traditional role in governing these rites of passage – it was now the government that dictated the rules of behaviour, the learning of children and the health of the citizenry. Doing so would help develop a single unified nation – the inhabitants of far-flung regions, speaking distinct dialects, would be bound into the central state. Where the eighteenth-century state had set apart 'us' from 'them', the nineteenth-century state, challenged by urbanization and industrialization, needed to bind its citizens together – it needed to create a more coherent 'us'.

The era of inward conquest can be seen as the beginnings of the state's dabbling with solidarity. Schools might not yet have been universal, but they began to include children whose parents could never have afforded to educate them. Prisons and policing may have stiffened the coercive hand of the state, but they also made day-to-day life more peaceful and predictable for citizens. But it was a double-edged sword – the more the state provided, the more citizens would expect from it. Authority led step by step to accountability. As citizens faced the common risks of modern urban life, demand grew from the public to shield them from uncertainty. And the growing wealth of the late nineteenth and early twentieth centuries meant there were enough resources to begin providing this.

By the start of the twentieth century, the solidaristic state had emerged. A key moment was the creation of public pensions, workers' compensation and sickness insurance under the authoritarian Chancellor of Germany, Otto von Bismarck. While citizens worried about risk, the German state worried about disorder and binding together a nation state formed just decades earlier. Solidarity was not always about charity – here it was about defining the German nation.

Similar systems began to crop up across Europe and beyond. In England, in 1906 the Liberal government developed a series of solidaristic programmes from old-age pensions to sick pay and subsidized medical treatment to the creation of unemployment offices and unemployment insurance. In America it took the Great Depression and Franklin Roosevelt's New Deal for a similar mass expansion of the state into the solidarity business through the Social Security Act, which again founded pensions and unemployment systems.

One major area of solidarity is mostly lacking from our journey so far. Although states built asylums and trained midwives during the nineteenth century, the medical profession remained largely independent. Surgical hospitals of the type we are all intimately familiar with today did not emerge until the start of the twentieth century – because of the new 'germ theory' of disease, with its emphasis on sterile hospital environments. Even after hospitals were built it took most countries until after the Second World War to develop nationalized healthcare provision and/or insurance, in Britain's case with the founding of the National Health Service in 1948, in America's case (only partially) with Medicare and Medicaid in 1965. The conquest of health meant the solidaristic state had reached its zenith.

Common to these last extensions of the solidaristic state was that they followed shocks experienced by the population at large. The Great Depression exposed citizens to widely shared new risks – with 25 per cent unemployment, as in the USA in 1933, almost anyone could lose their job. The World Wars both solidified common national identities and pushed citizens from different regions, classes and ethnicities together. And they forced countries to develop and expand income and corporation taxes to pay for war. Once peacetime came about, that fiscal apparatus could be turned to paying for solidarity instead.

Escaping the solidarity trap was possible because individuals' desire to avoid paying for solidarity they might not need was overwhelmed by both a massive economic shock that no one could avoid and by the national feeling created by warfare. The World Wars and Great Depression set in motion today's solidaristic state. At the turn of the twentieth century, government spending on social services was typically 1 or 2 per cent of national income. By the end of the Second World War, it was approaching double digits. And by the 1960s it was expanding ever more rapidly to reach around a fifth of national income in most rich countries.

Why did the solidaristic state expand so fast across the twentieth century? The state got into the business of helping society's less fortunate because society's less fortunate got into the business of electing the state. Most Western countries did not have a full male franchise until the First World War, and few had granted women the vote at all until that point. Many countries had banned or restricted trade unions through the nineteenth century.

Once the full population could both vote and organize, the democratic masses set their sights on solidarity. This meant the construction of our modern welfare states was deeply political. Ultimately, it meant taxing wealthier citizens to free poorer ones from the tyranny of the market – insuring them against unemployment, ill-health and old age.

Early welfare states in countries from Germany to Britain to America initially involved transferring money to people temporarily or permanently out of the labour market. These reforms were backed by trade unions, who recognized that privately organized 'mutual societies' could help the occasional unfortunate but were not viable when large swathes of workers were made unemployed by the vagaries of the business cycle. Only the government was large enough for this kind of insurance: social insurance.

Although all wealthy countries ended up spending large amounts on social insurance by the late twentieth century, the politics of social insurance played out in strikingly different ways. In some cases, such as the development of unemployment insurance in Britain, the policies were put into place by more-charitable liberal parties, as programmes aimed at the 'deserving poor'. In these cases, they were limited in scope and means-tested – 'safety net' as opposed to universal social insurance. Such programmes may have been well-meaning but they were also politically vulnerable as wealthier citizens paid, but didn't receive, benefits.

In Sweden and Denmark, by contrast, social democratic parties developed mass social insurance schemes, intended to encompass the broader working population, and consequently relying on much higher taxes. These parties formed so-called 'red–green' coalitions with farmers' parties to embed a universal system. Universalism was an effective way to buy the middle class into the welfare state since social insurance would benefit them as well.

Perhaps the most surprising example was the aforementioned creation of the German welfare state by Otto von Bismarck in the late nineteenth century. Social scientists still refer to many Continental European welfare states as 'Bismarckian'. Why was the Iron Chancellor responsible for German unemployment and sickness insurance? For Bismarck, such policies were a way to keep workers away from the threat of socialism, and to buy them into supporting the German Empire. The design of such systems was also conservative in nature – benefits were proportional to incomes, so wealthier people would receive higher levels of social insurance, a feature that the German welfare state retains today.

Solidarity takes quite different shapes across the industrialized world – a legacy of a century of distinct political trajectories. Still, in all countries the welfare state and who pays for it remains highly contentious, not least because of the dilemmas of the solidarity trap. Let's see how the trap plays out and what we can do about it.

11. The Solidarity Trap

Why is it so hard to care for each other? Much of our political polarization today is about the efforts we make to provide for each other. Political parties claim to value solidarity but have very different philosophies about how it should be provided. By families, churches and the community? Or by the state? In meagre amounts as a last resort? Or as a generous social right owed to all citizens?

Even when we agree we want a certain type of solidarity we might differ on who we think should receive it, or whether we really want to pay for it. Our politics fails because when we try and look after each other, we quickly run into the solidarity trap: *we only care about solidarity when we need it ourselves.*

Our chief problem is that we can't know our whole life story ahead of time. We don't know when we might be in trouble – out of work or out of sorts – and in need of public support. Thanks to optimism bias, many of us imagine we're unlikely to ever need help. But most of us will. And across our whole lifetimes it's often hard to know if we'll be a net contributor – a 'taker' or a 'maker'. Everyone would always like to have bought insurance after bad things have actually happened. But it can be harder to convince people to fix the roof while the sun is shining.

The boundaries of solidarity are another dilemma. Not everybody sees the same 'us'. Ethnic, religious, linguistic and national differences can be harsh limits to people's conceptions of solidarity. In extreme cases, people's animus towards the 'other' may prevent them from supporting policies that would directly benefit them.

Finally, many solidaristic policies are hard to create and enforce because we fundamentally lack information about our fellow citizens. Even our seemingly all-powerful states cannot really understand how 'risky' different people are – in terms of how likely they are to lose their job. On top of this, the people who we want to offer solidarity are moving targets. People respond to policies in ways that benefit themselves individually. So they may subvert the very aims of our solidaristic policies. Let's now turn to explore the uneasy contours of the solidarity trap.

Solidarity across time

The most basic dilemma of the solidarity trap is uncertainty about the future. When life is going well, we forget that there is a shadowy 'other' who might benefit from solidarity. You. Just in the future. Future You might have lost a secure job. Future You might get sick or develop cancer. Future You cannot be protected for ever against the whims of fate. So who is going to look out for Future You? Current You?

If we could know for sure the full journey of our lives, from cradle to grave, if we knew how much we would earn and what needs we would have at each point, then we could balance our spending and saving across our life. We could 'self-insure' by pre-saving during happy times to make up for the hardships of hard times. Make your good times less good and your bad times less bad. Dull perhaps, but sensible. But we cannot know whether we will be hale and healthy, or fragile and sickly, tomorrow. So, it's not possible to balance our saving and spending perfectly to keep ourselves perfectly and stably content. Our uncertainty about how our lives will go prevents us from fully self-insuring.

First, there are periods in people's lives when, although they will be richer in the future, they cannot access those resources today. If you could borrow while young and repay once old that would solve the problem. But you need to find someone to lend money to you. And in the absence of the book of your life that sets out with certainty what riches Future You will earn, Currently Poor You may have difficulty convincing a bank to lend to you.

This is the problem of credit constraints. If for some reason the bank is unwilling to lend you money – even though you are likely to repay it in the future – then your great plans may come to naught.

This is an inefficient outcome – if people cannot access money to make investments they could pay back later, then we are all poorer off. But you can see it from the perspective of the bank.

Many solidaristic aspects of the welfare state resolve credit constraints. The most obvious is higher education. Many people would be unable to convince banks to provide funding for education when the 'return on investment' was at least a decade hence. A bank cannot hold your education as collateral; that would mean imprisoning you in the vault. Hence, even in the wealthiest countries, governments subsidize university loans. Other forms of public spending follow a similar principle: day care, job training, parental-leave policies, even housing deposits. The government steps in to fund services or investments that people find impossible to pay up front.

Second, we have the problem of catastrophic risk. While credit constraints are about the difficulty of matching up current hard times to future good times, catastrophic risk is the opposite problem. Things are currently fine and will probably be fine in the future. But what if they're not fine? What if things are really, really bad in the future? So bad that it's impossible to save and prepare on your own?

Life-changing illness, permanent unemployment, and destitution cannot be self-insured against. Only the very richest can save the hundreds of thousands of pounds or dollars that lengthy cancer treatment or several years out of work might cost. Most people cannot. In the absence of support, they must suffer. You might wonder why they can't simply purchase private insurance against these risks, as we do against catastrophes such as our homes burning down.

The problem is some risks are uninsurable on private markets, for two reasons: adverse selection and moral hazard. Adverse selection occurs when the people keenest to buy insurance are also those who face the biggest risks of something going wrong. Unless insurers can figure out who these people are – which, to be fair, they are ruthlessly keen on doing – they face insuring only bad risks. Which defeats the point of insurance as a way of pooling risk. Moral hazard is the idea that people might behave riskily once you insure them. As an example, if I offered you permanent private unemployment insurance you might think, great, now's the time to start a risky career I've always dreamed of as a supermodel, actor or stuntman. And I would wisely decline to offer you that insurance.

When things can't be insured privately, the state steps in. Even the American healthcare system – warts and all – covered COVID treatment for the uninsured, at the height of the pandemic. Very few wealthy countries will tolerate people entering complete destitution if out of work – they provide some form of unemployment or disability insurance, though it may vary dramatically in its generosity. To imagine what the absence of state support might look like, think about the experience of non-documented immigrants who can't find work and don't qualify for benefits – an endless tour of friends' sofas and church soup kitchens.

Given that each of us faces both good times and bad, you might think we would internalize this and cast our ballots for politicians who pursue a stable policy that protects us when misfortune strikes. But people don't always think like this. Because miserable me tomorrow doesn't exist today and might never. And miserable me in the past can't be helped anyway.

There is a temptation we all face to pay as little tax as possible when things are going well, on the assumption that bad times won't come, or at least they won't come for us. People may suffer from an 'optimism bias' – downplaying the likelihood or cost of catastrophic outcomes. And by the time you are paying a lot of taxes, you've already made it, and you don't need to worry about credit constraints. So for many people present good fortune outweighs future or past ill-fortune. When things are going well, people may think that taxes only go to pay for welfare for the permanently poor, feckless or undeserving.

The solidarity trap is pervasive and tempting when you're on the up. Well-to-do taxpayers often believe that they are always on the wrong side of the tax and transfer system that supports public solidarity. But, surprisingly, that's not generally the case, at least for most people. As the late John Hills argued, there isn't actually an 'us' and 'them'. Just 'us' in the past and in the future.

Hills looked at the welfare system as it works in the United Kingdom. Other than having a universal healthcare system, the UK has ungenerous public spending, with meagre public pensions and unemployment insurance. What's more, a lot of public spending in the UK is 'means-tested' – it is targeted at poorer citizens. From the perspective of a fifty-something wealthy Brit, it might seem that the British welfare system doesn't help people like them. They may not be receiving much from it today.

But what is true today may be false across someone's lifetime. A snapshot of taxes and spending will almost always show that the currently rich spend a large amount on taxes and the currently poor receive a large amount of spending. However, this is misleading. Except for the richest few per cent in the economy, almost everyone else gets back from the state roughly what they put in.

That's for a few reasons. First, people who are currently rich are likely to be poorer in the future when they retire, at which point they will be highly dependent on the state for not only pensions but much higher healthcare costs. Second, many people who are currently rich benefited greatly from free public education as children, and in the case of Gen Xers and older also from free university education (he says wistfully, looking at his own children). Third, some benefits are proportional, either to income (furlough payments, parental-leave pay) or years of work (pensions). Most of us live double lives – sometimes we're makers, other times we're takers. But we don't always remember that when we come to vote.

What makes the solidarity trap worse is that governments face a similar dilemma to you and me. Developing sustainable pensions systems or effective public education and infrastructure also involves a trade-off between now and the future. Politicians have to raise taxes in the present to pay for a reformed system, the benefits of which will only appear in the future, when the politician is liable to be out of office. In an ideal world, governments would make sacrifices during national good times that would come to fruition when the country goes through hard times. But if a rival political party can take the credit for future policies and the party currently governing takes the hit for present taxes, you can see why it's hard to make long-term public investments. And if the democracy trap kicks in – through high levels of political polarization – making solidaristic policy for the long haul becomes even harder.

A classic example of how hard it is for governments to pay costs in the present and put off benefits is the creation of the US public-pensions system, Social Security, during the New Deal. The bill that initially passed in 1935 mandated Social Security contributions by individual taxpayers and businesses in 1937 but no benefits until 1942. Even then, pension benefits would be minimal and not rise to their maximum until the 1980s. The idea was to build up a large pool of reserves so that the programme could be self-sustaining even as life expectancy increased. The policy's designers also wanted to avoid the typical electoral use of benefits by politicians seeking to win elections, as had happened with Civil War pensions. All very worthy. How on earth did they convince President Franklin Delano Roosevelt, who would have elections to win, that voters should pay for five years before anyone would benefit?

FDR had the advantage of a Democratic supermajority in the Senate and House, one that was due to his popularity – so he was politically insulated and at little electoral risk. And the new contributions wouldn't kick in until after the 1936 presidential election. Even with this political buffer, the plan could not hold. Following a recession in 1937, the Republicans, who vehemently opposed the New Deal, made major gains in the 1938 midterm elections. By 1939 higher contribution rates had been postponed and the benefits brought forward two years. In other words, the costs were put off and the payouts hurried up. Here we see the fragility of political promises about long-term investment. When the political environment shifts, so too can those promises.

At least the Democrats were still in office when the first Social Security cheques rolled out and could garner some of the political benefits of the policy. Protecting Social Security became an important part of the Democrats' electoral offer, and by the 1950s the Republican President, Dwight Eisenhower, had largely accepted the policy. Other investment policies can come to fruition decades after the political party that introduced them has left office. The UK Labour government led by Tony Blair developed the idea of 'baby bonds' in its 2001 general election manifesto – each newborn would receive a voucher for £250 at birth and again at age seven, to be accessible only after turning eighteen. These amounts were doubled for low-income children. Baby bonds were intended to reduce wealth inequalities, provide resources for credit-constrained young people, and introduce them to the merits of savings and investment.

Very well intentioned. But it took until 2005 to introduce the policy, and once Labour had lost office in 2010, its Conservative–Liberal successors immediately abandoned it. It took until 2020 for the very first recipients of baby bonds to hit eighteen and open their accounts. At which point, the UK was onto its fourth Prime Minister after Tony Blair. The policy may have been commendable, but it was also politically unsound – it couldn't survive a change in government and the party introducing it couldn't claim credit. Just like us, politicians can't align the present and future. And, given all the myriad challenges of the democracy trap, they too fall into the solidarity trap. Our politics will fail when we can't learn how to align our present with our future.

Solidarity across people

The 'welfare queen' is the most notorious racial trope in American debates about the size of government. In the mid 1970s, as Ronald Reagan entered the field to run (at first unsuccessfully and then very successfully) as Republican candidate for President, he drew attention to the case of Linda Taylor, a fraudster who had illegally obtained twenty-three welfare cheques. Reagan saw Taylor as symptomatic of a wider 'culture' of welfare-dependent mothers, abusing the generosity of the American public either illegally through fraud or, more insidiously, through a willingness to rely on the charity of others rather than work. While Reagan never directly mentioned Taylor's name or race (Taylor herself identified variously as black, Hispanic and Jewish), the motif of the 'welfare queen' was largely applied to African American women, and the word 'welfare' increasingly took on racialized tones.

For decades, scholars of American politics have found that US voters view their country's welfare system through a racial lens.

The word 'welfare' came to mean a very specific part of the broader welfare state – payments to poor, unemployed families. Initially this was through the Aid to Families with Dependent Children (AFDC) system, founded as part of the New Deal, the Democratic Party's grand re-envisioning of American solidarity. But this was replaced by the current Temporary Aid to Needy Families (TANF) in 1997 after President Bill Clinton – also a Democrat – promised to 'end welfare as we know it'. Over sixty years, how did 'welfare' move from a core part of the Democratic Party's agenda to an unwanted policy?

Martin Gilens argues that welfare became stigmatized because during the 1950s and 1960s the 'poor became black'. He points to an apparent paradox – the proportion of poor American citizens who were black remained steady at one third between the late 1950s and the early 1990s. Yet news media coverage of poverty in America changed dramatically: the percentage of pictures of the poor that were of black people rose from under 20 per cent in the 1950s to over 70 per cent by the mid 1970s. The proportion of black people in news coverage of the poor was double their actual representation in that group.

Why was news media coverage of poverty in America so racialized? First, there was the Great Migration of African Americans from the rural South to the industrial North and Midwest during the mid twentieth century. This meant that white Americans were unable to ignore black poverty as it moved from faraway sharecropping fields in the Mississippi Delta to the major cities of the eastern seaboard and Great Lakes.

Second, the Civil Rights movement caused long-standing American cleavages over racial segregation and oppression to resurface – culminating in the presidential candidacy of the segregationist George Wallace and the assassination of Martin Luther King.

Third, African Americans were indeed using government-provided welfare more from the 1950s onwards. But the reason was not because they had become poorer or more dependent on the state. It was because when AFDC was initially introduced, it was managed by the states. And segregationist Southern states had withheld welfare from qualifying African Americans. By the 1960s, the federal government had agreed to match state payments, bringing more states, and more African Americans, into AFDC.

These three forces – proximity, politics and policy – are at the heart of many contemporary debates about the size and role of government. Solidarity is, definitionally, support for other people. But what happens when people don't treat one another equally? What if the majority group stigmatizes the minority? In this case, other people become 'the Other'.

Ethnic politics in contemporary America has often played out along a white/black ethnic divide, with increasing importance given to Hispanic and Asian ethnicities. But group differences are not always based on race. Sometimes religion is the defining divide, as in Northern Ireland, where politics traditionally centred on the tensions between the Protestant majority and Catholic minority. Sometimes language matters, as in Swiss politics, where French-, German- or Italian-speaking is the key divide. And sometimes ethnicity matters, as in the divide between Turks and Kurds in Turkey.

Ethnic conflict is not merely about skin colour but rather about differences that people have ascribed to others often at birth (race and ethnicity) or in their childhood (language and religion). When political scientists look at the effects of ethnic diversity on solidarity, we find that diversity, however defined, appears to alter people's willingness to spend resources supporting each other.

Why would ethnic diversity reduce solidaristic spending? One reason is poorer communication – with different languages it becomes harder to understand and trust one's neighbours. It also becomes harder to police bad behaviour – ethnic in-groups can potentially sanction one another for cheating and fraud, which becomes harder with many diverse groups. To give an example, in Kenyan primary schools public fundraising is markedly higher in ethnically homogeneous communities, where non-contributors can be more effectively shamed.

But let's be blunt and turn from in-group behaviour to attitudes towards ethnic out-groups. A simple reason that ethnic diversity seems to produce weaker solidarity is that sometimes different ethnic groups dislike one another. They may see each other as competing for the same public spending or have an active distaste for 'other' people receiving solidarity, regardless of whether they themselves receive it.

Where ethnic groups differ greatly in terms of their relative wealth, this anti-out-group attitude intensifies. Political scientists have found it is not ethnic diversity alone that dictates how much public solidarity goes round but rather the differences between ethnic groups in terms of their average income. Where there is a rich ethnic majority and a poor ethnic minority, solidarity for the poor in the form of public spending breaks down, as now money must cross both the class and the ethnic divide. This is most pronounced in Latin American countries, where the class structure is highly racialized. By contrast, where societies are ethnically diverse, but the different ethnicities are similarly wealthy, as in, for example, Estonia and Switzerland, there's little sign that public spending is lower.

Ethnic tensions over solidarity are heightened when we look at solidarity provided in kind rather than in cash. Public housing, schooling, hospital appointments and so forth are limited in supply. New groups of beneficiaries can place strain on the system. If those new groups happen to be immigrants or ethnically distinct, this can produce what political scientists call 'welfare chauvinism'. People demand solidarity but for them alone, not for others.

A good example is public housing. In 2003 the European Union insisted that non-EU immigrants not be excluded from public services. In Austria, where access to public housing was highly competitive, that had major political repercussions. The law change meant immigrants to Austria suddenly became eligible for public housing. Just under half of households in Vienna live in public housing, so this is a benefit that extends well into the middle class. People who anticipated getting this subsidized housing suddenly faced new competition and higher rents. And this had a political spillover, with the radical right receiving an extra five points of support in Viennese wards with high levels of public housing.

Do these findings about ethnic diversity and public spending imply that many or most people are racist? Not necessarily. Thomas

Schelling famously showed that ethnic segregation can emerge in a society that is largely non-racist. He developed a model in which individuals may be willing to live as an ethnic minority in their neighbourhood but subject to some limit, such as not being in a neighbourhood that was less than one sixth their particular ethnicity. If people can move freely, even a small individual preference for not being in a minority can quickly spill over into high levels of segregation.

Why? If a single person – perhaps unhappy with being the only person of their ethnicity in their neighbourhood – moves out, they also change the composition of the neighbourhood they move to. That, in turn, might make someone of a different ethnicity a minority in this new neighbourhood and encourage them to move. There is a 'chain reaction' as people sort into neighbourhoods that end up being highly segregated – *even if* most people were happy to be in a highly integrated neighbourhood to start. Segregation happens even though most people didn't individually desire it.

But doesn't this kind of 'structural' argument, which looks at diversity from above and abstracts people into distinct groups, veer dangerously into excusing people from their responsibility to treat people equally? It might also make differences across groups seem permanent – as if they can never be overcome and have to haunt us all to the end of the universe.

Perhaps we would do better to put responsibility where it belongs – in the heads of people who view the world through racial preferences and antagonisms. People who think about the world in a racialized way tend to see all types of policies through that lens. Political scientists call this 'ethnocentrism'. For example, when ethnocentric white people think about government help for the poor, they think it goes to black people and they become less supportive. Poorer white citizens who might benefit from welfare spending but who have ethnocentric preferences can end up opposing benefits like food stamps against their own material self-interest. And this goes both ways. Because the retirement scheme, Social Security, is associated in the American cultural mind with old white people, whites with greater ethnocentrism tend to want *more* spending on Social Security than their incomes or age would predict. Social Security is perceived as a policy for 'us' not 'them'.

Accordingly, ethnocentric poorer people will not necessarily be the great supporters of solidarity that we might predict. And, increasingly, this has led them to stop voting for the traditional left and to be attracted to populist-right parties, whose manifestos commit to excluding immigrants and outsiders from benefits. Does this mean that politics is failing, as people fail to vote for parties that would materially benefit them? Ultimately where you fall on that depends on whether you think 'cultural' voting reflects what people truly care about, or misinformation and culture wars. But, either way, it's not great news for solidarity.

If people are ethnocentric when it comes not only to immigrants but fellow citizens in their own country, what hope is there for global solidarity? Foreign aid has become increasingly politically contentious in the wealthiest countries of the world. There is a sharp split between the near consensus among political elites that foreign aid should be raised – up to a target of 0.7 per cent of national income – and mass opinion. Between 1972 and 2014 in the General Social Survey, consistently more than 60 per cent of Americans said the US spent too much on foreign aid. In terms of actual spending, the US spent only around 0.2 per cent of national income at the beginning of this period and under 0.1 per cent by the early 2000s. It is not entirely surprising the US was so far off the international target of 0.7 per cent of GDP given public opinion.

Support is higher in Europe, where foreign-aid spending is also higher, often meeting the 0.7 per cent target. About 50 per cent of Europeans support such spending but this support is never unconditional. Europeans whose individual financial circumstances have worsened are sharply less supportive of foreign aid. As we might expect, it's not only individual economic circumstances that shape attitudes to foreign aid. Attitudes to 'other people' may be just as important. People with ethnocentric views are 20 percentage points less likely to support foreign aid.

Are there ways to overcome ethnocentrism and encourage solidarity across racial divides? There just may be. But it involves heightening another identity – a shared one in the nation. National identities are often ethnic too – not least because many current countries were founded on ethnic lines, as with the former Yugoslavia. But they don't have to be. Inclusive nationalism seeks to bind all the ethnic, religious and linguistic groups within an identity that stresses solidarity within the nation. This is often easiest to do in those 'nations' that sit inside a larger country and seek to break away: Scotland and Catalonia are good examples. That kind of nationalism may, however, depend on resentment of the larger country: the UK or Spain.

Inclusive nationalism can be summoned even in the largest of countries by framing solidarity as a national issue and highlighting shared symbols. An interesting example comes from an online experiment in which Hindus in India were asked if they would like to donate to victims of a fire elsewhere in India.

Half of the respondents were given the name of a Hindu village and the other half a Muslim village. But each of those groups was also split randomly into two by whether people saw a map of India shaded in the colours of the national flag on the same webpage. This was intended to prime them to think of the nation as a whole. In the absence of the map flag, the respondents predictably preferred to share their earnings with their co-Hindus. But among those who saw the map flag, they were equally likely to give to Muslims or Hindus. And this difference was strongest among low-social-status Indians – the national prime very effectively wiped away ethnic differences among respondents who were 'low caste'.

Many people instinctively shun national symbols, thinking of them as divisive. And yet in the case of ethnic differences *within* countries, they can actually help us get towards solidarity. National political institutions and norms of national solidarity can overcome historical ingrained religious or ethnic distrust, though possibly at the cost of heightening aggressive nationalism. But there are still limits to solidarity. In the absence of a global government or 'map flag', we may be very distant from international solidarity, even when we are more generous to those at home.

Solidarity and information

Solidarity is about lifting up the unfortunate, about ensuring the community leaves no one behind. And so it depends on being able to identify who is in need of help and who is at greatest risk. But how can the state figure out who the needy are? We require a lot of information about who lives where and who needs what. And we have to prevent the targets of our solidarity from undermining or manipulating our best-laid plans.

Let's begin with the problem of getting information about citizens. There's an uneasy duality to the world we live in today. Big Tech knows a lot about us – our habits, our interests, our politics. Each time we accept cookies, we've sold off valuable information about ourselves. And that data is compiled, merged and cross-referenced with such efficiency that we find ourselves constantly creeped out by adverts appearing on the internet that seem eerily reminiscent of a discreet chat we just had with friends.

How about Big Government? Does it have the same reach as technology companies? That depends. Governments know a great deal about us through our tax codes or social security numbers. They know how much we formally earn, what government benefits we receive and what social insurance contributions we have made. They know about our family if we apply for child tax credits or parental leave. When we pass away, they know how much we left our descendants. And every decade they send us a census form asking who lives in our house.

Superficially, that's a lot of very personal information – but it has real limits. Governments know about us best in the inevitabilities of life: death and taxes. Death is hard to fake – outside plot twists in *Law and Order*. But taxes collected might not always accurately reflect taxes owed. Governments struggle to get citizens to report all their income. Even in Scandinavia, where the government has an incredible wealth of knowledge about its citizens through its 'citizen registers', the very rich are able to avoid taxation. Leaked documents from the Panama papers show the richest 0.01 per cent of households in Norway evade around a quarter of their taxes.

When the government distributes solidaristic payments – to poorer people – it would like to know whether people reporting low incomes really have low incomes. And when it collects taxes – from richer people – it would like to know whether people with high incomes are correctly reporting how much they earn. This gap between what the government knows and what's 'really' out there can undermine solidarity. If too many people claim benefits they don't 'deserve', then costs rise. If too few people pay the taxes they 'should', then revenues decline. And soon the government can't keep its solidaristic promises.

There's another even more insidious problem. How do we measure things that are simply not observable, even if we had the snoopiest of all tax agencies? Who has greater need of services? Who would benefit most from building a new park? Which school pupils would do best from a targeted intervention? Which businesses might be bankrupted by a regulatory change?

How can governments get an accurate account of public preferences? We know from our exploration of the democracy trap just how difficult it is to know what people want because they might strategically misrepresent their views. The fact that governments cannot see in our heads makes it tempting to misrepresent our own preferences or our own characteristics, in order to benefit from particular schemes.

The government might prefer, for example, only to subsidize ailing firms that have been legitimately hit by side-effects from a trade shock. But unless the government can get inside the company and explore its books, it may be hard to tell apart a company whose ill-fortune was self-inflicted and one that genuinely suffered through no fault of its own. A widespread recent example has been firms defrauding government to get hold of COVID support funds. The British government lost almost £6 billion through misrepresentation (almost 10 per cent of its overall payments). In America, one woman from Oklahoma was responsible for almost $44 million of COVID-19 relief scheme fraud.

The same applies to government policies targeted at people who have suffered from ill-fortune. Disability schemes have been a particularly contentious area. Since the early twentieth century, most industrialized countries have had some form of sickness- or injury-related benefit, often initially created to compensate people who had been injured at work. Over the decades, this has been expanded to people whose inability to work was not directly caused by work itself. But many disabilities are not easily observable, especially to distant government bureaucrats.

While governments are unlikely to bankrupt themselves by insuring bad risks, it might make programmes less politically sustainable, particularly if the public believes that welfare fraud is endemic. Although actual fraud on disability benefits in the UK amounts to around 0.3 per cent of total claims, the British public estimated over a third of such claims were fraudulent. This may be stunningly inaccurate, but, in a world where even the government finds information hard to come by, it isn't surprising. And this kind of misunderstanding poses real challenges for solidarity.

Governments also face the informational problem of moral hazard when people behave in risky ways when they think they're insured by the state against health risks or unemployment risks, and so forth. This is a common conservative critique of solidarity. With universal health insurance, the argument is made that it simply encourages poor health behaviours. If you have a National Health Service, then people will eat poorly, drink and smoke too much, and not take good care of themselves, knowing that the state will 'bail them out'.

If that were true, then we would see systematically better health behaviours from people, particularly the uninsured, in countries without universal healthcare. A quick comparison of obesity rates and general self-care in the United States and Europe should give us pause. In the USA, 37.3 per cent of the population were obese in 2016 and, despite America's fragmentary and expensive private healthcare system supposedly encouraging better health behaviours, 13 per cent of deaths could be attributed to obesity. By contrast, in Denmark and France, where all citizens are insured and the government pays the vast bulk of the expense, obesity rates were 21 per cent and 23 per cent, and the percentage of deaths attributed to obesity was just 7 per cent.

Unemployment insurance might be better grounds for the moral-hazard critique. Generous unemployment insurance in Continental Europe might mean people stay unemployed for longer, being unwilling to seek new work unless it matches their previous work conditions. Where unemployment insurance was meagre, people would have to seek work.

The moral-hazard critique of unemployment insurance is a commonly held belief as it meshes with intuitions people have about the merits of hard work. But is it accurate? It seems logical that more-generous unemployment benefits would reduce people's incentives to return to work. Yet, among wealthy countries, there is a positive relationship between the 'replacement rate' offered by benefits and overall employment. Countries such as Switzerland, Denmark and the Netherlands combine generous unemployment insurance with high employment.

There's another reason the state might want to guarantee generous unemployment insurance, *even if* it produces moral-hazard problems. And that's because people adjust their behaviour in response to government policies in good ways as well as bad. In countries with generous unemployment insurance such as Germany, Austria and Sweden, there is also a large group of blue-collar workers who have developed strong vocational skills working in high-end manufacturing. The types of skills these workers have acquired take decades to perfect and are tied very closely to specific firms and production processes. That seems like a risky investment. It's no coincidence that people are only willing to invest in these very 'specific' skills when they have the guarantee of generous unemployment insurance to fall back on. Sure, people are insured against risk, but that doesn't mean they will act in self-harming ways – they might also invest.

My colleague John Ahlquist and I ran an experiment in Oxford to see how well this argument holds up. We had people play a tedious game – moving sliders on a computer screen until they matched a given number. We made it more attractive by offering people the chance to invest some money beforehand in a 'skill' that would earn them more for every slider correctly placed. However, while they were in the lab they could be made unemployed – that meant they would have to sit and face the computer screen doing nothing for a while. So investing in the skill was risky. They might get the slider task back, but they might be offered a different task, where their investment in the skill didn't matter.

This was an attempt to mirror real-world working and unemployment risk in the lab. We at least picked up some of the mundanity of the less fun jobs I've had. The question that really interested us was what would happen if we gave people more-generous unemployment payouts during the periods of the game that they were unemployed? Would that make them more likely to make the investment in skills, as the 'specific skills' argument suggests? We found strong evidence that participants would choose to invest in the skill. Whereas only 50 per cent of people invested in the skill when they received no unemployment insurance, about three quarters did when they received 75 per cent of their previous earnings as insurance. Providing a safety net can encourage people to make costly but beneficial investments.

Moral hazard and investment are both dynamic problems. The government makes a policy and then people respond in ways that might complement it or, if you're unlucky, undermine it. That means policies intended to promote solidarity can end up weakening it.

One obvious example is attempts to get young people on the housing ladder by subsidizing first-time buyers. The British Help to Buy scheme provided a government loan of 20 per cent of the house's price to help first-time buyers put down a deposit on a newly built house. This feels like a benevolent policy aimed at improving access to housing. But it runs up immediately against the fact that house-sellers are aware of the policy. Knowing that more people can now afford houses, they can raise the price of their house cancelling out the extra amount that young buyers could afford. Affordability remains the same, young people continue to find it hard to own properties, and all the benefits have accrued to existing homeowners, who get to charge more money.

These kinds of dynamics exist across all areas of solidarity. Education policies, for example, are prey to being undermined by parents.

Because school districts are typically defined geographically and because parents can move across district borders without legal restriction, affluent parents often make sure to locate themselves in those areas that have the best-funded, or most elite, schools. Since parents may move in response to policies, this can make it very difficult for governments, local or national, to develop equalizing education policies.

The history of school bussing in the United States is a classic example, which connects closely to our earlier discussion of diversity. During the 1970s, many US school districts tried to racially integrate schools by bussing black students into white schools and vice versa. The response of a number of middle-class white parents was simply to pull their children out of the school district – either by privately educating their children or by moving house to a different district. Ultimately school segregation remained high because 'ethnocentric' parents subverted the policy to avoid their kids having to mix with those with different skin colours.

Similar patterns can occur when governments try to equalize schools along income lines. In my own work analysing education in England and Wales, I find that areas with higher house prices tend to have a very high variation in educational performance across local schools. High prices allow wealthy families to economically segregate themselves in those particular neighbourhoods with the most expensive housing and 'best' schools. Surely, though, you might think, this gives local education authorities the incentive to try to equalize across schools to prevent this kind of wealth-based segregation?

Not so fast. Middle-class parents have another card to play. Educational reforms over the past few decades in England and Wales have allowed schools to opt out of local government control. Although schools that opt out cannot keep geographic boundaries, richer parents can still limit the intake to 'people like them'. These schools are permitted non-academic selection procedures that can be gamed by cunning parents – religious preference, teaching specialties and so forth. In other words, if you can't segregate geographically, you segregate your school by other means.

Political economists call this kind of behaviour 'sorting': people will 'sort' into the types of places that have the types of taxes and public goods they want. This is, of course, anti-solidaristic. People are dividing to get what they want, rather than uniting. It reminds us of the equality trap – equal rights to move into more-expensive areas undermines equal outcomes. Whether or not it's egalitarian, it happens in a free country, so it's a basic challenge to all solidaristic policies.

Let's bring all of these informational challenges to solidarity together. First, we have the challenge of getting people to correctly state their income to determine both who gets more benefits and who pays more taxes. Next, we have the challenge of figuring out who really needs solidarity, especially when people have an incentive to misrepresent themselves. Finally, we have the dynamic challenge that we can't control how people will behave once we put a policy in place, and they may just end up subverting it. Are there ways to combat these challenges and achieve solidaristic policies? Surprisingly, there is one particularly simple solution – give the same thing to everyone. Let's see what it looks like.

12. Escaping the Solidarity Trap

Three letters have captured the imagination of reformers over the past decade – UBI. Universal Basic Income has brought together an unlikely coalition of supporters: from anti-poverty activists on the political left to Silicon Valley heavyweights on the libertarian right. And it's been experimented with across an incredible variety of geographic locations: from Oakland to Finland, Spain to Sierra Leone. It has been proposed as a solution to a litany of twenty-first-century problems: from bouncing back after COVID-19 to the replacement of workers with robots. Is UBI a miracle drug? Can it help us escape the solidarity trap?

We need to start with the abbreviation because UBI has the merit, rare among policies, of telling you what it actually is. Let's go in reverse because it's easiest to understand that way. The I (for Income) means the UBI is a cash transfer. That distinguishes it from other types of solidarity such as healthcare, food stamps and education, which are given in kind rather than in cash. Cash is easy for the government to distribute. You don't have to worry about the quality of the service provided because cash is cash.

Cash is also fungible: you can split it up and spend it on different things. There are no restrictions on what you can spend your UBI on. If you want to spend it all on fast food and alcohol, good for you. There's nothing, except the criminal justice system, stopping you from spending your UBI on illegal drugs. Of course, there's nothing, except perhaps the wisdom of age, preventing you from spending your state pension similarly. UBI is agnostic about how it's spent – for good or for ill.

The B (for Basic) means the UBI provides a baseline level of cash. It won't be enough for most people to live on. But everyone gets the same amount. That means there is no need for the government to try and figure out who deserves what. Everyone gets the same, regardless of need, merit or effort. But UBI also preserves existing inequalities. People who earned more will still earn more, plus the UBI and minus the taxes they pay. Since the amount is 'basic', it will have almost no impact for the very rich. For the very poor – they stay poorer than everyone else but now they have a chunk of cash to fall back on.

Finally, and most simply, the U (for Universal) means this is a benefit that *every* citizen in the country receives. There are no conditions to receiving a UBI. UBI is agnostic both in terms of how it is spent and how recipients behave. UBI proposals sometimes differ by whether they include children. Some proposals give a grant of money at eighteen rather than an annual flow of income. But a pure UBI goes to individuals not households (though presumably money for children is received by their parents, otherwise *Fortnite* will end up being 10 per cent of the economy). 'Citizen' does provide a restrictive element. It's easy to imagine that countries adopting a UBI might prevent recent immigrants from receiving it, partly for 'welfare chauvinist' reasons and partly to prevent mass immigration seeking access to the UBI.

The original UBI was introduced in 1974 in the Canadian province of Manitoba, where the small farming town of Dauphin allowed any family to opt unconditionally into receiving a flat annual benefit of around $14,000 in today's US dollars. Unlike a 'pure' UBI, any extra earnings that families made would be taxed at a higher rate, which meant the benefit was fully taxed away at around double its value. The pilot only lasted a couple of years, had some positive benefits on health outcomes and did not seem to reduce the hours people worked. So, broadly, the programme appeared successful. But it was also politically fragile; once the Conservative Party took control in 1979 it suspended the programme.

Since then, UBI schemes have generally been less generous, variable in funding or limited to poorer people. The Alaskan Permanent Fund gives around $1,600 annually to each permanent resident from oil revenues, but this figure jumps up and down with oil prices. The Finnish government introduced a pilot in 2015 which gave 2,000 unemployed working-age Finns around $7,500 per annum on top of their benefits and still guaranteed if they found a job. In Spain, a 2017

Barcelona pilot gave money to people in the city's poorest districts, and following COVID the government gave unconditional grants of $1,000 per month to poor families. The current panoply of UBI-like programmes is a mix of meagre, variable payments to everyone and more-generous payments to the poor.

A more ambitious UBI has been popular among a wide array of political groups: from technocrats to technologists to socialists. Well-known politicians from Andrew Yang to Jeremy Corbyn have made the case for introducing a national UBI and brought it to popular attention. These proposals are far greater in magnitude than what we've seen so far. Andrew Yang promised a purist UBI of $1,000 per month for each US citizen (called a 'freedom dividend'). The entrepreneur and CEO of Open AI, Sam Altman, has suggested that every American benefit from an 'American Equity Fund', funded by taxing companies and land at 2.5 per cent, that would pay each adult American $13,500 a year. In common is a view that UBI is more efficient and fairer than the political messiness of existing welfare programmes.

But does the UBI really help us escape the solidarity trap? Recall the problem that people experiencing good times weren't willing to pay for those going through a rough patch. A UBI is a form of consumption smoothing – you receive the same benefit from the government every year – in good times and bad times. At a minimum then, it should be there for you when times are tough.

What about solidarity across people? The UBI cannot be easily stigmatized as something that 'those people get' because everyone gets it. If ethnocentric people want to cut the UBI to hurt another ethnic group, they end up hurting themselves. Still, we've already seen there might be a problem with immigrants being denied access to the UBI – how many years would they have to be resident to receive it? How fair is it to tax immigrants to pay for a UBI they can't receive? It's also not clear that the UBI can't be stigmatized. The most obvious critique is that since everyone gets it, the lazy, the dissolute, the undeserving also receive it. *I* deserve my UBI but I'm not sure that *you* do. The biggest risk to the UBI is that it becomes politically unpopular, and that people end up associating it with 'those people' – the lazy and feckless – so the whole edifice collapses.

Where the UBI does most for us in escaping the solidarity trap is in resolving the information problem. The government doesn't have to know much about the residents of its country, other than who is and who isn't a citizen, to distribute the UBI. There should be very little bureaucratic overhead. And people can't take advantage of the policy design to gain more. It doesn't matter what neighbourhood you move to or what evidence you present to the government about your needs, you get the same. People can't sort into the UBI except by moving country.

The UBI also solves a future problem: advances in information technology might threaten the viability of the existing welfare state. Big data and artificial intelligence help insurers to avoid the adverse-selection problem – if insurers can tell who 'bad risks' are, they can refuse to offer them insurance. That in turn makes private insurance cheaper for good risks. And that creates a political problem for the welfare state – if 'good risks' can insure themselves privately, why would they support 'paying twice' for insurance by also funding social insurance out of taxation? Information dissolves the solidarity between good and bad risks. But a UBI is not subject to the same problem – having more information about people doesn't matter if you give them all the same thing.

Perhaps the key challenge for the proponents of UBI is cost. Typical UBI proposals in the United States, such as Andrew Yang's, presume a payment of $12,000 per annum. While the mean income in the US in 2019 was around $66,000, that's misleading since income in America is so unevenly distributed. The median income was just over half that, at $36,000, so three times the UBI. What about already existing social spending and services in America – from unemployment insurance to government-supported healthcare? According to the OECD, the United States spends around 19 per cent of national income on social spending in gross terms (it's a lot more in net terms – 29 per cent – we'll come to that in a moment). That's just over $12,000 per person. So UBI advocates are essentially asking for an extra welfare state. Or are they?

Conservatives are fans of the UBI for quite different reasons from socialists. In the minds of the former, the UBI provides a market-like way to replace the existing welfare state in its entirety. Gone are the alleged inefficiencies of the Social Security Administration or public housing projects or Medicaid, to be replaced by their cash equivalent. The UBI is still redistribution but on the market's terms, as people would need to buy private healthcare, rent private housing and replace food stamps with their UBI cheque. Some poorer people, perhaps with large young families in low-cost areas, would be better off. But many wouldn't, especially those with high health costs. We get solidarity in terms of cash, but we don't get solidarity in terms of the risks people face.

Of course, UBI doesn't have to replace the existing welfare state. But it does potentially undermine it politically. We know what the solidarity trap threatens – people are already loath to insure their future selves or people they see as 'others'. If offered a cash benefit instead of existing programmes with all their complexity and stigmatization, it's quite possible that people might be willing to support a UBI.

What welfare states have in their favour is the opposite of the novelty of a UBI. Welfare states have long-standing institutions and norms built up around them (with some negative connotations as well). Every existing pension, unemployment and transfer policy already has its own supporters, both its recipients and the bureaucracy set up around it. The UBI by contrast is politically untested and thus fragile. Who will defend it? Everyone? We can see from the original Manitoba UBI scheme that embryonic UBI schemes are politically easy to kill. Come a recession or change of government, a UBI might find itself without defenders.

One way to resolve these concerns is to emphasize universal benefits that everyone receives, but also to arrange – in a rather unsolidaristic way – that people with higher incomes get more. Walter Korpi and Joakim Palme advocate this particular model. They argue that countries with benefits that are proportional to income tend to have higher levels of income redistribution. In their own words, there is a 'paradox of redistribution' where 'the more we target benefits at the poor only and the more concerned we are with creating equality via equal public transfers to all, the less likely we are to reduce poverty and inequality'.

In Korpi and Palme's view, for solidarity to work you need to tie the middle class in. Tying benefits such as pensions or unemployment insurance to earnings increases the value of the welfare state to middle-class citizens and prevents them from opting out into private alternatives. That latter concern is particularly crucial. High-income people opting out of state-provided insurance means that the state inevitably ends up insuring all the bad risks.

What's more, because in Korpi and Palme's model middle-class people end up both paying high taxes *and* getting high benefits, the welfare system becomes more important to their day-to-day lives. Ironically, then, by giving the middle classes particularly generous – better indeed – benefits than the poor, you end up with a more politically sustainable and more solidaristic set of outcomes than if you just target charity at the poor.

Thus the alternative to UBI is to take the universalism and apply it to the welfare state as a whole. This has essentially been the Swedish model. The Swedish welfare state's very generosity is precisely what buys the middle class into supporting it. The Swedish welfare system is not a simple UBI-style cash transfer – it is a series of extensive social services, provided at high quality, and used eagerly by all citizens. This includes publicly provided and funded healthcare and pensions, as you might expect. But it also includes a range of public services that in America are only available, begrudgingly, for the poor – childcare, and employment assistance such as training, for example.

Childcare is a particularly stark example when one considers the differences a Swedish family face compared to their American counterparts. Swedish parents, no matter their income, have the fees they might pay for childcare capped by the government at a 'maxtaxa' – a maximum tax of around $175 per month. Children can start in childcare as young as twelve months old. Contrast this with paying for childcare for a twelve-month-old in America – the Economic Policy Institute estimates infant care in Massachusetts costs around $1,743 monthly – ten times as much. Even for a four-year-old, monthly costs are \$1,250. It's easy to see just how important publicly subsidized childcare is to even high-income Swedes.

The state clearly plays a highly conspicuous, cradle-to-grave role in the lives of everyday Swedes. Many English-speaking readers of this book might find that off-putting – a trip down the proverbial 'road to serfdom'. But we should be careful not to confuse the visibility of a welfare state with its size. I alluded earlier to the fact that the net amount that America spends on social spending and services is much larger than the gross amount. What does that accounting lingo mean in this case? Net spending includes parts of the welfare state that aren't obvious to the naked eye.

Come tax time many Americans are familiar with the byzantine litany of tax credits and deductions they can use to reduce the amount they owe Uncle Sam. From a European perspective, where taxes are deducted at source and few credits exist, this all seems very complicated. But it's where a third of the US welfare state lives, hiding out in a cave produced by the tax code.

Americans can deduct all kinds of expenses on social services that they purchase from private providers – the most obvious being healthcare payments (whether directly through an individual health savings account or implicitly through the tax deductibility of employer-provided healthcare). They can deduct educational expenses and childcare costs. They receive tax credits for having children, and, if poor, the Earned Income Tax Credit. They can even deduct the cost of interest on their mortgage (probably itself backed by the government's mortgage bank, Fannie Mae).

In other words, solidaristic measures are still provided by the American government – it's not quite the land of bootstraps of popular lore – but they are disguised through paying lower taxes rather than receiving higher spending. And because wealthier people pay higher taxes, these kinds of deductions and credits are more meaningful for them.

This submerged welfare state operates beyond the comprehension of the average American taxpayer, even as they benefit from it. And given the complexity of US tax-filing, I don't blame people for not dwelling on it. But it creates a disconnect between what people think the government does and what it is actually subsidizing and paying for. This disguise does not seem to benefit the US welfare state – rather than avoiding discontent, the current set-up seems to aggravate it. Those who especially benefit from the invisible welfare state – wealthy citizens with tax-deductible health insurance and mortgage interest – are ironically often most opposed to it.

This gap between the visible and the invisible welfare state is not an American phenomenon alone – Australia, for example, also has a large difference between gross and net spending – and it appears to distort how people connect politics and policy. In countries with less visible welfare states – like America – people find it harder to place political parties on an economic left–right spectrum or to connect their own policy preferences to parties. So, far from the Swedish welfare state being an easy target, standing out in a political crossfire and constantly under threat, its role is clearly understood by the Swedish voting public. Some of them like it more than others, usually the poorer members of society. But there is little disagreement about what it does.

This explains why visible, universal-welfare states, despite being expensive, seem to be most secure. Political promises to help the unfortunate are always at risk of being overturned by the fortunate. So they need to be embedded in highly visible institutions so that people can see what they are getting and can follow the logic of the system. The solidarity trap is much easier to solve when you can actually see how the system works for everyone.

Universalism isn't a solution for everything. What if there is an inherent limit to what we can provide? Some government services cannot be provided to everyone, at least not without fundamentally changing their essence. The most obvious example is elite public higher education, which is hard to universalize for two reasons. The first is logistical – a single prestigious bricks and mortar university cannot conceivably educate every high-school leaver in a state or country.

The second is more cynical – for an institution to be elite it cannot be universal. Of course, this raises the question of why we need elite institutions in the first place. Should the state play a role in assigning some students to more-prestigious education than others? That said, no country has a truly equal higher-education system where all institutions are considered uniformly prestigious. Even in those countries such as Sweden and Finland that claim a level university playing field, there are still implicit rankings that school-leavers and their parents are highly aware of.

Can you allocate a limited good fairly? Solidaristically, even? In the past, access to elite universities was highly correlated with family income because so few people attended university and there were relatively few universities. That meant that right-wing parties were traditionally the advocates of high state funding for universities. But as enrolments expanded across wealthy countries, it was the left-wing parties that increasingly became the proponents of greater funding for higher education and right-wing parties became sceptical – a sharp contrast to the 1960s. Mass higher-education enrolments create a new challenge for both types of political party, however, since elite universities still exist within a mass system. How should their entry be allocated now that they are not simply a finishing school for existing elites?

The answer from politicians of all stripes has tended to be 'by merit'. But the baseline for how to judge 'merit' is deeply contested. Should students be admitted purely on the basis of test scores? If so, doesn't that privilege the children of the rich, whose parents can more easily afford private tuition? And what about the concerns of ethnic minorities that standardized tests carry implicit racial bias? Moreover, should universities really only take pure academic performance into account? That might create an academic monoculture when perhaps a university should be more rounded and holistic – including people with wider abilities and backgrounds.

The end of affirmative action – race-based admissions preferences – in many American states brought these issues to a head. In California, once universities were prevented from taking ethnic composition of the student body into account, there was a striking shift in the demographics of the University of California (UC) system, with black and Hispanic students substantially reduced in number. As with so many other policy debates in the realm of solidarity, ethnic diversity became a battleground between conservatives and liberals.

The change forced on the UC system produced a policy response that was intended to avoid universities becoming a monoculture in more ways than one. The UC system operates a policy where any student in the top 9 per cent of performers across California's high schools is granted a place at a system university (not necessarily their top choice). That looks like a pure merit-based policy. But UC also instituted a policy that any student in the top 9 per cent of their high school (judged on past performances at that school) would also be admitted, through a policy called Eligibility in the Local Context (ELC). This was a similar design to an older policy in Texas called the Texas Top Ten Percent (TTP), which used performance within a particular high school as the eligibility criteria (for entry into the flagship University of Texas Austin (UT Austin)).

Do ELC and TTP help resolve the solidarity trap when it comes to allocating a scarce service fairly? There is good news and bad. Students who only qualified for the ELC were about 10 per cent more likely to attend a UC system university than less prestigious colleges. Half of these students were from under-represented minorities, and their SAT scores were substantially lower than for students entering through the standard route. So the ELC worked to widen the chances of students from schools whose students had been traditionally less likely to attend elite universities.

The TTP has similar beneficial impacts on these kinds of students. Students 'pulled in' to UT Austin were more likely to graduate and had somewhat higher medium-term earnings, while there was no effect on those students 'pushed out' (those who would have attended UT Austin in the absence of the scheme). A programme intended to improve equity also improved efficiency.

Despite the success of these programmes, the solidarity trap can still bite. For one thing, these new rules can be theoretically manipulated by strategically minded parents. Want your kid to get into a UC school or UT Austin? Why not move to a weaker school district, where they are likely to perform at the top of the class? The disadvantages to this strategy are immediately obvious: moving one's entire family is not simple, and there is no guarantee it would pay off. Nonetheless economists have found that about 5 per cent of families in Texas who could profitably move did so. And this, in turn, reduced the proportion of ethnic-minority students in the TTP group. So, like most solidaristic programmes, this one too can be gamed.

There is a further wrinkle in the design of these programmes. They promise to improve ethnic diversity because poorer high schools that benefit from such programmes tend to have dispropor-tionately large numbers of ethnic minorities. But for such programmes to permanently increase the ethnic diversity of universities, this would need to remain the same. In other words, such programmes could perniciously 'lock in' racial segregation across schools. Re-placing solidarity with segregation would be a tragic irony. These programmes would constantly have to be reformed and remade to address an evolving problem – no mean feat for government.

Escaping the solidarity trap requires us to expand 'us'. So many of our problems achieving solidarity come from a narrow conception of the common good, across time and across people. Our solutions may require us to change people's norms – who they think counts as part of the community. This means overcoming ethnic, religious and lin-guistic divisions within countries – no simple task. But the example of civic nationalism provides one escape path. Highlighting the national nature of solidarity can bind together different groups. That the British National Health Service is treated as a 'national religion' helps explain its continued popularity in a country with otherwise meagre benefits. Health services are particularly useful ways of changing norms since their staffing is typically very ethnically and regionally diverse, exposing patients to their country's diversity, while hopefully healing them.

We can also structure our institutions to buy more people into solidarity. Think, for example, of the universalistic Swedish welfare state, which succeeds because it is expansive and visible, not hidden away. If people understand what their taxes pay for, rather than hid-ing public funding through deductions, this transparency can underpin, not undermine, support. Advocates of greater public sup-port for solidarity need to be honest and open about what the public is paying for, rather than hiding it in the tax code.

And this is just as true for proponents of a Universal Basic Income. The UBI has many characteristics that help it escape the solidarity trap. But how a UBI combines with existing welfare state schemes needs to be addressed up front, rather than assuming the simplicity of a UBI makes the case for it alone. We cannot replace whole systems of solidarity overnight. Our common ground, our support for one another, needs to be clear, credible and trusted.

PART IV
Security

We can't avoid anarchy without risking tyranny

13. Lockdown: Saturday, 8 March 2020, Rome

'Enough with the fear-mongering about the coronavirus. You are scaring my mother!'

David Adler was in his apartment in San Lorenzo, a once working-class, now bohemian Roman neighbourhood beloved by local hipsters. The revelry was high outside. Although everybody knew the news from the north of Italy about the rapid spread of the coronavirus, Rome hadn't been hit by the epidemic and spring had been sunny and dry.

David was spending the year in Rome, from where he would commute to a fellowship at the European University Institute, nestled in the hills above Florence like a luxury hotel, albeit one overrun by graduate students. Living in Rome, working in Florence – David felt like 2020 was going to be a good year.

Online, things didn't look quite so rosy. As an American now based in Italy, David was trying to show his family back home that things in Rome remained normal, for now. His tweet about his mother, quoted above, shows the disconnect between the frenzied online world and his rather more relaxed experience on the streets of Rome.

He walked through the alleys of San Lorenzo, FaceTiming his brother back in San Francisco, live-streaming drunk Romans partying in the streets. It's not that people were unaware of the disaster unfolding north of them in Bergamo, in Milan, in Verona. Everybody could see the shadow of crisis drawing nearer. But the government had not yet blown the whistle. For now, things were normal.

The next day, Sunday, 9 March, Giuseppe Conte, the Italian Prime Minister, dressed smartly in a suit and blue tie, announced to the Italian public that the whole country should 'stay at home'. Staying at home was a simple message, to be enforced without exception or wiggle-room by the Italian police. Suddenly, Italians were to be quarantined, allowed to leave their homes only to purchase food, to exercise, or for essential work or health reasons.

For David, that meant being confined to a tiny apartment in Rome for two months. Through his window, he could gaze out on empty streets. He saw blue-uniformed *carabinieri* stopping each rare passer-by to check on their reasons for being outside and to usher them homewards if not satisfied. As restrictions tightened, the police became emboldened to impose the lockdown by force if necessary. In some cases, the show of force was comedic: videos circulated of the police using drones and quad bikes to capture a lone sunbather on a beach. In other cases, it was tragic, as when twelve prisoners died in prison riots that began when visitation rights were removed.

For the most part, Italians obeyed the lockdown rules, even when – despite these displays of heavy-handed policing – they might have got away with small violations. David and his fellow apartment-dwellers were allowed out to exercise but only within 200 metres of their door. Tracking every rogue jogger exceeding this limit was impossible, even for a country with one of the highest numbers of police officers per citizen in Europe (450 per 100,000) – more than twice as high as England or Sweden. The government had to rely on Italians policing themselves – either through their own conscience or because they suspected that nosy neighbours might inform on them. Which they often did.

As the days grew longer and gloriously Mediterranean, Romans stayed indoors, refraining from the leisurely evening *passeggiata* that marks spring evenings in San Lorenzo. The lockdown had mostly worked – cases dropped precipitously over the spring. But only by crushing the joyful anarchy of everyday Roman life.

A few months earlier in Wuhan, China, the city where the virus first emerged, the balance of order fell decidedly on the side of the police. Not yet realizing that the lockdown would soon encroach on their freedoms, Western TV viewers gawped disbelievingly at dystopian images of Wuhan's enforced quarantine.

The most striking image was of government workers welding shut the doors of a Wuhan apartment complex, forcing residents to stay in their flats. Like in urban Italy, most Wuhanese lived in large apartment buildings, which made it easier for authorities to monitor their comings and goings. But, unlike in Italy, the rules were unyielding. From January, Wuhanese citizens were allowed out only once every three days, one person at a time. Even if you were sick, you couldn't leave the building. To check into the hospital, you had to be approved by a neighbourhood committee. Across the city, large yellow barricades divided buildings and neighbourhoods from one another.

When the eleven million citizens of Wuhan were eventually permitted to leave their apartments in April, these yellow barricades were replaced by yellow codes. On their smartphones, citizens seeking to pass checkpoints had to present a QR code to a police scanner. A colour code would be assigned – green for free movement, yellow for a week of quarantine, red for two weeks. The public could be controlled forcibly at the gates of their apartment complexes by uniformed agents of the state. Or they could be controlled invisibly through code.

Whether blocked from leaving their apartment by a metal bar, or coerced by an app on their phone, Chinese citizens were forced to comply with the regulations whether they liked it or not. The state was aided by the memory of SARS, of which several thousand Chinese citizens had died in 2003, and, in rural areas, by a suspicion of outsiders. During Chinese New Year, fearful of the virus, farmers dug ditches around their villages, cutting off roads, to prevent unwanted arrivals. Even in Beijing and Shanghai, largely free of the virus, mobility was restricted. Yuan Yang, a *Financial Times* editor in Beijing, recalls that 'people in Beijing began to voluntarily self-isolate after Wuhan even before the state demanded it'. She recalls that residential committees in apartment blocks started to ban visitors off their own bats.

Both the state and its citizens chose security over freedom. It worked. By the end of the year, life had returned to normal in Wuhan – restrictions were lifted, shops were open, and people were out and about. By mid 2022, the total reported death count in China was just under 25,000, as opposed to 175,000 in Italy and over a million in the USA. China had repressed the pandemic – and its own citizens.

★

A quarter of the way around the world from Wuhan lies Sturgis, South Dakota. Every August, half a million motorcyclists meet for the annual Sturgis Rally. To put this in perspective, South Dakota's regular population is just shy of 900,000 people. With the virus surging, could the rally really go ahead?

During the coronavirus pandemic, the United States never had a single set of federal rules about social distancing. Each state set rules according to its own health needs and according to its local politics. And that meant that the 'laboratory of democracy' – as America's loose form of federalism is often called – faced the risk of a lab accident.

South Dakota is the kind of state that takes its freedom seriously. It views itself as a bootstrapping, self-reliant place. Face masks, 'stay at home' orders and other public-health rules were viewed with scepticism. It's also a very rural state, where social distancing was nothing beyond the norm. South Dakota's governor, Kristi Noem, argued that South Dakotans could be trusted to manage their own risks, that 'if folks want to wear a mask, they should be free to do so. Similarly, those who don't want to wear a mask shouldn't be shamed into wearing one. And government should not mandate it.'

The Sturgis motorcycle rally went ahead, with numbers only just below normal. But by September Noem was fending off claims that the rally had been a 'super spreader' event. The *New York Times* was featuring stories about participants who had been killed by the virus just weeks later. By early November, the number of weekly new cases was over 1.5 per cent of the state's population. Deaths, too, were rising, higher proportionally than in any other state in the union by December. Wide-open prairies and personal responsibility alone were no shield. Treating people 'like adults' hadn't stopped them becoming patients. In America, unlike Wuhan and Rome, the citizenry effectively protected their personal freedom. At the cost, by 2022, of a million lives.

Was liberty worth this level of insecurity? In each country, citizens had faced the security trap: *we can't avoid anarchy without risking tyranny*. But their choices had been very different.

★

All around the world government rules about social distancing butt up against the desire of citizens not to obey them. Locking people up in apartment complexes might delay the rule-breaking, but, once rules were relaxed, disorder soon followed. David Adler recalls that for a week after the Italian lockdown ended people behaved cautiously, blinded by their newfound freedom like people exiting an afternoon movie. He noted that during the lockdown 'political authority had been so heavily securitized you were always feeling invisible boundaries. But once the lockdown ended, those boundaries vanished, and people acted like kids at university breaking rules without their parents around.'

So within a week Italians were back at bars and house parties, footloose and mask-free. Actually, to be precise, they did have their masks with them. But as David recalls, when he returned to the streets of San Lorenzo, his Italian neighbours were out partying once more, but this time 'they were wearing their masks rolled up around their arms'.

Lockdowns are hard on people. We are social animals. And we also have jobs. Not everyone can easily obey the rules and keep their lives going. A taxi-driver living in a high-rise flat with her parents, spouse and children is not someone who can easily socially isolate either in her work life or when she returns home. For a university professor like me, able to work from home – by which I mean spend hours on Zoom – and with a house with a garden, social isolation was, if not fun, both possible and bearable. That's not true of everybody.

But sometimes people's different behaviour in lockdown was not down to where they worked or lived but their political ideology. In particular, what mattered in how willing they were to tolerate the near tyranny of lockdown was trust. In October 2020 I surveyed over 1,600 Britons to understand what drove their choices about social distancing. One of the strongest predictors of people's social distancing behaviours was whether they voted to leave the European Union in 2016's so-called 'Brexit' referendum. Brexiters wanted distance from Brussels, but not each other. They were also less likely to trust the government's scientific advisers and to want to take a vaccine. It seems that when people trust the government less in general, they also trust it less in a pandemic.

The same kinds of patterns held up in how people behaved. Using information collected by Google from people's mobile phone locations, we find that in Britain areas that voted to leave the European Union had much lower levels of staying at home, even adjusting for local wealth and demographics. Similarly, in the United States, counties that voted for Trump in the 2016 presidential election stayed at home less during the pandemic. And even in the high-trust Scandinavian countries of Denmark and Sweden, lower-trust areas with high populist voting had less social distancing.

Those who don't trust the government in normal circumstances also turned out not to trust the government during an exceptional moment. And often, as in the Chinese case, there are good reasons to be sceptical of state power. On the other hand, as in South Dakota, if we are free to do whatever we like, we may end up harming those around us.

In 2019 no democratic government could have imagined what it would ask of its citizens the next year. Nor that it would have to call in the police, even the military, to enforce these rules. But viruses place governments on a wartime footing. They force the state to reckon with perhaps its primary goal – to ensure the security of its citizens, especially when those citizens won't behave themselves. Security, though, is balanced on a knife-edge. How can a state provide it without falling prey to the great temptations that authority gives those who are in charge? Can we escape the security trap and avoid the perils of both anarchy and tyranny?

14. What is Security?

Every day I wake up in my own bed, having slept soundly – well, sometimes soundly, but certainly not with one eye open. I reach over for my phone – in the same place as usual – check the news and my email. I look through my clothes for something to wear, walk downstairs, turn on the kettle, toast a bagel. I jump into my car, waiting in the drive. I drop the kids off and head into central Oxford and my workplace. The journey is slow, too much traffic, but it's uneventful. And it's like that almost every day.

This all seems normal, tedious, quotidian. Is it? Why am I able to sleep through the night without jerking awake at rustling, hooting or howling? My clothes, my phone, my internet connection: they're all there just as they were the day before. So, thankfully, is my car. Even though I left it outside my house. Maybe I didn't even lock it. My daily drive into work is more or less always the same. When I stop the car in traffic, I'm not wondering if someone is going to approach it trying to sell me something, or rip me off, or point a gun at me. My life might sound a bit boring, but it is certainly secure.

I'm lucky. If you're reading this book, chances are you are too. We live in a kind of bubble. We don't see it but we are surrounded on all sides by a protective forcefield. It's not only us – the forcefield extends to our property. I know it's possible that I could come home to a burgled, ransacked house. If I do, I'll be shocked, fearful and probably a little self-pitying. Somehow, despite the potential for danger on all sides, by and large our bodies and our possessions remain untouched, unsullied and safe.

What should really shock us is that this state of affairs is normal. Billions of people – large majorities in wealthy countries, and increasingly most people throughout the developing world – are able to live in this safe bubble. This is a remarkable, totally unique experience by the standards of most of human history. And, sadly, it's not the world that many people live in today – in poorer communities, in countries without stable government, such day-to-day safety is fleeting. A thousand years ago it was something to be hoped for but rarely relied upon. And yet, in the past few centuries, at least in the wealthy world, it's increasingly something we take for granted. It is the air our society breathes.

What does the world look like without this forcefield? Without security we are in a state of *anarchy*: the absence of authority.

A world without authority is one where there is no 'third party' which can enforce rules, agreements, rights or peace. Each of us is on our own. An anarchical society is a self-help society. But not a warm, sweater-wearing, yoga at the community centre kind of self-help. Under anarchy we cannot rely on anyone else or on any written agreement we have made.

The only way to survive in a world without authority is to assume the worst. Maybe someone will attack me in the middle of the night, so I *do* need to sleep with one eye open. Perhaps my possessions will be where I left them, but perhaps they will have been stolen or spoiled. I might be able to travel from place to place in peace – but I might not be able to make it from my house to the university unscathed. And if I do manage to get to my Oxford college, there's no guarantee that it won't be on fire.

For Thomas Hobbes, society was teetering on the brink of a return to an anarchical 'state of nature'. 'State of nature' is sadly not as appealing as it might first sound. Nature lacks third parties. The 'law of the jungle' is a misnomer – there is no law because there are no rules or judges to enforce them. I cannot trust anyone's promises. All there is, is self-preservation.

If you've heard of Thomas Hobbes, you'll likely remember one quote – outside society, in the state of nature, 'the life of man [is] solitary, poor, nasty, brutish and short'. Which is not exactly a great advertisement for the state of nature.

What did Hobbes mean? Hobbes built his theory of society from the ground up – reading his most famous work, *Leviathan*, you can't help but be impressed by the ambition. Hobbes begins by considering the core of the human dilemma – our fear of violent death. In Hobbes's telling, in the absence of society, we are all alone, driven by impulse, desire and fear to secure everything we can; constantly fighting to protect ourselves from death. The persistent threat of attack by others would mean we could never escape the vagaries of day-to-day life. Always looking over our shoulders means never looking forward. We could not plan, we could not invest, we'd barely be able to live.

But there is a way out of this endless war of man against man. If we could create a guardian who could keep us safe and protect our agreements, then we would be able to look to the future. To do so we'd need to create a 'social contract' that bound us all to follow the authority of a single sovereign. For Hobbes this sovereign would both act on our behalf and force absolute obedience from each of us. The frontispiece of Hobbes's *Leviathan* shows that sovereign as a regal giant made up of the bodies of the citizens, like one of those posters of Barack Obama made up of tiny different photos of him.

But there is a tension at the heart of Hobbes's solution. The figure of the sovereign protects us all because it has absolute power over us. That should leave us feeling uneasy. We no longer need to look over our shoulders at our fellow citizens – a third party exists who will punish their infractions, and ours too. But how can we trust the sovereign? Who enforces rules on the sovereign? Does anyone?

Hobbes provided a blueprint for a new kind of absolutist state, whose sovereign authority could not be questioned and must be obeyed. That tension we feel when we read Hobbes is the security trap: *we can't avoid anarchy without risking tyranny.*

Given the risk of tyranny, why is security a good thing? We can't guarantee that it gives us the opposite of Hobbes, that it makes our lives 'sociable, rich, kind, sophisticated and long'. But it may set us on a path towards those goals.

The first benefit of security is immediate – *we can focus on things beyond simply staying alive.* When we can't be sure that we won't be suddenly attacked, we have to be constantly prepared to defend ourselves, or even to strike pre-emptively. Studies of the mental health of civilians during civil wars, or even just in areas with high crime, show just how exhausting – mentally and physically – constant alertness can be.

External disorder can produce internal disorder – a chaotic environment produces a chaotic mind. Sociologists have long examined how high crime rates and perceived disorder affect people's mental health. Disorder might be tangible – graffiti and vandalism – or more intangible, such as the sense that people don't watch out for each other. People who perceive high levels of disorder are much more likely to report psychological distress – fear, anxiety and depression. This can even affect unborn children. Epidemiologists studying pregnant women in Raleigh, North Carolina, found that women who lived in a high-crime neighbourhood were 50 per cent more likely to have a pre-term birth.

There's a well-known quote, often misattributed to Thomas Jefferson, that 'the price of liberty is eternal vigilance'. The problem is, individual people cannot be 'eternally vigilant' without becoming exhausted. But when we know we will be protected, then we can live a little. And in the long run we might be able to plan.

The second benefit of security is allowing us to *invest for the long term*. Security makes things predictable. If I don't have to worry about being attacked, robbed or murdered today then I likely won't have to tomorrow either. And nor will the people around me. I can devote my energies to tasks where I have to endure the costs today for the benefits tomorrow – in other words, investments, such as planting fields, building roads, receiving an education. Since the origins of early agriculture, civilization has advanced, step by step, technology by technology, by being able to plan over the long run. But that required security provided by a sovereign: a chief, a monarch and, eventually, a parliament.

Mancur Olson characterized the stability provided by a sovereign as the emergence of a 'stationary bandit'. That doesn't sound especially promising, but Olson contrasts this with a world of 'roving bandits'. In the absence of stable rule, people are prey to being robbed, exploited or killed by any malign actor who passes by. These roving bandits move on after their pillaging, looking for another sucker, leaving destruction in their wake.

Contrast this with an overbearing but stable ruler, be it a king or a chieftain. This ruler may be venal, ruthless and expropriating, but they do best by encouraging the local farmers and townsfolk to plan for the long run and invest. Then, when those investments come to fruition, the ruler takes their slice at the point of a sword. The stationary ruler may be just as malign as a roving bandit, but their incentives are to protect those under their power, even if just to reap the reward from their efforts. Security may be exploitative but it does create investment. In the West today we aren't ruled by chiefs or monarchs, but we retain the strong arm of the sovereign state, through laws, courts and the police. And the army if we need it.

Thirdly, and finally, security creates *trust*. The promises we make to each other don't carry weight on their own. A contract cannot enforce itself. We rely on other people to carry out what they promised to do. And if they fail to do so, either because they are incompetent or because they are devious and never intended to in the first place, then we may be out of luck. If we are worried people are untrustworthy, we might never enter into agreements to start with. And so we all end up poorer and more isolated.

What we need is a third-party enforcer. Someone or something that can make sure that contracts and agreements are abided by. Now we can go out with confidence and make deals with others, even those we've never met before and never will again. Think, for example, of eBay. The early internet was a web of anonymous users without central control. Not a high-trust environment. eBay's innovation was to act as a third party that could guarantee transactions on the second-hand market emerging on the internet of the 1990s. By turfing out rogue sellers and providing secure payment mechanisms, it was able to bridge over the anarchy of the early internet. What's more, behind eBay lurked the weight of the US legal system, and behind that the 800-pound gorilla of the US government. It took security to create trust on the internet.

Most of us now live in a world where we are secure in our own homes – personal security – and in our own countries – national security. So two cheers for security. What about the third? Unfortunately, there isn't one. We might be able to make promises to other citizens with the state as guarantor – but the logic stops at that point. We can't enforce any promises that the sovereign makes to us. They're the one who's sovereign, after all. And, even worse, there is no guarantor of security between countries – no *international security*. Nation states still live in a condition of anarchy, as the recent war in Ukraine so starkly demonstrates. No outside force can make them follow agreements, abide by their promises or stop attacking one another. We can sign treaties such as the one that established NATO, but we cannot guarantee, when push comes to shove, they'll work.

We live in a world marked by local security but global insecurity. Countries may not be looking over their shoulders nightly but they need to remain vigilant. And this is costly – it means expensive armies and military technology. Planning for the future becomes harder when you cannot be sure that alliances won't shift and you'll be suddenly vulnerable. And deals with other states may be struck but don't stay stuck – for example, the US opting in, out and in again to the Paris climate agreement depending on its changing political weather. Likewise, if treaties don't have global buy-in, they may be ineffective. Breaking treaties may be frowned upon but there is no court to force a country to follow rules it won't follow. There is only the threat of force or sanctions from other countries.

Would we want global security if it meant giving up national sovereignty? The recent political successes of nationalist movements and politicians in countries from Italy to the UK to India suggests not. Still, while there is no definitive global sovereign, we do live in a more secure international environment than our ancestors. How did we get there?

Building Leviathan

Justice is not new: we simply used to have to enforce it ourselves. Before the modern police existed, providing security was in the hands of the general public. Indeed, it was an obligation. And as one might imagine, it didn't always provide much security. Over the centuries we have developed a wide array of institutions to embed the promise of security. Our modern criminal justice system fulfils a huge number of roles: keeping public order, investigating crimes, and capturing, prosecuting and imprisoning perpetrators. It's true that the ability of our police, judicial and prison services to perform these roles fairly or effectively fluctuates wildly. But it is a step change from the world before 1800.

We often think of classical Greece and Rome as precursors to the modern state, with assemblies, laws, rules and regulations. Yet when it came to the enforcement of these laws, things were less organized, at least at first. In classical Athens, before the rise of Solon the lawmaker, and in Republican Rome, it was up to private citizens to investigate crimes and to capture wrongdoers. Over a thousand years later in medieval England, little had changed on that account.

It's the middle of the fifteenth century. Place yourself in the position of a poor villager, farming a strip of land on the estate of a nobleman in rural England. A shout rings out that a pig has been stolen. What happens next? There is no local policeman to turn to, nor porcine detective unit to track the case of the missing squealer. What you might not expect is that you, as a villager, would be held responsible for the apprehension of the pig thief. The village, on discovering the missing pig, would raise a 'hue and cry'. This meant that the villagers should stop what they were doing, hunt down the miscreant and escort them to the local magistrate – the nobleman.

Justice was communal and organic. There was security of sorts – any ill-doer might be caught by their fellow villagers and tried and punished by local elites – but it was amateur and haphazard. And since villagers were not paid to police, their incentives to do a good job were shaky – local custom and tradition could only get you so far in preventing or prosecuting crimes.

By the early nineteenth century, an embryonic police emerged but it too was amateur. 'Constables' were local officers appointed under this system to staff the night watch of towns. The role was typically unpaid and undesirable. The writer Daniel Defoe described being a constable as 'an unsupportable hardship' that 'takes up so much of a man's time that his own affairs are frequently totally neglected, too often to his ruin'. Community self-policing was ramshackle. It would not survive the coming of industrial cities.

If you thought this era of policing sounded amateur and arbitrary, wait until you hear about punishment. Today, after people have been caught and tried for crimes, they are typically sent to jail for a fixed(ish) term. There are many reasons to be sceptical about the functionality of prison systems today but modern prisons are at least a fairly uniform sort of punishment. In my office I have a wonderful book on prison architecture, the kind of thing I like to have on display to keep students on their toes. The book's many blueprints and photos show that from London to Moscow, Havana to Hubei, prisons around the world are built along very standard lines, and perform a very similar role, although with varying degrees of corruption, hygiene and safety.

Early prisons were not places where prisoners sat out a multi-year sentence. They were what we might think of as 'jails': holding houses for people whose punishment would be rather less humane. How were 'criminals' (and I use scare quotes deliberately) punished then? Either through physical punishment, from lashing to torture to execution; or through banishment, shaming, exile or transportation. Prison was not the punishment; it was where you went to wait for a less desirable punishment.

To get a sense of how rare long-term imprisonment was, in England between 1826 and 1833, of just under 100,000 punishments handed out, almost 50,000 of those were sentences under six months. Only forty-six people in England were given a jail term of over three years! What were the rest of the punishments? Almost 10,000 people were executed, 2,000 were whipped or fined, and around 25,000 were 'transported', largely to Australian prison colonies. Things in Continental Europe weren't much better – French and Spanish convicts were sent to row for years on end in the prison galley ships of the Mediterranean.

Today we expect prisons to do a number of different things to ensure our security. Yes, there is still a motivation to punish for the sake of punishment – as deterrence, justice or sometimes bloodlust.

But we also use prisons as fences – to separate us from those who we fear will threaten our security. Finally, we have some perhaps more noble aspirations. Prisons can be used to rehabilitate criminals, to remould them into reformed citizens, who no longer threaten collective security when released. This aim of prison is fundamentally pretty new.

Given the historical ferocity of other punishments, it's unsurprising that the origins of the modern prison lay in the desire of religious do-gooders to rehabilitate prisoners through repentance, rather than engage in the bloodier alternatives. The ancestors of modern prisons are two experiments conducted in early nineteenth-century America: Eastern State Penitentiary in Philadelphia and Auburn in New York State.

Eastern State Penitentiary was founded by local Quakers, whose intention was to provide an ideal institution for, you guessed it, penitence. That goal would be best achieved by treating prisoners like monks. They inhabited single cells, where they dwelt in complete solitude. Inmates were not allowed to communicate in any way. Guards wore socks over their shoes to prevent any sound, all the better to hear attempts by inmates to talk to one another. Prisoners were referred to by number, not name, and when let out of their cells had to wear full face masks. The prison was designed on a 'radial' model – a hub and spoke setup, made famous by Jeremy Bentham as the 'panopticon' – the all-seeing, all-disciplining prison. All prisoners could be observed by guards sitting at the hub of the jail. Bentham called his design 'an iron cage, glazed', with 'an invisible omniscience'.

This is a rather sharp turn in the security state. The prisoners were being protected and 'improved' by an unchallengeable, omniscient authority. For Michel Foucault, this meant moving from the 'spectacle' of public executions and shaming to a system that would force inmates to internalize the discipline of the state. There is a certain irony that prisons became the model of security because jails, workhouses and mental asylums had previously been models of disorder. A century earlier, prison guards were expected to earn their incomes from selling beer to the jailed. Asylums charged entry fees for visitors to come and gawk at the chaos within. The modern word 'bedlam' comes from the chaotic state of affairs at Royal Bethlehem Hospital for those deemed mentally ill, essentially treated as a macabre tourist attraction by the curious citizens of London.

From disorder came a regimented order in both prisons and police. Ultimately the Pennsylvania system of solitary, silent prisoners was unaffordable. The Auburn model of prisons, embodied by – still silent – teams of prisoners living and working together became the norm. Eventually prisoners were even allowed to speak. Mass imprisonment replaced physical punishment and transportation. Grand stone prisons were built in booming industrial cities to house thousands, ultimately millions, of the long-term imprisoned.

As punishment changed, so too did the forces that put people behind bars. From the early nineteenth century, countries developed recognizably modern police forces. Rather than each citizen being responsible for staffing the night watch – or apprehending our pig thief – a cadre of uniformed, trained, professionalized police took over these roles. The key novelty with the modern police in England and America was that they were made up of the very citizenry of the country they sought to protect. They were not a mere extension of the military but an attempt at self-government.

For Americans or Englishmen at the dawn of the nineteenth century, a permanent police force looked like a dangerous step back towards the absolutism associated with Hobbes and a step away from cherished liberties. The 'police' were associated with the guards of Continental Europe, patrolling the capital and apprehending political enemies of the monarchy. Or, in the case of the *gendarmeries* of France, Belgium and Italy (the now famous *carabinieri*), they were military units roving the countryside in search of bandits. The Continental police force was really a domestic military – securing internal order just as their comrades in the infantry would secure external order.

Even the word 'police' had different overtones on the Continent. Whereas in English we distinguish the concepts of 'politics', 'policy' and 'police' – their French and German equivalents were more muddied. What 'police' meant to an eighteenth-century German was general management of the public – everything from public order and crime prevention to checking weights and measures or deciding the kinds of clothes people could wear during festivals. This was all part of the concept of having a 'well-ordered police state' – a phrase that many of us in the modern world would find sinister.

Today, this concept of 'police' seems to us to be overstepping how we guarantee our security. And our ancestors in the English-speaking world saw it as a threat to long-standing liberties. The *Daily Universal Register* declared sniffily in 1785 that 'Our constitution can admit nothing like a French police; and many foreigners have declared they would rather lose their money to an English thief, than their liberty to a *Lieutenant de Police*.' And yet, with the Industrial Revolution and the rise of the modern city came ever-growing disorder. So what to do?

New York, London, Boston and Manchester in 1800 were considered crime-ridden and anarchic. How long could fears about absolutism derail developing the police? The solution was to develop a 'civilian police', a recognizable force with a uniform and strict rules and principles of operation. This was ultimately about self-government – New Yorkers policing New Yorkers. From the emergence of London's 'bobbies', named after their founder, Robert Peel, in 1829 there followed a springtime budding of city civilian police forces across the world – Toronto in 1834, New York in 1844, Amsterdam in 1851.

The civilian police was a solution to both the absence of security and to its dark reflection, the tyranny of security. It was a way of escaping the security trap. Anarchy could be contained by making policing regular and impersonal – a civilian police was supposed to enforce rules without exception or favour: it had to treat people equally. But a ruthless military could also treat people equally – equally badly by enforcing martial law. So in itself that's not enough. How could the police themselves be constrained? They needed to be part of the society they would exert authority over, and ultimately that society needed to be able to constrain them. If the police force became too powerful, the government would have to be able to curtail its power by defunding it. In other words, for the promise of security to be self-enforcing, the people need to be able to guard the guardians.

The story I've set out about the emergence of order looks too good to be true, doesn't it? Well, it is. While modern prisons and policing have indeed supplanted the chaos of 200 years ago, they have not always – indeed they have rarely – lived up to their promise of creating security without feeding tyranny. Corruption is rife in many police departments and prison wings. Ethnic minorities, urban residents, poorer citizens are not always treated equally and fairly. Regarding the first two levels of security, personal and national, we've not resolved all of our problems. But the invention of the police went a long way to bringing the kind of security Thomas Hobbes thought was necessary for life to not be 'nasty, brutish and short'.

So much for *personal* and *national* security. What about the third level of security: *international security*? You could have read the past few paragraphs and been forgiven for thinking, isn't this missing the point? Sure, it may be safer to cross the street without being pickpocketed in Whitechapel or Hell's Kitchen than a hundred years ago. But what else happened in the last hundred years?

The two World Wars of the first half of the twentieth century vastly exceeded any previous conflicts in their bloodiness and geographic reach. There were no uniformed police to step in and pull apart Imperial Germany and Edwardian Britain, Nazi Germany and Third Republic France, or Imperial Japan and New Deal America. It seems silly to even imagine one. The twentieth century's myriad of bad actors couldn't be simply apprehended, tried and imprisoned. Who exactly could stop these armies, arrest these leaders? Countries lived in Hobbes's anarchy. Far from relying on a third party, it was a self-help system. Alliances might prevent countries from truly going it alone but adversaries remained unchained.

We are seventy-five years on from the end of the Second World War. Has anything really changed? Are we not now safer and, if so, is that because somehow we have created security internationally, through diplomacy, agreements and norms of engagement?

The answer is a typically academic 'it depends'. A few years back, Steven Pinker, a man with an eye for a smouldering academic debate ready to be stoked, published a book, *The Better Angels of Our Nature*, in which he claimed that today we really do live in a much safer, more peaceful world, unimaginable even decades ago. Pinker argued that war had in fact been in decline for centuries and that it was, like a five-year-old iPhone, becoming obsolete. Pinker claims that scientific and intellectual enlightenment over the past few hundred years has drawn us from the abyss of war.

Unfortunately for this extremely attractive thesis, it's not really clear that warfare has declined. Bear Braumoeller argues there are reasons to question both Pinker's theory and his data. Pinker argues that Enlightenment ideas underpinned new beliefs in reason and equality and – if you read your Immanuel Kant – in the possibility of 'perpetual peace'. The problem with this argument is that the Enlightenment did not just give us Kant – it gave us Hobbes and Hegel, with their conceptions of the strong state; it gave us Rousseau and Herder and their development of cultural cohesion and nationalism; and it gave us Karl Marx, who believed in inter-class conflict. The Enlightenment was a time period, not a discrete set of ideas that everybody agreed on. Those competing ideas included the need for powerful state bureaucracies, racial and national 'purity', and the never-ceasing conflict between classes – none of this screams pacifism the way Pinker suggests.

But it's not just this partial view of the Enlightenment that should give us caution about the decline of war. Taking the long view, on almost every measure conflict was higher between 1900 and the end of the Cold War than the whole of the nineteenth century. It's true that since 1990 interstate war has declined. But that's because the guns have pointed inwards. Civil wars have become far more common since 1990 and, what's worse, they tend to last far longer than conflicts between nations. Finally, wealthy democracies have been engaging in a two-decade-long conflict against non-state actors – al-Qaeda, the Taliban and most recently ISIS. So even if it's no longer the case that we worry as much about Great Power war, it's certainly not the case that the militaries of America, France, Britain or China are gathering dust. In fact, as Braumoeller notes, if we include these 'internationalized civil wars', 2016 was the most conflict-heavy year since 1945.

What we can say is that countries – particularly the larger ones – were, until very recently, less likely to go to war with one another than fifty years ago. Is this security? And if it is, did we create it with the equivalent of an international police force? No and no. The United Nations, itself a napkin sketch of what a world government might look like, has mobilized peacekeeping forces. For conflicts among smaller nations, for whom the UN might actually loom as a credible threat, or for some civil wars, the blue helmets of peacekeepers might substitute for the blue uniforms of a police force. But, even then, UN peacekeepers failed to prevent genocide in Bosnia, Rwanda and Myanmar, to name just three examples among many. As for the big players, they can largely ignore the warnings of the UN – as happened when the United States invaded Iraq.

Of course, the Russian invasion of Ukraine in 2022 has changed conventional wisdom about the likelihood of serious interstate war. If anything, the rarity of cross-border conflict and the annexation of territory had led military analysts to become complacent. The tragic litany of war crimes committed by Russian soldiers, from Bucha to Mariupol, reminds us that civilians too are not immune to the recurrence of violence and malice. And it shows us that international security remains an oxymoron.

15. The Security Trap

Our boring, peaceful lives actually teeter on a knife-edge. If we want to maintain order, we run the risk of losing control to our guardians, but if we remove our guardians we can easily slip back into disorder. We face the security trap: *we can't avoid anarchy without risking tyranny*.

The problem of tyranny is how to prevent the people we put in charge of security from overstepping the mark. It's a problem about *them*. We need to control this particular group of people somehow, even though they have a monopoly on the use of physical force. If we civilians cannot constrain the police or the military, how on earth can we expect them not to exceed their authority? If there were some higher force that we could call on, perhaps they could threaten our protectors if they stepped out of line. But if that's the case, what's to stop this higher power from themselves exploiting their lofty position? Like an infernal set of Russian dolls, each time we find a higher power, we have to ask who will control them? We face the eternal question expressed by the Roman poet Juvenal: *who will guard the guardians?*

Let's now turn to the second face of the security trap – anarchy – a problem not about *them* but about *us*. If no one is watching us, or no one can punish us, why bother following the rules? If there's no Big Brother will we behave or will we run riot? Almost no system of security can monitor all our behaviours all the time, certainly not if we were truly committed to getting around it. In the real world, some level of anarchy will always creep in.

Escaping the security trap, then, means edging along a ridge between the sheer drop of tyranny on one side and anarchy on the other, trying to adjust our institutions – from policing to prisons to the military – so that they are strong enough to defend us but not so strong they will exploit us. To stop our politics from failing we will have to figure out how to keep out balance.

Tyranny

Juvenal's question – 'who guards the guardians?' – gets to the heart of the security trap. The question in itself suggests we might face an infinite loop.

The problem of tyranny stems from the fact that each layer of guardians we add needs to be powerful enough to control all the layers below them. So every time we think we have gained security, we have actually employed an even more powerful – and potentially less controllable – force. And, in doing so, we may have created problems far larger than the ones we began with.

Game theorists have long been interested in Juvenal's question and sought possible solutions to the never-ending spiral of guardians. One is stopping the spiral by forcing it into a circle. If each of us is willing to punish miscreants, and someone else is willing to punish us, we are all simultaneously givers and recipients of punishment. We can avoid the problem of infinite regress by having the guardians guard each other.

It's a neat solution to the security trap but it's not entirely satisfying. It faces the 'O-Ring' problem: the rubber ring used in the joints of the rocket boosters of the ill-fated space shuttle *Challenger*. These rings were made brittle by the low – for Florida – temperatures. On launch day they failed to hold. And so the entire US space programme was capsized by the failure of a simple piece of rubber. Lots of economic and political problems face this same 'weakest link' dilemma: the whole shebang collapses if one actor doesn't fulfil their responsibilities.

The circular solution to the security trap is similarly fragile – if I fail to punish who I'm supposed to punish, then I break the circle and it falls apart. Democratic elections could reinforce this circle – and hence make us less reliant on every individual fulfilling their responsibility. Elections can act as the 'intervenor' of last resort. A new mayor, elected to 'clean the house', can punish corrupt cops if the courts themselves are too venal to do so. It's a nice idea. But the experience of democratic politics in America in constraining the police suggests it is far from a perfect solution.

The Black Lives Matter movement may have resurged following the murder of George Floyd, but it first came to mass attention after the 2014 shooting in Ferguson, Missouri, of the African American teenager Michael Brown by a white police officer, Darren Wilson. As lawyers, journalists, protestors and politicians descended on Ferguson, its police department suddenly found its behaviour sharply illuminated. It did not look attractive under the harsh glare of the media's spotlight.

The most damning indictment of the Ferguson police department comes from the United States Department of Justice. In painstaking detail over one hundred pages the Department meticulously lays out its charge sheet. The Ferguson PD, often in cahoots with city government and local courts, was accused of essentially running a protection racket. The city relied on court fines for revenues, so it encouraged the police department to issue fines for the most minor offences and then for the courts to issue further fines and summonses for failure to pay the initial fines on time, pushing the citizens of Ferguson into mountains of debt.

One example, cited in the Justice Department's investigation, is of an African American man who was arrested for sitting in his car by a playground, cooling off after a basketball game. He was approached by an officer who accused him of being a paedophile and demanded to search his car. When the man cited his constitutional rights not to be searched without due cause, he was arrested at gunpoint and charged with eight misdemeanours including providing a false name – he gave his name as Mike not Michael – and not wearing a seatbelt – the car was parked. He was fined, taken to court and ultimately lost his job.

This kind of hair-trigger policing, where the most minor of imagined infractions resulted in fines, court summonses and job losses, was the basic modus operandi of the Ferguson Police Department. The department's interests appeared to be in squeezing cash out of its citizens and intimidating, not protecting, them. To quote verbatim from the Department of Justice report, 'many officers appear to see some residents, especially those who live in Ferguson's predominantly African American neighborhoods, less as constituents to be protected than as potential offenders and sources of revenue'. A police force whose ostensible role was to protect citizens appeared to view them through an 'us against them' lens – largely defined by race. The Ferguson police department was over 90 per cent white and the community it 'protected' was two thirds black. Not only did it appear to treat African American citizens differently; it saw them as 'potential offenders' – so the people to be protected by the police were viewed as people to protect the police from, or to extort.

How did the city of Ferguson end up with this horrific inversion of security – with guardians who preyed on those they guarded? Missouri's racial politics are clearly a major part of the story: thirty years ago, Ferguson's population was three quarters white and its police force appears to have viewed local demographic change as both a criminal threat and a revenue opportunity. The police were not only driven by apparent racial animus but also by the profit motive. That in turn was caused by America's highly decentralized criminal justice system, which meant both city and police force were self-funding and dependent on finding new revenue streams. No state or federal oversight was forthcoming until Ferguson had made worldwide headlines.

This revenue drive also coincided with the availability of military-grade weaponry from the US Department of Defense, which was selling off vehicles, guns and even aircraft as the wars in Iraq and Afghanistan wound down. In Ferguson this led to shocking pictures of police officers in full body armour, driving armoured Humvees and throwing stun grenades at protestors. And here we have the piling of security trap upon security trap, as tools created to ostensibly secure the protection of American citizens from threats abroad were turned on the very same citizens in their home towns.

Anarchy

We would all love to avoid heavy-handed rule enforcement by the uniformed agents of the state like in Ferguson. The problem is that when given an inch we take a mile. We all benefit from everyone else following the rules but appear unable to follow them ourselves if we think no one is watching. Anarchy is a state of temptation. And it's a costly one – if we can't trust others, we'll devote our precious resources to keeping safe: we'll fail to make agreements, fail to thrive.

We can think about our incentives to follow the rules, or let anarchy rip instead, in three ways. First, we have legal rules and norms, enforced by the state. If we know we will be observed breaking a legal rule, we know we are very likely to be punished. This is Hobbes's Leviathan leaning over and tapping us pointedly on the shoulder. Still, much of the time people break legal rules because they don't think they will be observed.

In that case, the government can try and 'randomize' enforcement. Whenever you pass through the 'nothing to declare' gate at customs you are running this gauntlet. While customs officers will stop certain passengers based on their own suspicions, related to their baggage, departure point or (with great room for abuse) appearance, a number of people will be stopped and have their bags searched entirely at random. This is a probabilistic legal rule – you might or might not be caught by an agent of the law, depending essentially on whether you get lucky. If you speed on the public highway, fudge your taxes or carry drugs into a nightclub, you are taking your chances. We can allow quite a lot of anarchy, provided that there is both a real and known probability of being caught and the punishment for the infraction is serious enough. A little risk of severe consequences can stop a lot of wrongdoing.

Second, we might follow the rules even in the absence of legal enforcement, if we think we will earn the opprobrium of our friends and families for breaking them. This is the realm of social norms. Sometimes we might face a social norm when we break a legal rule but the cops aren't there to see it. For instance, if we are with our family and they alone see us steal a bar of chocolate. At other times, social norms make us behave ourselves even if we are not violating an actual law – they are in part what prevent people from insulting passers-by, pushing people on public transport and starting fights.

What social norms rely on is information – we need to know who is behaving and who isn't – and some form of group identity – I can't

easily constrain bad behaviour in society at large, but I might be able
to punish or reward people in my group. That in turn relies on groups
punishing those members who don't punish rule-breakers.

It's not hard to see how such a system can both hold together
norms among groups but also lead to cycles of revenge, shunning and
even honour killings. In northern Albania, the code of Kanun com-
pels villagers to engage in violent retaliation until revenge has been
meted out and the village is considered 'cleansed'. Failing to fulfil
Kanun means shunning and humiliation by the rest of the village.
Social norms can indeed create order under anarchy, but is security
through cycles of revenge much security at all?

Finally, we have moral norms: rules and principles we follow even
though no one is watching. This might mean stopping at a red light
on a country lane in the middle of nowhere, with no possibility of
being caught. Or paying for eggs at an unmanned farm stall by the
side of the road. In a perfect world, we could rely on moral norms
constraining our behaviour in anarchy. We would all follow Immanuel Kant's 'categorical imperative' – to behave in a way that could be
formulated as a universal law: our moral behaviour would itself
be lawlike. But relying on individual morality is risky. What if you
wind up being exploited by your less moral fellow citizens?

Another way to control ourselves and prevent anarchy is 'quasi-
moral norms'. These come into play when people can't witness what
we do but we can witness what others do, at least in the aggregate.
Antanas Mockus – a mathematician-philosopher who was mayor of
Bogotá, Colombia – provides an entertaining example. Like many
landlocked cities, Bogotá had a problem with accessing water. To
deal with water shortages, Mockus had a total water consumption
show nightly on network TV. Even though the government couldn't
monitor individual citizens, everyone could see that aggregate water
consumption was down. You might think that would encourage each
person to free-ride, knowing that others were doing the hard work
of using less water. Instead, people could see that others were not
choosing to free-ride and accordingly also chose to not take hour-
long showers. It didn't hurt that Mockus himself appeared on TV
showering and turning the water off while he soaped, to model good

behaviour. Perhaps not something we'd want to see from all our leaders but effective nonetheless.

Mockus also used social norms to try to shape behaviour among Bogotá's anarchic drivers. Eleonora Pasotti interviewed Mockus about his unusual strategies. Mockus had two types of vehicular anarchy to deal with: cars vs cars and cars vs pedestrians. To deal with the former he printed out 350,000 cards with thumbs-up or thumbs-down signs that motorists could wave at each other when happy or, more often, mad with each other. The idea was to curb road rage through citizens enforcing social norms on each other – both respect and shame – though it's easy to see how this might backfire.

Cars versus pedestrians is a more unbalanced battle. Drivers in Bogotá typically ignored traffic police when they tried to prevent drivers from blocking intersections. Mockus's idea was – believe it or not – to replace cops with mimes. Marcel Marceau-type mimes. Mimes were able to reinforce the norm in ways that the police couldn't. According to one of Mockus's aides, 'the mime showed the zebra lines and indicated to the driver he was running over the citizens. It was a game, a typically playful artistic activity, but it empowered citizen conscience.' Sometimes enforcing a norm is about sparking surprise.

Anarchic traffic is one thing, but what happens when there is no government at all? For centuries, citizens of wealthy countries haven't had to think about this question, as the nation state controlled every square mile of Europe, North America and Japan. But government collapses still occur and sometimes they are not quickly remedied. The country of Somalia has lacked any functioning government at all since 1991. That year marked the collapse of Major-General Mohamed Siad Barre's two-decade dictatorship. Following a civil war, Barre was toppled in a *coup*. But there was no *d'état* to follow. The country immediately faced the secession of its northwestern provinces and later its eastern ones. The remainder of the country lacked any kind of central government at all and was carved up by rival warlords.

What happens to security when the state packs up? Essentially, it becomes privatized. Mogadishu, Somalia's capital, became 'protected' by private security companies. At times such companies have been successful at keeping the peace, but there were no functioning courts to enforce agreements. So they would regularly face the challenge of new actors seeking profit and power. Rival warlords hired private armies, made up of impoverished teenagers. They would act like Olson's roving bandits – seizing previously government-owned institutions from ports to airfields and taxing citizens. Business leaders, tired of paying protection fees, tried to end the chaos by supporting an Islamist movement. But soon the Islamists were themselves seized by a radical wing who declared war on Ethiopia. They too were removed from power and Somalia remains split between the areas nominally controlled by a central government established in 2012, regions occupied by Islamist militias and the breakaway regions.

To be sure, Somalia is not a great advertisement for anarchy. But even here there are shades of grey. It depends what we are comparing contemporary Somalia to. Compared to more-stable East African countries – Ethiopia and Kenya, for example – Somalia is insecure and poor. But compared to Siad Barre's dictatorship, life may well have improved for regular Somalis. Peter Leeson has argued that anarchy trumped tyranny in Somalia. Somalia's life expectancy, infant mortality, sanitation and access to telephones all improved between 1990 and 2005, even compared to its neighbours. Its main export trade – in livestock – also boomed during the 1990s. While recognizing Somalia's many continuing problems, Leeson argues that swapping tyranny for anarchy was arguably worth it. Sometimes too little authority might be better than too much. But for most Somalis anarchy has been something to escape – the UN estimated that by 2015 two million Somalis had emigrated, often only to refugee camps across the border.

The problem with order

Scandinavians live in some of the richest, and safest, countries in the world. They don't have to worry too much about the trade-off between tyranny and anarchy that faces Somalis. But is this kind of security all it's cracked up to be?

The 'Law of Jante' is a tongue-in-cheek set of rules about Danish life, drawn up by the novelist Aksel Sandemose in the 1930s. The 'Law' has a series of ten rules from 'You're not to think *you* are anything special' to 'You're not to think *you* can teach *us* anything.' Sandemose was mocking the conformity of daily life in small Danish towns – fitting in was paramount, standing out was suspicious. And social norms would be used politely but ruthlessly to ensure obedience. Nonconformists, rebels, anyone who got too big for their boots, would be shunned or shamed. There was nothing anarchic about Jantean life, nor anything tyrannical. It was entirely secure and ordered. But to many of us this kind of order seems stultifying

The Law of Jante is particularly ill-suited to encouraging individual excellence or acknowledging success. The famous Swedish actor Alexander Skarsgård joked on *The Late Show* with Stephen Colbert that the Law of Jante forbade him from acknowledging publicly that he had won a Golden Globe. But at other times this kind of conformism prevents people from acknowledging very minor achievements – from travelling to visit one's parents to reading a highbrow novel.

Jante might, however, be beneficial in creating social cohesion: the bedrock of Scandinavian social trust, which underpins the region's extensive welfare state and low levels of crime. But when two Norwegian sociologists looked at whether agreement with the Law of Jante actually led to more 'generalized trust' in other citizens, they discovered that, among individuals, the more Jante sentiment one had, the *less* one trusted others. So it's possible that conformity can build an ordered society in which it *looks like* everyone trusts each other, but that is actually built on the back of individual anxiety about shadowy rule-breakers.

Robert Putnam, in his famous study *Bowling Alone*, called this the 'dark side of social capital'. Social capital is the kind of thing that do-gooding multinational companies like to talk about in their annual reports. It means the stock of mutual trust in society that acts like both a social glue to bind everyone together and an economic solvent to dissolve mistrust around making deals. For Putnam, it was the absence of social capital in southern Italy that explained its political and economic woes and its reliance on 'amoral familism' – a code of ethics where only your family should be considered important and everyone else viewed as potential threats or patsies. The absence of social capital looks like the cases of anarchy we've discussed.

But social capital is not always a good thing. As Putnam notes, high-trust communities such as those in Scandinavia, or its American offshoot, my old home state of Minnesota, can be conformist and unwelcoming. If people have high social capital but are intolerant of out-groups, we can end up with closed-mindedness and sectarianism.

Too much order not only produces conformity; it can also lead to stagnation. Fast economic growth often obeys the maxim that to 'make an omelette you need to break a few eggs'. Those eggs are existing businesses. Joseph Schumpeter famously argued growth comes through 'creative destruction'. Technological advances undermine existing companies, who are then driven out of business.

As an economic idea this has its merits but there is a political problem. Why would powerful people owning those existing companies let this kind of disruption happen? Why would they want to be 'creatively destroyed'? Political elites, especially those in the pocket of wealthy industrialists, often try to block such technologies. Conformist societies may also be especially unwilling to tolerate new technologies and so their industries may become sclerotic. So wherever new ideas can be easily blocked, whether by dictators or conformists, we'll see stagnation.

If order can be stultifying, perhaps it's not surprising that historically many people have sought to escape it, preferring to live outside, on the frontier. James C. Scott calls this 'the art of not being governed'. Being governed can mean being violently oppressed but it can also mean being observed and rationalized. Scott argues that states seek to control and order their citizens – not as Hobbesian overlords threatening tyranny but as obsessive collectors, striving to categorize every last person, every last inch of nature.

Our last names come from the state's earliest attempts to understand us, through the national census. In small villages, because everyone knew everyone else, first names would suffice. John, the butcher's son, would do if you needed to separate out two Johns. That's not ideal for a census-taker though. They can't jot down 'butcher's son' in the margins. And so they might assign last names to each John. This John is the son of Peter, so he's John Peterson. That John is a butcher, so he's called John Butcher. Once John could be told apart from John, they could be recorded by the state, to be called on for taxes or military service, or punished by the courts. Order had been created but very much on the state's terms.

That kind of order has not always been attractive to those upon whom it has been imposed. Until the late twentieth century there was an easy solution to that: run away. Most governments could not really exert sovereignty outside large, well-populated plains and valleys. Marginal physical locations – the mountains, swamps, islands, deserts and deltas – were difficult for the state to monitor or patrol. And so citizens who chafed at the state's demands for their money or lives would quietly vanish into the margins.

Scott points to the imagined country of Zomia – a real place but without real political borders: it's the hill country of Southeast Asia, crossing into Myanmar, Thailand, Cambodia, Laos, Vietnam, China and India. This region until recently proved stubbornly ungovernable. Distances of a mere dozen miles might take days to traverse for the armed agents of the state. And so, per Scott, 'avoiding the state was, until the last few centuries, a real option'. People could resist the entreaties of order by heading for the hills. There would still be trade with the cities but on their own terms – they were 'barbarians by design', avoiding the sharp social hierarchy of the lowlands. And the hill country was not anarchy. It produced a wide variety of political forms – some egalitarian, others unequal chiefdoms – though, in all cases, they lacked the tools of tyranny: a standing army or tax officials.

Is it possible for us today to re-create the freedoms of Scott's now-vanishing Zomia? Does it mean sacrificing order for anarchy. Can we retain security while still encouraging the innovative energy of creative destruction? Over the past decade, a movement has emerged to break away from the international order of sovereign states. The idea of 'charter cities' is to provide a place for creative destruction to unleash its promise, free from the overbearing state.

Charter cities experiment with the rules we create to govern our behaviour. When politicians change rules, they alter our behaviour – for example, congestion charging in London and in Stockholm. If the outcome of these little social experiments is good – clean air in inner cities' rather jammed streets filled with cursing drivers – then because ideas can be passed on for free, successful rules can be adopted elsewhere. What we need for this to work though are lots of experiments. And you know who is bad at experimenting? Large, conformist, well-ordered nation states. Cities, by contrast, are far more flexible.

A striking example is Hong Kong and its counterpart over the border with mainland China, Shenzhen. When the Chinese Communist Party developed a special export zone in Shenzhen in 1980, the zone had just 30,000 citizens – a set of small fishing and rural villages. By 2015 it had grown to China's fifth-largest city, with over eleven million residents. I visited Shenzhen myself in 2005, as part of a British review of education policy, and it seemed an impossible, gleaming fortress of skyscrapers. Shenzhen's model was about learning the rules that made Hong Kong successful and implementing them in a special zone outside normal national restrictions. A deliberate site of disorder if you will.

The concept of charter cities follows this model. Charter city advocates suggest that developing countries issue charters to found cities along similar models in unpopulated parts of their coastlines. Here rules, or even systems of government, can be experimented with and picked, discarded or kept, depending on what works.

Would it succeed? Despite great publicity at the start of the charter city initiative, there has not yet been great progress in convincing developing countries to benefit from the energy of disorder. Part of this is political – few nation states like to be told to relinquish sovereignty, particularly to a city that could then embarrass them by outpacing the rest of the country. And where the country creating charter cities is authoritarian, the liberties granted to the cities may easily be taken back. Rather than Shenzhen becoming more like Hong Kong, the crackdown by the Chinese Communist Party on free speech in both cities is making Hong Kong more like Shenzhen. Autocrats generally prefer tyranny to anarchy.

Another problem is logistical – finding space on a coastline for millions of new citizens, let alone funding it, is an almost unimaginable venture for all but the most optimistic. Many recent charter city plans developed by Western economists in countries from Madagascar to Honduras to El Salvador have come to nothing. Finally, there are also critiques of the project on its own terms. Is this yet another neo-colonial adventure in the developing world? Will the 'meta-rules' just be some form of libertarian technocracy that only listens to tech elites? These issues could be overcome but require enormous numbers of safeguards for the new citizens which might, in the minds of charter city proponents, dilute the whole agenda of experimenting with rules. Instead of a charter city you may just end up with a dirty, overcrowded, chaotic but otherwise pretty normal city.

16. Escaping the Security Trap

For most of us, moving to a charter city does not seem a viable solution to the dilemmas of the security trap. We care about preventing *our* police from overstepping their bounds. We want *our* streets to be ordered and *our* fellow citizens to behave. So what can we do if we want to escape this trap?

The security trap presents us with two problems — the threat of tyranny and the chaos of anarchy. It is tempting to think we can resolve both problems without the mess of politics. But the alternatives are not promising. When society seems anarchic, there are often calls for a 'strong leader' who can ignore politics and get things done. But, once in office, such leaders, from Vladimir Putin in Russia to Recep Tayyip Erdoğan in Turkey, crack down on peaceful protest and neuter any opposition. And so instead of anarchy we get tyranny.

Adopting a market model can't help us escape the security trap either. Markets work most effectively when people freely and voluntarily exchange goods and services, with the ability to refuse any deal they don't like. But anarchy doesn't respect existing property rights. And the provision of security doesn't look much like a market. The threat of force can compel people to accept deals they don't want. Security is also a basic need — if the threat of violence is existential, people will pay whatever they must to be safe. Finally, nothing prevents private security from extorting further money from their customers, particularly if they are the only 'local provider'. Markets don't work under anarchy; and they could bring us tyranny.

What about technology? New information technologies permit us to monitor both ourselves — preventing anarchy — and our guardians — constraining tyranny. But we'll need to be careful. If we're not, technological advances to solve one problem might worsen the other. Technology cannot see the full picture — machine learning, artificial intelligence and remote sensing are just algorithms — amoral and neutral – and if they aim to reduce anarchy they might just bring us tyranny. Technology does not exist in a politics-free world.

Let's begin with how we escape anarchy. Anarchy is like a liquid seeping into our lives through the smallest of cracks in our security. Where we cannot observe misbehaviour, we should expect anarchy. So one obvious place to begin is to improve our powers of observation. Before the last few decades, that basically meant increasing the number of observers, which in turn meant hiring more police. Or, in the Communist world, increasing the number of informers.

The advent of closed-circuit television (CCTV), and computer algorithms that can interpret this feast of visual data through facial recognition, has fundamentally altered the costs and viability of observation. Take a rather familiar example: speed cameras. Thirty years ago, to catch someone speeding required someone else to speed – the police car that would catch them up. Radar speed guns initially needed a trained police officer to use them and a police car to chase down the offender.

Speed cameras combined with automatic number plate recognition systems have made the physical police officer obsolete for traffic enforcement. A camera can now measure speed, photograph the offending vehicle and decode the number plate, meaning that the role of police officers is reduced to sending out the tickets. We may hate them, but speed cameras work: the presence of cameras has reduced crashes and injuries by 40 per cent in the UK. Cameras introduced in school safety zones in Seattle have reduced speeding by half. When people think they are being observed, they drive more safely, if resentfully.

Can the logic of speed cameras be extended more widely, to other places where people behave badly when they think they are not being watched? Well, if you live in London they already have! Britons are used to being gazed upon by myriads of CCTV cameras, nestled like all-seeing pigeons on every lamppost and bus shelter. But hitherto these largely played a deterrent role – put up outside supermarkets to scare off thieves.

Those same cameras are now employed more proactively by police in London using facial-recognition technology. Such technologies initially took a still image and matched it to a database. That's useful for investigators but only 'after the fact'. The innovation in London is to make that process live – cameras can immediately identify people on police watchlists as they walk past. Observation happens in real time, akin to having an eagled-eyed police officer, with a particularly sharp memory for faces, stationed at every corner.

However, such systems have not always been accurate in the past. An independent review of London's facial-recognition technology found a wide array of concerns. First, the legal status of the technology was unclear, especially given recent legislation on human rights and data protection. Second, it's not even clear that the technology works properly. In a pilot study, conducted at the huge Westfield Stratford shopping centre, forty-two individuals were recognized by the system as being on the police watchlist but in only eight cases had the AI system accurately identified them.

Even more fundamental is the question of whether facial-recognition technologies can work within a democratic society. The biggest new adopters of AI surveillance technology are, like London's police, in wealthy democracies. But, at the same time, the biggest producer of these technologies is an increasingly wealthy autocracy, China. Huawei currently provides these technologies to over fifty countries. Huawei claims it will not share data with the Chinese government, but that contradicts Chinese laws requiring such state access.

The most well-known system of citizen-monitoring, combining databases of citizen records with facial recognition, is China's emerging 'social credit' system. This refers to a whole archipelago of systems from private Chinese social media corporations to small cities to central databases that collate information on Chinese citizens, which can be used to sanction or reward them. The idea of social credit is that bad behaviours, such as failing to pay fines, public disorderliness or traffic violations can be tallied up against a citizen's social credit, whereas 'desirable' actions such as volunteer work or blood donation would increase their credit.

What does extra credit get you? That's a little less clear. But it appears to mean discounts on travel, more library books or shout-outs by the local press. As Yuan Yang at the *Financial Times* told me, the social credit system sounds more all-encompassing and centralized than its reality. The system is locally implemented and most cities don't have a social credit system at all. And, at least in terms of the benefits of accruing 'credit', it's more like a store loyalty scheme – the message from the state is, as Yang puts it, 'here's a nice sticker'. And the system is held together by a slightly ramshackle network of local governments and agencies, relying on the labour power of hundreds of low-level officials rather than technological wizardry.

The real traction comes from the so-called 'blacklist'. This is a nationally held list, assembled by Chinese regulatory agencies, of people who have violated legal or regulatory rules. Being on the blacklist has real consequences – not being allowed to fly or having one's children banned from prestigious schools. And here is where the twentieth-century world of blacklists has combined with the twenty-first-century world of artificial intelligence – people on the blacklist can be captured by camera and monitored, their details shared by private companies with the state. They cannot simply run for the hills.

It's easy to see how social credit could bleed into tyranny – an abusive state could blacklist political undesirables as easily as it does scoff-laws. But for many Chinese people the social credit system is perceived as necessary to deal with anarchy. It is hard sometimes to comprehend just how quickly China has industrialized. In 1980 20 per cent of China's population lived in urban areas – just under 200 million people. Today 60 per cent of Chinese people, over 800 million people, do so. The modern security regimes of America, of Britain, of France, began during the industrial era, as new cities were filled with uncountable, anonymous migrants from the countryside and old systems of order collapsed. Xin Yuan Wang, an anthropologist at University College London, has interviewed Chinese citizens about how they feel about social credit. And she argues that for many it is a necessary and desirable way for the government to try and create trust out of thin air in an era of rapid urbanization.

According to Wang, long-standing rural understandings of individual trustworthiness and of social relations were strained as people moved to the cities. Urban residents did not know who to trust, bereft of traditional ties and social norms that could bind people into communities. Wang quotes an interviewee stating, 'living in China is tiring . . . you have to be vigilant and always on guard against others'. The social credit system is perceived as a solution to this problem. Most fascinating of all, Wang finds that many Chinese people believe that the West already has a social credit system. There are widespread myths about people in Europe being denied jobs for long-ago fare-dodging episodes and confusion about the difference between the widely known concept of 'credit scores' (for mortgages) in America and the government keeping a 'social credit' tally.

With the end of the frontier, it is much harder for Americans and Europeans to simply vanish into the mists if they have gone bankrupt or committed a crime. Nowadays, credit ratings, criminal records and tax histories can be easily collected and merged on computers. And that information can be combined by police forces with new geographic crime prediction technologies to squeeze out the last gasps of anarchy.

Data science is the new cavalry of crime prevention. Algorithms of ever-greater complexity and processing power are now being used by tech firms to predict likely crime rates in areas as small as 500 metres squared, basically a city block. These companies merge previous crime locations and use geographic prediction technologies to provide information to police forces on where they think crime is likely to occur.

Exactly how accurate such algorithms actually are is up for debate – in some cases, they are basically moving averages of previous crime. One obvious problem with this approach is that it creates positive feedback – areas that had crime are expected to have more crime – and that produces 'state dependence' – where you initially arrest people determines where you arrest people in the future. If police forces have been disproportionately active in poorer communities or those with high numbers of ethnic minorities an algorithm might keep sending them back. This in turn means that policing becomes less neutral, less uniform, more prone to reinforcing its own bias. And given the state of some police forces, that's a problem. Where once was anarchy can tyranny grow.

Let's now turn to that issue – the misbehaviour of the very people who are supposed to protect us. We've seen that AI technologies are likely to be very effective at overcoming anarchy, but it's pretty obvious how they can also be used – or misused – to strengthen the powers of the state. As I noted earlier, technology itself is neutral. We need to harness it, if we are to bind the hand that guards us.

Unsurprisingly, the United States has been ground zero for debates about whether and how to restrain the police. The killings of George Floyd and Breonna Taylor in 2020 were sadly not a recent phenomenon. In the early 1990s, the beating of Rodney King threw a national spotlight on police violence. Police reform movements have been active for decades. But so too has police violence. What can be done?

When we think about how to reform the police, we can set out the options on a spectrum from technological changes to police operations to a full reimagination of how to maintain public order, possibly without the police. In each case we have to keep in mind the security trap – our solutions might end up replacing tyranny with anarchy. Or they might even reinforce tyranny inadvertently.

Let's begin with technological innovations that could restrain the police in the same way that facial recognition constrains the public. The most widespread recent technology adopted, sometimes rather reluctantly, by the police is body-worn cameras. These devices are attached to police officers' chests or headgear and are supposed to be turned on before engagements with the public from traffic stops to using firearms. Importantly, these devices are 'always on' – they store the thirty seconds of video that occurred before a police officer turns them on, reducing, though not eliminating, the temptation officers might have to turn them on immediately after engaging fire. The data is uploaded to encrypted databases in police departments and stored for several months.

What are the supposed benefits of body-worn cameras? Most obviously they provide documentary evidence of what police officers were actually doing when they stop motorists, unholster their guns or question suspects. These cameras are directly useful in terms of adjudicating the rights and wrongs of police engagements with the public.

But it's the indirect effects of body-worn cameras that are more interesting, and more promising. If police officers know that all their engagements are being filmed then, perhaps, they will change their behaviour. Future video evidence means present-day restraint. In turn, citizens knowing that police officers are wearing cameras ought to give them more confidence that they will be treated respectfully, or at least lawfully, by the police. When cameras are on we have much lower uncertainty about each other and, hopefully, this will increase trust and improve behaviour.

That's the theory. Does it work? Body-worn cameras lend themselves quite well to social scientific analysis because their use can be randomized within police departments. Some officers get randomly assigned cameras on duty, others not. Then we look at whether the officers with cameras are less likely to use force. A year-long 2012 experiment with the entire police department in Rialto, California, randomized camera-wearing across shifts. During camera-wearing shifts, use-of-force incidents dropped by a half. But randomizing shifts rather than officers means that all police officers were wearing cameras at some point. And it turns out there was a spillover effect – police officers on non-camera-wearing shifts were also less likely to use force than in previous years. It seems there was a cultural shift where officers always behaved *as if* they were wearing cameras, even when they weren't.

Strong evidence has been found that body cameras do seem to restrain whole police departments, even when not everyone is wearing one. Looking at the differential rollout of body-worn cameras from 2014, cameras appear to reduce police use of force, particularly homicide, by half. And negative sentiment towards local police departments on Twitter and the number of searches for 'Black Lives Matter' on Google both declined after the introduction of body-worn cameras by those departments.

So are there downsides to cameras? While cameras might root out or restrain 'bad apples', might they also make it harder for 'good apples' to police? Monitoring the police could make them more cautious, make criminals more confident and ultimately lead to higher crime rates. Then the FBI's Director, James Comey, wondered in 2015: 'in today's *YouTube* world, are officers reluctant to get out of their cars and do the work that controls violent crime'. That would indeed be bad, but a randomized study of police in Spokane, Washington, found no evidence at all of police passivity when wearing cameras.

And maybe our guardians just don't care if they're being filmed. We know, in horrifying detail, exactly what happened during the murder of George Floyd by officer Derek Chauvin because of video released from the body-worn camera of one of Chauvin's fellow officers, Tou Thao. It's true that the images of Floyd's death made viscerally clear just how brutal the police could be. A police force on film could not just issue mealy-mouthed denials and hope the problem went away. But the problem is that even though Chauvin knew he was on film, he did not moderate his behaviour. What's more, it was the cameras held by passers-by on their smartphones, not the body-worn cameras of Chauvin's colleagues, that produced the videos that sparked international disgust. In the absence of this video evidence from civilians it's hard to be sure that the footage from the body-worn cameras would ever have been released.

We might also argue that problems with the police go beyond just the use of force to the way they treat local communities more generally. Recall that in Ferguson, Missouri, the problem was not only police violence but a police culture that saw the citizens they were sworn to serve and protect as a constant threat or source of revenue.

The most full-scale vision for reforming the police promises revolution not evolution. 2020 saw the emergence of the slogan 'Defund the Police'. What the slogan actually means has been a heated topic. For some, it's a slogan that stands in for a series of police reforms, including cameras, the removal of immunity, and departmental re-organizations. For others it literally means cutting funding, possibly completely, to police forces. What might that involve?

The full-fat Defund the Police model would replace police functions with employees from other social services: social workers, psychiatrists, drug rehabilitation specialists. And it entails some level of community self-policing. For proponents of this argument, the police actually galvanize crime by criminalizing behaviour in poor areas that would be ignored in richer ones, by responding violently to protests or by heavily fining citizens, pushing them into poverty. Look at Western Europe, they say, where police spending is far lower and yet so too is crime. And they ask whether spending more on the police is not just worsening the problem rather than resolving it.

So could American crime and police violence both be reduced by cutting police spending? Or would anarchy emerge in its wake? Simply cutting police spending without addressing America's wider social problems is unlikely to cut crime. But to mimic European social welfare systems would require an unprecedented – at least for America – surge in overall public spending, far beyond the savings one could make in the criminal justice system alone. In other words, for security you might need solidarity. And America, to put it mildly, is not always solidaristic.

So far, we've talked about ways of escaping the security trap in terms of *personal* or *national* security. We've left the big challenge until last – *international* security. It's no surprise that wishing for 'world peace' has become associated with trite remarks at beauty contests – it seems like such an obviously desirable and hopelessly unachievable goal. And even though thinkers like Steven Pinker argue we live in a much more peaceful world than our ancestors, as we saw earlier, that claim is fiercely contested because there are still so many civil wars, terrorist attacks and border flare-ups – all of which have proliferated since the end of the Cold War. So what can we do to reduce war and international conflict?

We can begin to counter international anarchy by simply cooperating, either informally or formally. Sometimes informal cooperation is enough to help us maintain peaceful relations; at other times we want to 'put a ring on it', by signing a treaty or codifying an alliance. Informal cooperation may be as simple as trading with one another or having similar political systems. One of the few laws of political science is that democracies don't go to war with one another. This is the idea of the 'democratic peace' – a term established enough to be used by Presidents Clinton, Bush and Obama.

There's quite a list of reasons to think that war is unlikely to break out between democracies. Democracies better represent the will of the very people who will be sent out to fight; they are better at negotiating with one another because their political systems are all about debate and give-and-take; and democratic leaders fear the public-opinion consequences of entering into costly wars.

Democracies also tend to have free markets and trade with one another, which makes war more costly – this is sometimes termed the 'capitalist peace'. This latter argument formed the basis of the *New York Times* columnist Thomas Friedman's famous 'golden arches' theory – that no two countries with a McDonald's had ever gone to war. Sadly, this theory lies buried beneath the rubble of the NATO bombing of Serbia, and the various conflicts between Russia and Georgia and Ukraine. Shockingly enough, the pacifying power of fast food failed to resolve these conflicts peacefully.

Arguments about economic interdependence preventing war have a rather tragic history. One of the most famous books in international relations, *The Great Illusion*, was written by Norman Angell in 1909 and argued that international trade and investment made war and plunder pointless. The book was not well timed. Still, it's not hard to believe that greater economic relations have some benefits for peace – war is generally bad for business, not least because of the taxes needed to pay for it and the inflationary pressures it produces.

So where does this leave us in terms of solutions? Well, they would have to be pretty big ones – promoting democracy abroad with a view in part to promoting peace. That's not impossible: it has been a part of American foreign policy since the 1990s. Organizations such as the National Endowment for Democracy in America, the Konrad Adenauer Foundation in Germany and international organizations from the European Union to the World Bank have placed democracy promotion abroad as key goals. But, as you can imagine, hectoring voices from rich countries have not always been heeded. And the experience of the Iraq and Afghanistan wars, along with aggressive pushback from Russia and China, has cast a shadow over democracy promotion. Still, the absence of war in democratic Latin America, or among recent democracies in Africa, suggests there's life in the democratic peace yet.

A more direct way of securing peace among nations is signing collective-security agreements with one another. That's basically what NATO is – not only do members agree not to engage in conflict with one another but they also commit to collectively defend any member under attack from an outsider. This is why NATO for example got involved in Afghanistan after 9/11 and why Greece and Turkey have remained at peace (if tenuously) since the Second World War.

NATO's structure also explains why Ukraine, not a NATO member, and the Baltic states, members since 2004, have had such different experiences of Russian military aggression under Vladimir Putin. NATO being a collective-security agreement requires the United States, France, the United Kingdom and the other members to defend Estonia, Latvia or Lithuania if attacked. Although President Trump loudly pronounced his dissatisfaction with NATO, calling it 'obsolete', even under his watch a Russian invasion of the Baltics was effectively deterred.

By contrast Ukraine's relationship with Western military powers has been a much looser military alliance. Since 2008 NATO has pledged that Ukraine will become a member, but the alliance never offered a Membership Action Plan, its standard 'on-boarding' process. Tim Frye calls this 'the worst of all worlds' since it disappointed Ukraine, highlighted splits within NATO and deepened Russian paranoia. Crucially it meant that Western allies had made no binding commitments to Ukraine. Nothing Ukraine could do alone made any difference – in 2019 the Ukrainian parliament changed the constitution to make joining easier; in 2020 Ukraine became an 'enhanced opportunity partner' of NATO.

But none of this was membership. And in an anarchical world all those other agreements with NATO members were uncashable cheques. Russia did not invade Ukraine because of NATO expansionism, despite its self-justifications. The US ambassador to Russia under Barack Obama, Michael McFaul, claimed there was not a 'single serious conversation about NATO expansion between Obama and a Russian official'. Nor were Putin's claims that Ukraine wasn't a real country shared by average Russians – in January 2020 over 80 per cent of Russians believed Ukraine should be independent. Russia invaded because Vladimir Putin personally sought to remove unfriendly leadership in a neighbouring country, to seize territory occupied by Russian speakers and to violently announce Russia's continued position as a world power. And he could do so because Ukraine was not a NATO member and so NATO allies were not forced to defend it.

What we learn from the Russian invasion of Ukraine is that formal treaties matter, at least among allies. They are the only credible signal that can be sent under anarchy. And being 'on the way to membership', treated as an ally, even sent weapons, is not the same as being an actual member. NATO membership has kept the Baltics free. NATO non-membership keeps Ukraine, as well as Georgia and Moldova, in the shadowland of anarchy and empty promises.

Treaties among allies might seem like playing on easy mode. What about among enemies? Can signing a piece of paper really prevent adversaries doing what they want in the absence of a global judge, jury and executioner who could bang heads together?

The experience of nuclear- and chemical-arms treaties suggests maybe it can. The most successful arms control treaties of our time have been nuclear-arms treaties. From the late 1960s onwards, a litany of abbreviations entered international relations – the NPT, the SALT treaties, the START agreement. And they largely achieved their goals of non-proliferation and arms reductions, even if they didn't end the Cold War directly.

The other most lethal weapon of the twentieth century was chemical weapons – they were used in combat during the First World War with the horrific consequences of over a million casualties. And yet by and large they have barely been used since, except by dictators such as Saddam Hussein and Bashar al-Assad gassing their own people.

Why not? Here the reason for peace – or at least less vile warfare – seems to be our own norms and the treaties that embody them. The Geneva Protocol outlawed the use, though not possession, of chemical weapons. The 1993 Chemical Weapons Convention prohibits their development. A 'taboo' against using chemical weapons has emerged and it has largely stuck. Today we even discuss whether states have a legal 'duty of care' to citizens during wartime, one that can be ruled on in international tribunals like that set up following the Yugoslav wars. So even if we cannot legislate war away, international cooperation does give us optimism that we might be able to constrain our worst impulses.

Nuclear and chemical weapons were of course both examples of new military technologies. And so, we might ask ourselves, was it the cooperation that mattered in preventing their use? Or something about the technology itself? Could it even be the case that the more advanced – and lethal – our technologies, the less likely war is to actually occur? That would be fortunate, if not entirely reassuring.

Nuclear weapons are the most emphatically destructive force mankind has developed. And yet many scholars of international relations argue they are responsible for the lack of a Third World War. The reason is that nukes lead to Mutually Assured Destruction (aptly abbreviated as MAD). If you have what's called 'second-strike capability' – launching your own missiles before you've been annihilated by someone else's missiles – then you will deter your adversary from ever launching a first strike. In other words, if your enemy knows both of you will be 'mutually destroyed' if they launch their nukes, then they won't attack first.

Thus, we have the irony that the most lethal weaponry possible actually maintains the peace – unless somebody makes a mistake. The most famous 'near miss' of our era was when Stanislav Petrov, a Russian lieutenant-colonel, decided *not* to engage in second-strike attacks on the US when his early-warning system displayed incoming American nuclear missiles. He guessed right – the 'missiles' were actually sunlight glinting off high-altitude clouds. And so today we are alive and you can read this book. And that's the danger of MAD – it secures the peace *if* everything goes right.

What military technologies will shape the next fifty years and will they underpin – or undermine – peace among nations? As with body-worn cameras and social credit, new weapons systems take advantage of technological advances in our ability to capture imagery and process data. Drones are the new eyes of the military. They allow both mass surveillance and pinpoint targeting. Artificial intelligence enables militaries to process terabytes of this information to find and – to put it bluntly – eliminate targets.

The most interesting technological development combines drones with artificial intelligence – the creation of so-called Lethal Autonomous Weapons Systems (ironically abbreviated as LAWS). If you are thinking of *The Terminator* or *Robocop* – wrong size, right idea. Weapons are usually lethal, so that's nothing new. The autonomous part is. It means that the weapon itself is given the ability to choose a target, move to it and terminate it, without direct human interference. This feels like science fiction but that's increasingly not the case. The American MQ-9 Reaper, introduced in 2007 to autonomously fly to designated targets and then dispatch its payload, has now been fitted with AI capabilities that allow it to choose targets itself, waiting only for human permission. Humans retaining that permission is the thin blue line between this particular guardian being unguardable.

What do LAWS mean for the possibility of peace through deterrence? Can we prevent our robot friends from mutually destroying us? While we retain control of the final decision to engage, nervousness about the accuracy of LAWS may actually restrain combat – in 2003 automated US Patriot missiles ended up killing American troops because of faulty information. It's possible that fear of getting it wrong may prevent conflict. But even if LAWS become infallible, their use could still deter conflict. By their nature they are hard to observe – drones are small and it's impossible to know what AI systems they have operating them. Which means they are useful for deterrence. If you tell your adversary that you have LAWS, which you will use if attacked, it's very hard to know if you're bluffing and the consequences may be dire. Like nuclear weapons, the sheer lethality of LAWS may ironically help secure peace. Well, at least until the robots break free of our control.

From our safety on the street, against criminals and sometimes against the police themselves, to our safety from global annihilation, solutions to the security trap require us to constantly battle against the twin perils of anarchy and tyranny.

We can solve some of our problems ourselves. Our day-to-day security rests on trusting others. Our streets don't have to be anarchic if we are willing to give way to one another. We might not even need mime artists directing traffic. The social norms we develop organically to exclude or shame people who violate the rules may be stifling but they do provide certainty in our day-to-day lives. However, the new anonymous online world threatens to disrupt our ability to enforce norms, as regular Twitter users will know well. We may need some form of central authority that, with great discretion, moderates our interactions. Our decentralized online financial transactions are, except for the Wild West of cryptocurrency, usually governed by central eBay-style guarantors. Whether we are willing to accept our speech being governed that way is a different matter.

We are now living in a world of ceaseless mass surveillance thanks to the development of video technology and artificial intelligence. As the panopticon views everywhere we go and everything we post online, anarchy is slowly squeezed out of our day-to-day lives. This might well increase our security if criminals are caught on CCTV, or terrorists smoked out of online chatgroups. But it's easy to see how surveillance tips into tyranny, along the lines of China's social credit model. If it's too late to reverse this, we need to design institutions that balance against those watching us. If we are to create institutions to observe us in order to end anarchy we must simultaneously create ones that observe our guardians.

The advent of body-worn cameras may prevent the police from exploiting their power over the citizenry, though this did not prevent the murder of George Floyd. But we may need to go beyond this. We need transparency over the new tools of observation used by the state: public disclosure of the algorithms used to predict crime, oversight of the use of real-time facial recognition, use of satellite imagery of military engagements.

If we are to keep consent-based policing and a civilian-led military, we will need clear methods of accountability and political intervention against cover-ups by the police or security services. And that means empowering and trusting politicians to enforce this oversight. At the international level, it means continued development of the legal framework to punish war crimes, even when – especially when – Great Powers resist. But it will be an unceasing challenge – the very people we want to enforce these rules are the ones we need protection from. The security trap is all-pervasive.

PART V

Prosperity

What makes us richer in the short run makes us poorer over the long haul

17. Paris: Saturday, 12 December 2015

Laurent Fabius was late. It was the closing moment of the Paris Agreement on Climate Change, a crucial, perhaps last-gasp, moment for global cooperation on reducing greenhouse gas emissions. The French Prime Minister had been at the centre of two weeks of heated negotiations, conducted in the extraordinary surroundings of an old military airfield, with temporary tents erected to cater for the negotiations of over 190 countries.

The last such meeting in Copenhagen in 2009 had been an abject failure – no binding commitments had been made, cooperation against climate change had steered off track. But Paris had gone far better. The big players – the big carbon emitters – had stayed engaged. For once, the USA and China and India and Russia had stayed on course. But where was Laurent Fabius? It was now past 7 p.m. – the meeting was expected to have wrapped up ninety minutes earlier.

Fabius dashed onstage at 7.13 p.m. He had corralled all the Paris attendee countries around the same objective, to commit to reducing carbon emissions and keeping global temperatures in check. Now was the moment to strike. But the politics of ameliorating climate change are far from simple. Fabius had tried to charm the attendees – to get India onside he had sent all delegates a gift book of Indian and French philosophical quotations. Diplomacy was key to difficult negotiations – as Fabius said, 'states are no cold monsters'. But there had already been dissension – the South African negotiator, speaking on behalf of over one hundred developing countries and China, had claimed the draft report was 'like apartheid' and that poorer countries had been 'disenfranchised'.

The diplomacy would be especially challenging because of a need for consensus. Meaning all 197 parties to the United Nations Framework Convention on Climate Change needed to agree. Any country could bring the whole process to a halt. All it had to do was raise a vocal objection. And just as the conference reached its climax, the Nicaraguan delegate stood to do just that.

Fabius reached the lectern and spoke quickly into the microphone. He appeared flustered to the audience and the Nicaraguans were wondering what had happened to their objection. It was being ignored. Fabius rapidly announced: 'I am looking at the room, I see the reaction is positive, the Paris climate accord is accepted.' And with that he brought down the gavel in his hand and the Paris Agreement was official. Over Nicaragua's objections.

Well, almost. The Americans had already noticed that the word 'shall' had sneaked into the document, implying legal commitments that might derail the entire agreement since it would mean Congress, held by the anti-Paris Agreement Republican Party, would need to be involved. French delegates quickly reassured delegates this was a simple 'technical error' and 'shall' would be replaced by 'should', making all things right in the world. Unlike Copenhagen, Paris had been a roaring success. It had raised hopes for a collective solution to sustainable global prosperity. But did it actually mean anything?

Climate change is humanity's hardest political problem. If we can make progress with climate change, then just maybe we can resolve our other collective challenges. Climate change is also quite literally a global problem – it affects all of us and it may require all of us to act in concert to mitigate it. There's no global government that can take charge of this problem, just nation states, each with its own energy consumption and production needs combined with often legitimate historical grievances. Somehow the Paris Agreement had brought all the major players into the same room – well, tent – to agree on a path forward. But it had done so by jettisoning many of the things that make international agreements work: binding commitments, sanctions and enforcement.

The Paris Agreement was designed in response to the perceived failures of its predecessor, the Kyoto Protocol, and to the collapsed negotiations at Copenhagen. The Kyoto Protocol, adopted in 1997, was the first attempt at a binding global agreement on reducing carbon emissions. Kyoto mandated that developed countries would need to sign up to specified reductions in greenhouse gas emissions. Countries that failed to meet these targets would be officially sanctioned with financial penalties. It was a legally binding treaty with an enforcement branch. Sounds strong and effective? It wasn't.

Kyoto faced an immediate problem after its adoption. Although the United States had signed it, that didn't mean it would be legally binding on the US. First it would have to be ratified by the US Senate. That was the problem. During the Kyoto negotiation process the Senate legislated that the US must not sign a treaty mandating emissions reductions by the US but not by developing countries. That is exactly what Kyoto had done. So the Kyoto Protocol never even made it to the Senate for ratification.

Why were US politicians so against Kyoto? Perhaps because of lobbying from energy companies or distrust of climate change science. But the real bone of contention was that America would need to make sacrifices to control climate change while other countries wouldn't. This gets us to the heart of why climate change is so challenging politically. To resolve it, people need to make individual sacrifices today for the sake of our collective future. But that's not in their immediate interest. And this sets in motion the prosperity trap: *what makes us richer in the short run makes us poorer over the long haul.*

Earlier in this book, I introduced the 'tragedy of the commons' with the case of cod fishing. If fishermen can't agree to restrain themselves, they can completely deplete fish stocks. We're now figuratively fishing in a bigger pool. The earth's atmosphere is the largest commons of all. When one country produces carbon emissions, those emissions don't confine themselves to national borders. Emissions are natural cosmopolitans, they have wanderlust. As they permeate the atmosphere, they contribute to the global stock of greenhouse gases that heat up the earth for everyone, regardless of how many emissions they have produced.

To reduce global emissions, we have to bring everyone on-board. Slowing down emissions is costly. It's not just the cost of producing solar panels or wind turbines; whole industries, not least the fossil fuel sector, need to be fundamentally transformed or, more likely, shut down. And that means making sacrifices by consigning coalminers to unemployment or decommissioning factories.

But unless every country does this, it may be all for naught. If some countries pay the costs of net zero policies, while others do nothing, the earth continues to heat. Even worse, there's a temptation for smaller countries – from Bangladesh to Brunei to Britain – to do nothing and free-ride on the efforts of others. After all, if everyone else is pursuing net zero, I might be tempted to guzzle gas, knowing my effect on the global climate will be negligible. But if everyone thinks like that, emissions will rise uncontrollably. Climate change is the greatest collective action problem of all.

The United States is not a small player. Cutting its emissions, which in 1990 amounted to about 22 per cent of the global total, would have made a tangible difference to global warming. But by 2017 its emissions were barely higher than two decades earlier and now they only constituted 12.6 per cent of global emissions. The new polluters were those same developing countries that were not bound by Kyoto to reduce emissions – China (up from 11 per cent in 1990 to 25.9 per cent of global emissions in 2017) and increasingly India (up from 2 per cent to 7.3 per cent). But from the Chinese and Indian perspective, wasn't that fair? The US – and European countries – had been pumping out pollution for decades. They had 'had their turn', now it was the turn of the developing world. Was that really 'free-riding'? Or fairness?

The US failure to sign may have fatally weakened Kyoto but it wasn't the only saboteur. Canada bailed out of Kyoto in 2011 as it became clear it had no chance of reaching its targets, not least because it had begun extracting lucrative oil from Alberta's tar sands. The main countries who met their commitments were in Eastern Europe, benefiting from the closing of Communist factories and power plants. Countries followed Kyoto when it was easy, and left the treaty if it proved hard.

The Paris Agreement, on the other hand, worked through discretion and deliberate vagueness. Each country had discretion to set its own targets for carbon reduction, ideally ambitious ones. There was no global attempt to set targets for countries – this was bottom-up rather than top-down. The only collective goal was an outcome – a rise in global temperatures of no more than 1.5°C. Global temperature changes in the future are not a binding commitment – they're an ambition. Emissions reductions were now a discretionary national matter.

The vagueness came from the fact that emissions targets were also non-binding. Whether a country would or wouldn't seek to meet them was unknown. And although all countries made the same over-all commitment to lower global temperatures, developing countries did not have to have the same emissions targets as developed coun-tries. This had helped bring South Africa, China and other concerned industrializing nations onside. Countries simply report every five years on their targets and develop new, hopefully more ambitious ones. The idea was to create a ratchet effect that pulls countries towards net zero. But there's no emissions police; no court of emis-sions arbitration. The big players – the USA, China, India – would never have permitted it.

The Paris Agreement marked a change of strategy for the inter-national community when it came to climate change. Binding international cooperation proved impossible. Countries were unwill-ing to accept the heavy short-term costs of meeting emissions targets or the absolute authority of international law. But there was some agreed direction for the long haul, however frail. A partial escape from the prosperity trap. Perhaps this was a more realistic approach than its failed predecessors. Maybe the United States would at least stay on board this time.

On 8 November 2016 even that hope looked to be at an end. Don-ald J. Trump was now President-Elect. On 1 June the next year Trump announced he would begin the process of leaving the Paris Agreement, as he had promised during his campaign. Environmen-talists across the world were heartbroken. It felt like they were back to square one. But . . . perhaps they weren't.

A little-noticed aspect of the Paris Agreement had stipulated that any signatories could not begin the process of leaving the agreement until three years after signing. This would prevent short-term polit-ical volatility from derailing the agreement. It would then take another full year for the process to be completed. Four full years. Right up to the end of a first Trump term. How very convenient . . . Perhaps sustainable prosperity wasn't doomed after all.

18. What is Prosperity?

What is prosperity and where does it come from? Put simply, it's about 'the good life'. Having enough to be content. Perhaps also securing a better life for one's children and grandchildren. Those of us in the wealthy countries of the world have become used both to high levels of material comfort and an ever-growing economy. Not everyone shares this comfort. Nor is economic growth guaranteed. And, of course, 'more stuff' is not the sole source of human happiness. But compared to our ancestors of just a century ago – literally, our great-grandparents – we live in a world of unimaginable riches.

Historical experience tells us that this prosperity is not guaranteed. Many places have gone through reversals of fortune, as once wealthy civilizations and countries declined. The world today is undoubtedly far richer than the world of 1500. But where once Tenochtitlán, Cairo and Beijing stood as the largest and wealthiest cities we now have New York, Tokyo and, well, Beijing.

Places rise and fall because economic policies that are tempting in the short run can undermine sustainable growth. All countries, all cities, face the risks of the prosperity trap – *what makes us richer in the short run makes us poorer over the long haul.*

Before we can understand why we get caught in the prosperity trap, we need to establish what we mean by prosperity. The most common measure, gross domestic product (GDP), is not a bad place to start, though we'll shortly see its limits. GDP can be thought about in three ways, which ought to be equivalent: the total value of all production in an economy; the total sum of incomes to workers and business-owners; or the total amount of spending on consumption, investment and government, plus exports (minus imports). In other words, the value of things produced nationally should equal the money citizens earn, which should equal what people spend on domestic production.

When we talk about rich countries versus poor countries, we are usually referring to GDP per person. That means we are comparing average incomes. However, comparing how rich countries are by simply doing a currency exchange like in a bureau de change is misleading. If all goods and services were traded internationally that might make sense but many are not and are much cheaper in poorer countries. A famous example of this is the *Economist*'s Big Mac index. Most of the cost of a Big Mac comes from the local cost of doing business. You will be pleased to know that Big Macs are not actually internationally traded on ships around the world. In January 2022 a Big Mac cost $5.81 in the USA. But in India and South Africa, where local wages and costs are much lower, a Big Mac costs the equivalent of $2.50. By contrast, in expensive Switzerland a Big Mac would set you back seven bucks.

Statisticians use Purchasing Power Parity adjustment, which goes well beyond Big Macs, to account for lower prices in poorer countries. The IMF estimates for 2020 that if you translated rupees into dollars at the prevailing exchange rate, Indian income per head was just under $2,000, whereas adjusting for the cost of living across the country as a whole, it more than tripled to around $6,500. By contrast, Switzerland's income per head of $86,489 declined to $72,874 once purchasing power was considered.

Comparing prosperity across countries is challenging. That is even more the case across time, especially over the very long run. Our modern concept of GDP is not even a century old – its initial development was during the Great Depression, as politicians and economists struggled to figure out how much poorer their countries were getting. That means it is hard to work out how rich modern countries were centuries, sometimes even decades, ago. We simply don't have the raw data. Instead, we have the incredible efforts of economic historians such as the late Angus Maddison who painstakingly used data from scattered historical sources to try and estimate GDP per head two millennia ago.

Despite its ubiquity, GDP has come under concerted attack in recent years. Why? The first problem is what GDP excludes. Markets that are not under the formal view of government – from grey markets such as informal nannies to fully illicit markets such as narcotics – don't make it into the GDP numbers. When Italian statistical authorities decided to include estimates of this 'informal' production in 1987, they boosted national income overnight by 20 per cent, pushing Italy's GDP past that of the UK.

GDP also excludes production that occurs in the household itself. Billions of hours of labour in housework, childcare, caring for sick and elderly relatives is from the perspective of GDP non-existent or, worse, viewed as 'leisure'. This means that the more we outsource to the market tasks previously performed by the family – cooking, cleaning, childrearing – the more we raise GDP – even if there is no extra labour really being performed in aggregate. There has been an understandable feminist pushback against GDP, given the systematic undervaluation of work typically performed by women for centuries.

GDP is also a limited way of understanding human happiness and welfare. In Amartya Sen's view, what matters to people's prosperity is not income per se but the capabilities it provides them to live life as they want to. Income certainly helps people afford the means of existence and to access opportunities. But there are other ways of getting to those ends.

Education and good health may be necessary for people to both understand and seize opportunities. The Human Development Index (HDI) includes not only GDP but also life expectancy and educational attainment. This shifts around how we rank countries – Qatar drops from sixth to forty-fifth whereas Sweden rises from twenty-seventh to seventh. Our long-term prosperity ultimately depends more on the long-term health and education of the population than on short-term national income. So taking HDI seriously might help us avoid the prosperity trap by focusing on what matters for growth over the long haul.

GDP can also be attacked for what it includes. Many market activities are harmful. Fossil fuel extraction enters GDP as a positive, but the pollution it causes, whether to nearby streams or to the carbon stock in the atmosphere, is not deducted. In the 1940s Simon Kuznets argued for a prosperity index that measured human welfare, not production. That would mean excluding activities that were harmful in the aggregate, including military production. The problem with excluding such activities is of course that soldiers and coalminers are consumers too – removing their production means national production, income and expenditure no longer match up.

We can see embodied in GDP a germ of the prosperity trap. Generations of political scientists have found that economic growth just before elections boosts the chances of incumbent politicians. That, however, incentivizes subsidizing energy production or military build-ups even if they are clearly harmful over the long haul, because the long run is presumably after any forthcoming election.

To counter this short-term/long-term mismatch, Martin Weitzman developed the concept of Net National Product. The NNP can be thought of as the potential annual return we could get on the country's current stock of capital, including its natural resources. If we consume more than the NNP, we are spending today at the cost of reducing tomorrow's seed corn. Drawing down on fossil fuels and other fixed resources is a form of depreciation of our natural bounty, which ought to be deducted from national income. Hence the NNP can be viewed as a measure of the *sustainability* of growth.

Sustainable growth is the core way that environmental political economists think about prosperity. Sustainability was originally defined by the United Nations' Bruntland Commission in 1987 as 'development that meets the needs of the present without compromising the ability of future generations to meet their own needs'. Not a shabby definition of the risks of the prosperity trap. But sustainability can be surprisingly hard to achieve, especially for countries reliant on natural resources.

A group of economists led by Kenneth Arrow – he of Arrow's theorem – found in 2004 that many countries in sub-Saharan Africa and, perhaps unsurprisingly, the Middle East were not meeting the sustainability criterion, so heavy was their investment in natural-resource depletion. The World Bank found that countries from Nigeria to Azerbaijan to Burundi had negative 'genuine savings' in 2000 once the depletion of their natural resources had been taken into account. It argued that Nigeria's capital stock was one fifth of what it might have been had rents from these resources been more carefully exploited and saved.

Even in defining and measuring prosperity we face the prosperity trap — how can we value the future when we are incentivized to undermine it in the short run? We are not the first to face challenges of balancing short-term temptations and long-term sustainability; the history of economic development is a history of our ancestors wrestling with the prosperity trap.

The history of prosperity

How did we get so rich? Some people reading this book may not feel especially affluent. Others may be reading it in business class. But all of us live in a world of what would have seemed impossible abundance centuries, perhaps even decades, ago. The world's richest person in the early nineteenth century, Nathan de Rothschild, died from an abscess that could have been cured today with an antibiotic costing pennies. Rothschild's misfortune, and our relative fortune, depend both on technological and scientific advances and on the massive investment since then in producing and distributing goods.

It's not only in medicine that the average citizen today can experience more prosperity than historical millionaires. In my hand I hold an electronic box that allows me to access almost all human knowledge. I can talk instantaneously to a friend in San Diego, while finding the optimal way to arrive at the restaurant I just booked. I can see annoyed responses from around the world to an ill-judged tweet I just sent out. From the perspective of the not-so-distant past, we live in an age of miracles.

In that past, every day was much the same. People were more or less as wealthy as their distant ancestors, or their unborn descendants. This was the era of the Malthusian Trap, named after the Reverend Thomas Malthus (1766–1834). Malthus argued humanity was doomed to eternal poverty. Most people would only ever earn enough to cover their day-to-day subsistence. If people received higher wages, through technological growth, they would just respond by having children. Since population growth was exponential, at some point it would pass the capacity of agricultural technology to sustain it. At which point mortality would have to rise – directly through famine, or indirectly through disease and war. Rather disconcertingly, Malthus referred to these as 'positive checks'.

We can see early hints here of the prosperity trap. Clearly populations as a whole would be better off by slowing down their propensity to produce offspring (quite a euphemism), but from the perspective of an individual family they can't prevent others from having children, and every extra child they have could be set to work for the family's benefit. Or perhaps they just like having children. Either way, their individual incentives and society's are misaligned. Doom is inevitable.

Today we do not live in a Malthusian world. We can feed the exponentially increasing population of the world, which during the last one hundred years has quadrupled to eight billion. What did Malthus get wrong? Two things. First, something Malthus doubted was possible – people could reduce the number of children they had voluntarily. Malthus, with the prejudices common to his era, felt this might be possible among the European 'upper orders' but not among poorer citizens or outside Europe. Second, our ability to feed, clothe, shelter and provide for an exponentially growing population has somehow been able to outpace it.

Let us return to the world before 1800, when both incomes and population remained constrained. Angus Maddison estimated the global average income in the first millennium was around $450 per person per year (in US dollars valued at their 1990 levels). Enough to stay alive and just that. From 1000 to 1820, this rose to $670. But some slight regional differences had emerged: incomes in Africa and Asia varied between $400 and $600, whereas in Western Europe, and in its English-speaking colonial offshoots, incomes per head had broached $1,200 per annum. Still, in terms of annual growth rates over this period this was the difference between literally zero growth and 0.14 per cent per annum in 'booming' Western Europe.

And then, suddenly, an actual boom. One that wasn't simply reversed by Malthusian checks like famine. One that continued to grow. Not that fast by contemporary standards – even in go-go Western Europe incomes only grew by 1 per cent a year in the middle of the nineteenth century. But growth compounds. Western Europe hit average incomes of $4,000 by the First World War, and after the catastrophe of the interwar years incomes rose to $12,000 by 1970 and $20,000 by the 1990s.

Between 1820 and 1998, Western Europe saw annual growth more than ten times higher than the previous eight centuries – from 0.14 per cent to 1.51 per cent. Even higher rates of long-term growth occurred in the English-speaking colonial offshoots of Europe, and especially Japan too. A growth rate of 1.51 per cent looks mediocre from a modern perspective, but it meant that, by the twenty-first century, Europeans were over fifteen times as rich as they were in 1820.

When we turn to other parts of the world the story is quite different. Latin America and Eastern Europe grew but at a substantially slower rate. Asia outside Japan grew at under 1 per cent per year from 1820 to 1992, and Africa at 0.67 per cent a year. Over two centuries, the Western European rate would make you twenty times richer; the African rate just under four times richer. Today, countries such as Norway, Switzerland and the USA have average incomes over $60,000. Mozambique, Liberia and the Democratic Republic of the Congo under $1,500 (adjusted for purchasing power). A forty-fold difference. There has been, as Lant Pritchett termed it, 'divergence, big time'.

Why? Scholars who study economic growth think about countries as giant 'production functions', where inputs like labour (workers) and capital (machines and factories) produce national output. Bluntly, there are two ways to increase GDP in this setup – you either increase the sheer amount of inputs, through population growth or building up the capital stock; or you increase the effectiveness of the inputs, by improving your labour and capital stock through education or technology. Traditionally growth theory emphasized the former – countries would become richer when they had higher savings rates, which would build up the capital stock. While this is slightly moralistic, it fits the logic of the prosperity trap – countries that avoid the temptations of consuming in the present and invest more have a stronger future.

More recently, economists have emphasized the importance of generating ideas and being able to effectively use technology through higher investment in education. This growth snowballs because technological ideas can be replicated cost-free, which means all firms can benefit whether they invented the idea or not. Think of the discovery of electromagnetic waves by James Maxwell, which enabled innovations from the radio to the television to the microwave.

But such growth depends on people being willing to innovate in the short run, even when they can't capture all the long-term benefits of innovation. At the individual level, unless you or I are a Newton, a Maxwell or an Edison, it's unlikely that our own choices will make a huge difference to collective growth. Or that, even if they did, we could individually capture the benefits we had produced for everyone else. So there's an incentive for us to consume now and benefit from a wealthier country later, built on the savings and innovation of others. But if we all do this, we fail to innovate and remain poorer in perpetuity. Again, the prosperity trap rears its head because what makes sense for us in the short run harms us over the long haul.

How does this help us answer why some countries are richer than others? Sure, some places might have saved or educated more. But what starts the wheels in motion? How do countries solve the prosperity trap? In particular, how do we stop people choosing short-term temptations over long-term growth? Enter politics.

The most influential account of how politics affects growth comes from Daron Acemoglu and James Robinson, who argue that today's differences in income can be traced back to AD 1500 and the political institutions established then. That sounds a little bloodless. By 'established', I mean imposed at the point of a musket by European colonizers. These political institutions could be inclusive of all people living in a colony or they could be exclusive to a small cadre of colonists, leaving the original population unrepresented politically. Where you got inclusive institutions, you ended up with long-term growth; where you had exclusive ones, long-term stagnation. Politics makes growth.

The political institutions Europeans created in colonies depended on how many Europeans lived there. Where mortality from tropical disease was high, European colonists were less likely to survive. In such places, a small, sickly European elite set about extracting as much labour and resources as possible from the established population, using slavery or indentured labour.

Politically, this produced highly exclusive institutions that solely represented the interests of the tiny imperial cadre. Economically, it meant using forced labour, producing immediate riches in tobacco, silver and sugar. But there was limited investment in industrial capital or in education, and hence economic decline in the long run. Extractive institutions produced a 'reversal of fortune' where those places outside Europe with large and wealthy populations – Aztec Mexico, Mughal India – declined dramatically under extractive European rule to become impoverished by the late nineteenth century.

By contrast, where disease was low, European colonizers appeared en masse and demanded political institutions that would safeguard their private property. This meant inclusive political institutions, including voting and property rights that ultimately enabled widespread prosperity. But only among Europeans. You might note that in the largest of all these low-disease, high-European-immigration colonies – the United States of America – inclusive institutions did emerge, but only if you were not enslaved.

We can see the prosperity trap throughout this story. Where there were immediate riches to exploit, Europeans seized them avariciously and often violently, producing untold wealth in the sixteenth century. But, as the decades passed, they failed to invest in political and economic institutions that might create sustainable long-term wealth – not only in the unfortunate colonies of Latin America but also in some of the most rapacious colonizers, Portugal and Spain.

The story of why some of Europe rapidly industrialized, whereas other parts remained agricultural and poor, in the mid twentieth century cannot be told through the history of colonialism alone. Where once Venice and Madrid, Lisbon and Constantinople, had been Europe's richest cities, by 1800 they had been usurped by London, Amsterdam and Antwerp. Why did the Industrial Revolution begin in Manchester, not Madrid?

Again, political institutions that solved the prosperity trap are key. A stark example is the sudden rise of England to economic superpower. Economic historians point to the so-called Glorious Revolution of 1688 in England as a crucial moment, when England's Parliament replaced the Catholic King James II with his Protestant daughter, Mary, and her Dutch husband, William. What began as a religious skirmish had epochal economic consequences.

After 1688 the monarchy lost its ability to unilaterally make financial demands on the public. The English Civil War of the 1640s had been precipitated by royal monopolies and 'forced loans' from the King to finance royal expenses. This rent-seeking and expropriation by the monarch was anathema to Parliament, which represented the wealthy landed and merchant classes, who were targeted by forced loans and who resented the monarch's granting royal charters to favoured firms. So the arrival of William and Mary was accompanied by a new set of checks on the monarchy and the emergence of parliamentary supremacy.

Although British monarchs were now in parliamentary chains, ironically their ability to raise taxes was improved because Parliament passed laws to guarantee that monarchs couldn't alter the terms of loans arbitrarily. Government spending rose from just over a million pounds per annum on the eve of the Revolution to £7 million by 1750. Debt rose from a million pounds to an eye-watering £78 million. And this was sustainable because the interest rate charged to the crown dropped from 14 to 3 per cent. English wealth-holders were far more willing to lend to a constrained monarch. Political promises could now be trusted.

This trust spilled over into the development of elaborate capital markets, the value of London's Stock Exchange increasing thirtyfold by the 1720s. By constraining the monarch, widespread wealth could proliferate. Keeping the monarch away from the temptations of short-term expropriation provided the seedbed for long-term prosperity, perhaps even the very Industrial Revolution that led to Britain escaping the Malthusian Trap.

What is the lesson of these long-passed historical episodes for us today? That we ignore politics at our peril when we think about growth. Political institutions establish who gets to participate in the economy and under what conditions. They shape our incentives to succumb to short-term temptations rather than long-term investment. And they make our political promises not to cut and run more or less credible. They can help us escape the prosperity trap, or lead us straight into it.

19. The Prosperity Trap

Tomorrow, we want to be prosperous. But today can tempt us away from tomorrow. The sugar hit of today's riches leads us astray. And our short-term temptations can add up to long-term stagnation, even ruin. The prosperity trap hinges on the dilemma that *what makes us richer in the short run makes us poorer over the long haul.*

The prosperity trap emerges even though cooperation with other people would make us better off in the long run. There is often an immediate payoff to cheating, reneging or otherwise taking advantage. Unless we constrain ourselves somehow, tie our own hands, we will be drawn to the short-term temptations of free-riding on the efforts of others. And if even only one of us cuts corners, the whole house of cards can fall. Many cooperative outcomes that we *know* are good for us – refraining from emitting carbon, paying our taxes for public services – can quite quickly be ripped asunder.

The prosperity trap can also emerge even if we don't need to cooperate. Sometimes we can all benefit immediately from some valuable resource, be it oil or diamonds, or some other manna from heaven. But like Aesop's proverbial grasshopper, we fail to think about whether these boons will last, and what we'll do when they're gone. And the wealth created from resources might distort our politics in all kinds of dysfunctional ways. We're not doomed to a 'resource curse' – Norway, for example, has used its oil riches carefully, building up a sovereign wealth fund worth a quarter of a million dollars per Norwegian. But oil can also bring civil war – Nigeria – authoritarianism – Saudi Arabia – and folly – the Qatar World Cup.

The final form of the prosperity trap comes when we successfully coordinate, but our very doing so creates a false sense of prosperity that is unsustainable. Financial manias – and the ensuing panics – are a classic example. We might agree at any point in time that we all greatly value tulips, or condos in Phoenix, or cryptocurrency. Until that's not the case, it makes sense to buy in – the financial value of an asset is after all what people are willing to pay for it. But if we have misunderstood the fundamental value of the asset, or its likely future value, we may find that doubt sets in, and with it a sudden collapse. These bubbles emerge because we seem ineluctably drawn to believe 'this time is different'. Can we find ways to stop these manias in their path or at least to prevent doubts seeding panics?

Collective action

A spectre has haunted all the previous chapters of this book: the spectre of collective action. Each trap was set by the clash between our individual interests and our collective goals. For democracy, it was our incentive to undermine collective voting by manipulating our votes. For equality, it was the tension between equal individual freedoms and equal collective outcomes. For solidarity, it was our individual desire to only bail out the collective when we could be sure of benefiting ourselves. And for security, it was the individual temptation to avoid collective rules when they weren't convenient for us.

With prosperity though we dive into the heart of the collective action problem. Prosperity is about growth – about each generation being better off than the one before. This needn't necessarily mean higher economic growth. But it does mean ever-rising human happiness. The crucial thing about prosperity is that everyone can be made better off than they currently are.

We call this happy outcome 'positive sum'. Imagine a political event – we sign a trade deal, we pass an environmental bill, we cut taxes. A positive-sum outcome is one where, if we tallied up how much better or worse off everyone was afterwards, the sum would be positive. On average, people would be better off after the event, even if some lost out. If that's the case, we could – emphasis on *could* – make everyone better off by reallocating some of the winners' gains to the losers.

A 'negative sum' outcome is one where collectively people are made worse off, even though some might be better off. You might think that surely people would seek to avoid such collectively poor outcomes. Oh, you sweet summer child. This book has been about the unfortunate ubiquity of negative-sum outcomes, caused by individual self-interest undermining collective goals.

A final case is when the winners' wins exactly balance the losers' losses. This world of zero-sum outcomes is how most sports and games work. Think about the humble coin toss at the start of a football match. A coin can land in one of only two ways. We have a winning team and a losing team. But zero-sum games also proliferate in politics. The classic example is territory – it can only belong to one sovereign country at a time. A peaceful transfer of territory is zero sum. So is voting – in Canada or the USA, you can only vote for one candidate. If you switch voting in the following election, there is a winner (the new candidate) and a loser (the incumbent).

Now let's turn to prosperity. How should we think about positive-sum, negative-sum and zero-sum outcomes here? We can get positive-sum outcomes in the economy in two ways. First, we figure out how to produce more stuff, either by discovery (Look, a well of oil!), by effort (Work harder, peasants!) or by invention (Eureka!). Second, we find a way to shift the stuff we have around already in a way that makes everyone happier. These are the fabled 'gains from trade'.

Producing more and allocating things better involve some kind of cooperation between people – collectively investing in research and design or discovery, reducing barriers to trade, developing legal systems so we can trust each other, and so forth. We don't have to have central planning – individual effort and self-interest could be doing most of our work – but we do need a collective framework to stabilize this.

What about zero- and negative-sum economic outcomes? For zero-sum outcomes it's easiest to think of splitting the proverbial pie by dividing something that is fixed in quantity. The most obvious analogy is land. As jovial realtors say, they ain't making any more of it (tell that to the Dutch). Take for example the division of rural land between peasants and their feudal overlords. When landlords enclosed land previously held in common by the peasants, this was a straight zero-sum transfer from the villagers to the landlord. Any fixed good – oil, diamonds, natural gas – is going to have the same quality: there's only so much of it, and if one person has it another doesn't.

In zero-sum situations, nobody would voluntarily agree to being the loser. Zero-sum outcomes, let alone negative-sum ones, are not going to happen in an ideal-type market economy, where all transactions are voluntary. But they can still happen in politics. Throughout much of human history might has made right. Violence, rather than voluntary market exchange, was what mattered. And that meant the economy was in fact often negative sum. In the course of seizing land, blood got spilled. Both sides could have been better off if the land had just been handed over without bloodshed, even if there had still been a clear winner and loser. But it was not to be. In a world where most valuable resources are scarce and fixed in supply, and violence is the way of solving disagreement, there will be minimal growth and constant conflict. Not a recipe for prosperity.

Prosperity and positive-sum interactions between people go hand in hand. And zero-sum (or, God forbid, negative-sum) outcomes sound bad. But even when we could have positive-sum outcomes in theory, we might fail to achieve them in practice. Our individual self-interest might override a collectively beneficial goal.

The classic example of the difficulty of getting to positive-sum outcomes is the infamous Prisoner's Dilemma. The standard exposition is two prisoners deciding whether to grass on each other or stay shtum, but it can be used to describe all kinds of political and economic dilemmas. The Prisoner's Dilemma shows how hard it is to secure collective cooperation among the players involved, when there is an individual incentive to defect from cooperation – in other words, to cheat.

During the Cold War people often spoke about the US–Soviet arms race as a Prisoner's Dilemma. In any two-player Prisoner's Dilemma, each side has just two choices – to cooperate or to defect. In an arms race, cooperating would be refraining from building new nuclear weapons. Defecting would be building them. What makes something a Prisoner's Dilemma is how the best choice each side can make depends on what the other side chooses to do.

Building nuclear weapons was obviously costly and increased the threat of something going wrong and ending up with an accidental nuclear war. Both the US and the Soviets would have been better off if each side cooperated and refrained from building more nukes than if they both defected and carried on the arms race. But the problem each faced was that if one side refrained from building nuclear weapons while the other side did so in secret, they would be at a serious strategic disadvantage. Given this risk, both sides defected, and the arms race went on. Both sides *could* be better off by cooperating. But their individual incentive is always to defect, whatever the other side does. So they do.

The Prisoner's Dilemma also characterizes many social situations that share certain characteristics: no communication; no trust; no way of signing a contract; and being a one-off decision. The Prisoner's Dilemma is best at explaining human behaviour in the anarchic situations we saw in the last chapter on security, such as clan violence in Albania. If there is no third-party enforcement of agreements and no ability to build relationships, then the Prisoner's Dilemma will be prevalent. This explains why prosperity can be so hard to kickstart in places experiencing civil war, or where there is massive mistrust among ethnic or religious groups, or indeed among nations.

But the Prisoner's Dilemma can also be a useful description of less obviously violent economic situations. Whenever we can't fully know who others are, or tie them to a contract, and there are benefits from cheating, we should expect cooperation to collapse. Marketplaces where buyers and sellers meet anonymously or irregularly, from Craigslist and street corner vendors to the illicit trade in drugs or stolen goods, will be ones where there is a great temptation for both sides to defect.

Even governments face the Prisoner's Dilemma. For example, in countries with high levels of corruption and low levels of trust, getting people to pay their taxes can be challenging. If everyone paid their taxes, there would be more money to go round and the country could run an efficient modern bureaucracy – a positive-sum outcome. But each taxpayer would be better off evading taxes and letting others pay. And knowing this everyone wants to avoid being the patsy and we end up with widespread tax evasion.

In southern Italy, for example, tax audits of self-employed workers show that around two thirds of their income is 'concealed' from tax authorities. Economists have found that each individual Italian taxpayer responds not only to their own risk of audit but what they see others doing – a change in the auditing rate has triple the effect across society that it has on any single taxpayer. Tax-dodging is contagious.

Taxation is especially challenging because it involves far more than two players. The more players we have, the greater the benefits of us all cooperating, but also the easier it is for any one of us to cheat and get away with it. After all, if only I dodge my taxes, it barely reduces the government's revenue. But if everyone thinks like that, revenue collapses and we all end up with nothing.

This is the 'collective action problem'. When we need to make individual contributions to a collective goal, everyone will have an incentive to free-ride on the collective effort. But, like a loose zip, as one person defects, the other contributions come unstuck too and we slide down to nothing. We know we should stick to the collective plan but for each of us individually it's not worth it, especially if we suspect that others will free-ride too.

Climate change is the collective action problem par excellence. Every country needs to commit to reducing carbon emission because global temperature rises depend on global emission levels. But each country, especially small ones, could carry on polluting while benefiting from a stable global climate, as long as everyone else still cooperates. But everyone else is in the same situation. No one wants to pay the cost of bailing out polluting industries, especially if there's no point in doing so because everyone else keeps polluting.

Is there nothing we can do? Well, if we are stuck in a single, short Prisoner's Dilemma among multiple countries or people, maybe not much. But recall the characteristics of a Prisoner's Dilemma. It's not just the incentive to defect. It's also the single-shot nature of it. And the absence of third-party monitoring and enforcement. And the absence of communication and trust. So, what would happen if we tried to alter each of these developing laws, institutions and policies to shackle our worst impulses?

Let's start with the one-off nature of a Prisoner's Dilemma. Most encounters we have in life are repeated. Friends, clients, employees and employers – we engage in these relationships multiple times – perhaps our entire lifetime. Even internationally, countries don't encounter each other in simple one-offs. If you screw over an ally or trick an adversary, they'll remember it tomorrow. Diplomacy happens over the long run. We meet and we meet again, hashing out our differences. So what happens to the dark world of a one-shot Prisoner's Dilemma if we repeat it?

From darkness there comes light. Maybe. If we repeat the Prisoner's Dilemma endlessly then something called the 'folk theorem' comes into play: there's always a strategy that can maintain cooperation. For example, we could use a 'grim trigger' strategy. That sounds ominous . . . The 'grim trigger' strategy requires us, if we are cheated, to defect for ever as punishment. We cooperate as long as everyone else does, but if they don't then we unleash the dogs of war. Now that we all know the cost of cheating, we're incentivized to stay on track.

This seems a rather draconian tactic to employ. Can we really commit to punishing people for ever for what might be a rather minor transgression? How is this better than endless defection from the beginning? There is, fortunately, an alternative – 'Tit for Tat': cooperate if others cooperate but defect if they defect, deciding to cooperate again *only* if the chastened opponent starts to cooperate again. In other words, this strategy rewards good behaviour and punishes bad behaviour.

Tit for Tat can emerge in the most unlikely of situations. Robert Axelrod, who developed the strategy, points to the tacit agreement of German and British troops in the trenches during the First World War not to shoot at each other during certain periods, including the first wartime Christmas, despite orders from their superiors to do so.

This kind of cooperation in an otherwise violent, anarchic situation can continue for centuries. The borderlands between medieval England and Scotland, called the 'Marches', were largely lawless between the thirteenth and sixteenth centuries. The clans who lived in these areas engaged in perpetual 'reiving', the practice of raiding territory across the border for livestock and pillaging nearby villages.

Reiving ought to have been negative sum and have produced poverty and starvation, along with the customary theft and murder. But over time cross-border laws were developed, called the *Leges Marchiarum*. The laws did not, because they could not, end the practice of reiving. But they codified ways of loosely cooperating that relied on the reciprocity of Tit for Tat. If a reiver had unjustly killed someone on the other side of the border, the laws called for the practice of 'manbote' – if that person was caught they would be sent across the border, either to be executed or, more lucratively, to be ransomed. If livestock were stolen, the thieves could be pursued across the border, and locals on the other side would be compelled to help track them – a practice called 'hot trod'.

Finally, and most compellingly reminiscent of Tit for Tat, 'days of truce' would regularly occur when both sides would meet to settle disputes. Assize courts would be set up to pass sentence on lawbreakers but with an interesting twist – the English would choose the Scottish jurors and vice versa. This practice forced reciprocal behaviour. If the other side chose fairly, so would you. If they tried to rig the jury, you would do likewise. Although England and Scotland were almost constantly hostile with one another, the *Leges Marchiarum* kept that anarchy partially contained from their creation in 1249 until the union of the English and Scottish crowns in 1603.

What can we do with this apparent fountain of eternal cooperation? Well, it provides us with a way to build effective trust in situations where there is an incentive to cheat: keep long time horizons on the table. That means, perhaps counterintuitively, it's better to lengthen our relations with people we don't trust. If we make and keep making promises day after day, as long as we don't keep breaking them, we don't have to rely on some (absent) third party enforcing them. We can rely on time instead.

In fact, drawing relations to a close definitively has very bad consequences in the Prisoner's Dilemma. If we know we are meeting someone for the last time, then we can get away with cheating. But knowing that spoils all the previous interactions, since now in the penultimate time we meet we will also cheat, and the time before that, and so forth back to the beginning.

This is one of the reasons that term limits on politicians can backfire. If the politician knows that there is nothing they can do to be rewarded, and no way of punishing them, in their final term in office, then they may 'defect' by feathering their own nest. But knowing all politicians will face this temptation means that in all earlier elections voters face candidates who will ultimately betray them. So, in initial elections, voters might be forgiven for assuming that all politicians will be the same, and be willing to elect someone who is corrupt both now and later.

Lengthening our relationship with potential opponents flips the prosperity trap on its head. What makes us richer over the long haul stops us from succumbing to temptation in the short run. Our collective goals can win out because they always beat immediate self-interest, provided the other guy is willing to punish us. Hence, it's better to negotiate with someone who is willing to play hard but fair with you because they will keep you in line – provided you're willing to do the same. Sadly, despite the unimpeachable logic of Tit for Tat, it has proved remarkably useless for me as a parenting strategy – which raises the morbid question of whether my children really think this is an indefinite relationship.

Extending our time horizons is one solution to securing prosperity. But it won't work everywhere. For example, it doesn't help us in anonymous interactions. So what alternatives do we have? An obvious one is third-party enforcement. If we can be monitored by the police or punished by the courts when we transgress, then we can outsource the enforcement of cooperation. We don't have to make threats and promises about what we'll do in the future – we rely on the law.

But if politics is just a promise, and hence not always enforceable by third parties, that won't help us in political situations. We'll need different plans. One is to pay people to cooperate rather than free-ride. This idea comes from Mancur Olson, who did something rather provocative for a social scientist – he denied the possibility that groups of people could act coherently.

Olson argued that even if everyone in a group agrees on what they want, each will have the incentive to free-ride on the efforts of other group members to secure that goal. Imagine you are an employee covered by wage-bargaining agreements. Wouldn't it be lovely to get a wage boost but not go on strike? Or you're a group of oil-producing countries trying to restrict supply to keep prices high. Wouldn't it be tempting to sneak out a few highly priced barrels?

How do you get groups to work together and avoid the ever-present temptation of free-riding? Sticks and carrots. The stick is a norm of punishing group members who don't toe the line. This could be done by establishing an institution that sets rules and fines for free-riders. Union membership rules are one example. Or we could implement the kinds of social norms we met in the security trap, from Albanian norms of revenge to the conformism of Scandinavian villages.

The carrots are called 'selective incentives' by Olson – goodies that you only receive if you contribute. Again, institutions are one way of making our promises concrete – rules about access to club benefits such as the union bar or swimming pool. Or we can use norms – funerals and gifts to the family of the deceased in organized crime groups.

But, Olson notes, now we have another problem. Who oversees the sticks and carrots? Who is going to pay for the selective incentives? Who is going to pay the costs of monitoring and punishing group members who free-ride? We have just pushed the collective action problem back one notch.

Olson argued that groups would only effectively secure their collective goals if at least one member was large or rich enough to pay for the goal themselves. This member would secure such a benefit from the goal that they would pay for it regardless – which means that other members get to free-ride anyway! This was a decent description of NATO during the Cold War – the United States received enough benefits from keeping the NATO alliance during the Cold War for it to tolerate paying the lion's share of the costs, meaning that Germany, Italy, the Netherlands, etc., could free-ride under the American security umbrella. Perhaps Donald Trump had read Olson . . .

The collective action problem occurs whenever we find it hard to monitor others, in politics high and low. As an example of the latter, whenever you buy a ball of Italian buffalo mozzarella you might fairly ask how you know whether the milk in the cheese really does come from the buffalo stalking the swamps of Naples, as opposed to the mass cattle dairy farms of northern Italy. Cow milk is cheaper and could be added to buffalo milk without most of us being able to detect it in our cheese. This was a particular challenge for buffalo mozzarella producers in southern Italy, where social trust was low and organized crime and corruption common.

The solution that producers came up with to prevent adulteration with dairy milk resembles Olson's. The big buffalo mozzarella producers paid the costs of forming a consortium that insisted each piece of cheese was wrapped in paper with the manufacturer's name, which solved the monitoring problem. They lobbied the government for a trademark DOC label (like that used for French wines) to provide a selective incentive for producers.

But, even then, small producers might try to free-ride on the branding of the DOC and adulterate their cheese – in the early 1990s testing showed over a third of the mozzarella was adulterated. So Olson's punishment principle came into play – a first offence for producers led to a fine, a third to being turfed out of the consortium. The plan was costly, but it worked – adulteration was under 10 per cent by the late 1990s. So now you can buy your expensive buffalo mozzarella with confidence.

Let's return to the defining issue of our century – climate change. Here is the most extreme version of the prosperity trap. Over the long haul we may heat the planet to unsustainable levels, but our short-term incentives are often to pollute and emit to live the lives we have become accustomed to.

What have we learned from this tour of the Prisoner's Dilemma and how can it help us resolve the impending crisis? The first major climate agreement – the Kyoto Protocol of 1997 – failed. Superficially, the Kyoto Protocol solved the collective action problem. It had a monitoring and verification system to make sure countries did what they promised. It had enforcement mechanisms to prevent backsliding and free-riding, such as fining non-compliant countries and banning them from emissions trading. Finally, it envisaged regular meetings to update emissions targets, lengthening the shadow of the future.

So why didn't it work? First, international enforcement is an oxymoron – the international system is anarchic, there is no hierarchy that can enforce punishment. Rather than pay its fine, Canada simply left the Kyoto Protocol. Second, the costs of following the rules are very high, particularly for certain countries. Big energy producers such as the Gulf states and America, and major industrial countries such as China, have every incentive to obstruct collective action. They are not just free-riders but saboteurs.

The Paris Agreement, by contrast, has much wider acceptance. But can it work? It lacks the monitoring and enforcement capacity of Kyoto. But it does emphasize the shadow of the future. Countries must re-establish emissions targets every five years; they have to keep seeing each other driving down their emissions. Naming and shaming may not have legal effect, but it still motivates politicians' egos and maybe their behaviour.

The Prisoner's Dilemma only explains some aspects of the politics of climate change. It assumes parties face the same costs and benefits from contributing to collective action. But there are massive differences across countries in who wins and who loses from global warming or its abatement. Major energy producers in Northern climates – Russia and Canada – might actually benefit from climate change as previously frozen land becomes viable for agriculture, while being economically hurt by emissions reduction. Others, including low-lying island states such as Seychelles or Maldives, are threatened by the rising seas accompanying climate change and do not have emissions-producing industries to protect. We might be able to better handle climate change by allying together the losers and buying off – or politically defeating – the winners from it.

This also applies to businesses and industries. Sure, energy companies will be hit by emissions reductions, unless they can move quickly to focus on renewables. But the insurance industry and the financial sector will be hurt by the losses caused by climate change, as seen in the German floods and Greek firestorms of summer 2021. For some countries or industries, the benefits of acting alone may even outweigh the costs of doing so.

Finally, as climate change advances, more and more people become negatively affected, increasing the size of the environmental coalition. As renewable energy technologies advance, they become ever cheaper, and early investors in them may see increasing returns. And norms among the general public, at least in democracies, appear to be pushing towards environmentalism, placing growing pressure on recalcitrant politicians.

This is a type of 'catalytic cooperation' – once it gets going it becomes self-reinforcing. The Paris Agreement aligns with this bottom-up approach to securing our collective prosperity – it might just be a promise that lasts. Whether that promise is enough to prevent fundamental changes to the earth's climate and all the disruption and dismay that portends – on that the jury is out.

The resource curse

The history of global prosperity has largely been about creating new wealth. But what about those lucky places where wealth sits in the ground, ready to be tapped? Digging things up is simple relative to the complex webs of cooperation and trust on which sectors like finance, pharmaceuticals and high tech depend. And it can be done by a single company or by the state, which should reduce the risks of firms or people failing to cooperate.

When we look around the world at those fortunate places that have massive reserves of valuable resources, what do we see? Sometimes we do indeed see the fruits of natural wealth – the gleaming towers of Dubai. Other times we see endemic conflict – the diamond wars of Sierra Leone, the failed oil-rich states of Libya and Iraq. Even where there is both wealth and peace, such as in the UAE, it's built on imported, poorly treated labour, while citizens while away their hours in well-remunerated but pointless government jobs. And, in most cases, control of natural resources goes hand in hand with authoritarian political systems.

The mismatch between natural blessings and human suffering is called the resource curse. The resource curse is like one of Aesop's fables, though without the talking animals: wealth creates temptations, to which people tragically succumb. But this is different from the problems of the Prisoner's Dilemma. There we couldn't cooperate to secure wealth. Here it's the wealth itself that poisons us.

It is the prosperity trap in new form. Here, sudden prosperity creates all kinds of short-term temptations, pushing us towards our immediate self-interest and away from our long-term collective goals.

Let's begin with the most basic problem of discovering new resources – they divert you from other sectors in your economy. A famous example is the Netherlands' experience of discovering vast natural-gas deposits in the 1960s – the 'Dutch Disease' as it became known. As the Dutch exploited these new finds, investment surged into the extractive industries. This boosted national income, pushing up the prices of goods and property and the wages of workers.

That was good for a lot of people, especially real-estate agents. But it was bad for manufacturing companies that produced goods sold internationally, where higher costs mean lower sales. They had to keep wages and prices down. So they lost workers to other sectors where wages were rising. Even worse, flows of money from abroad into the resources sector pushed up the value of the currency. So now manufacturing firms seeking to export became less competitive and bankruptcies proliferated.

A second problem is that resource prices are highly volatile. Think about oil. A barrel of West Texas crude was around $20 in 2000, climbed to $140 by early 2008, before crashing to just over $40 during the financial crisis. When the coronavirus hit it nosedived from $60 to $20. As the pandemic ended and Russia invaded Ukraine it was back above $110. And this is a resource whose price is supposed to be moderated by the international cartel OPEC.

Volatility means resource-dependent countries are highly exposed to shocks to international demand and supply. And it's not just oil: gas, copper, coffee and a host of other volatile exports can tie a country's welfare to global whims. During its early years of independence in the 1960s and early 1970s, Zambia had an enormous economic boom led by copper, which accounted for 95 per cent of its exports. This was an optimistic era, in which young Zambians formed 'Zamrock' bands and Zambia set up its first airline. But the price of copper halved by 1975 and Zambia rapidly became one of the world's most heavily indebted countries. It took until 2005 for average incomes to recover.

This is not a new story. At the end of the nineteenth century, European wheat farmers were decimated as first the United States, then Canada, Argentina, Australia and Russia entered global wheat markets, massively increasing supply and causing a collapse in prices. The very same European farmers put out of business became the new sets of impoverished immigrants to the wheat-producing giants.

Volatility plays havoc with politics. When resource exports are key to national income, it is not surprising that governments will come to rely heavily on them for balancing the budget. But this reliance is dangerous. Tax revenues from resources shoot up during global booms but collapse precipitously during hard times, just when they are needed to provide unemployment relief. Oil-rich countries sometimes abandon standard income tax systems during boom times. Saudi Arabia's Income Tax Department produced almost half of the country's revenues in the 1950s but less than 2 per cent by 1978. When the oil boom stops, resource-rich countries can end up with highly imbalanced tax systems that depend on very volatile oil prices, rather than more-stable income and consumption patterns.

Resources sectors are also highly politically influential, securing subsidies, tax reliefs and preferential access to credit. Depending on a politically connected sector to provide tax revenues is dangerous business – it's easy to end up with highly profitable resource sectors that pay a pittance in taxes. For example, in the United States, oil and gas companies pay a substantially lower tax rate than that paid by other corporations.

The Dutch Disease and volatility are, at heart, economic problems. But the political sector is not hermetically sealed off from what's going on in the economy. Because natural resources tend to require large-scale investments and need heavy security, they are 'natural' places for the state to get involved. And when it does, the outcomes aren't pretty.

Michael Ross argues that oil and other natural resources become political handicaps. First, revenues from natural resources turn states into 'rentiers', reliant on unearned income – like a parodic Victorian investor, lazing on the chaise longue, watching investment returns roll in. Why is unearned income bad for democracy? First, it means you can buy off your disgruntled citizenry. More bread, more circuses. If you use the income to pay all your citizens six-figure salaries for superfluous jobs at the oil ministry, they might be less demanding of political rights, particularly since regime change threatens their cushy jobs. What's more, you can keep taxes low. When citizens are taxed, they tend to care who is in charge. When they aren't, we get 'no taxation with no representation', to mangle the famous American call for independence.

Secondly, natural resources provide authoritarian regimes with the revenues to pay for security. Against their own citizens as well as threats from abroad. It becomes cheaper to maintain an authoritarian regime. You can have both guns *and* butter. Oman, Saudi Arabia, Kuwait and the UAE all spend over 5 per cent of national income on the military; over 8 per cent in the case of the former two. The USA spends 3.5 per cent of national income, the UK, 2.2 per cent and Japan just 1 per cent of national income. It's true that the Gulf is not a docile place in terms of international relations; there are external threats. But the military is not a single-use product – it can easily be turned against a rebellious citizenry.

Finally, natural resources mean that countries end up neglecting other sectors of the economy that might in the long run be beneficial both for national prosperity *and* for democratic reforms. Natural resources are an extractive industry, quite literally. Extractive economic institutions go hand in hand with extractive political institutions run on behalf of a small elite. Digging up resources may be technologically complex, but it is sociologically simple – you just need a few people in the right location with the right tools. By contrast service sector industries such as finance, software development and marketing are sociologically complex – you need lots of decentralized, highly educated workers interacting, outside the purview of the state. It's much harder for an authoritarian state to successfully promote these kinds of industries.

Extractive industries don't require a large skilled workforce and also typically employ only men. So countries dependent on natural resources characteristically spend less on education, particularly for girls. In my own work, I find oil exporters spend 1.5 per cent of national income less on education than other countries – around a third less spending. And because natural-resource industries disproportionately employ men, women are not only less present in the labour force but also lack political influence. In the Middle East, almost a quarter of oil-less Tunisia's parliamentarians in 2003 were female; oil-rich Saudi Arabia, Kuwait, Qatar and the UAE had none. While female political representation is low in the Middle East that's not necessarily because regimes are Islamic (witness Tunisia) but because of oil.

Let's go back to the prosperity trap. The malign effects of resource booms on democracy happen because it's always easier for leaders controlling those resources to make short-term decisions rather than long-term ones that would be better for the country, especially when the oil inevitably runs out. If you're constantly worried about the short-term political survival of your dictatorship or dynasty, there's a temptation to spend your seemingly endless resources on buying off your citizenry or repressing them. If you're a citizen of these countries, it's simpler to take the immediate money or job rather than risk regime change, even if the latter might be better in the long run.

Finally, if as a government you focus on the immediate benefits of natural resources that literally stream out of the earth, then the gradual, tedious groundwork of developing reliable legal, educational and financial systems seems unattractive. Natural resources are a quick fix for short-term survival. Rather than engage in the hard work of making and securing political promises, resource-rich countries simply open the oil taps. What these states need is more, not less, politics.

Over the past few decades, some oil-rich states, such as Qatar and the UAE, have tried to move beyond the resource curse. They have done so by trying to reshape their citizens. States have of course long sought to shape the hearts and minds of their citizens. What is novel is that the Gulf states are attempting to wean citizens off almost unimaginable resource wealth, while not destabilizing their authoritarian political regimes.

The rulers of these countries are trying to create entrepreneurial citizens for the day the oil wells run dry. They do so by massive investment in education, including the wholesale adoption of Western syllabi and the construction of major new university partnerships, including New York University Abu Dhabi and Carnegie Mellon Qatar. They also rely on spectacle – the construction of the Burj Khalifa, the Louvre and Guggenheim art museums in Abu Dhabi, and massive global events from the UAE's Festival of Thinking to Qatar's successful World Cup bid.

Yet it's not clear these strategies have worked as intended or that they ever could. Far from creating entrepreneurial citizens who, unlike their American and European counterparts, are content to be deprived of political rights, they have created 'entitled patriots'. Citizens are happy not to rock the boat about regime change and have become increasingly nationalistic (witness the cold war between Qatar and the UAE). But they have not been willing to abandon the security of high public salaries for superfluous bureaucratic jobs. And the entire regime's viability is based on the backs of poorly paid migrant workers, denied political and economic rights. Curses, it seems, are hard to shake.

Manias and panics

As long as there have been modern financial markets there have been bubbles. Countless examples are related as modern-day fables about the excesses of amateur investors piling into everything from tulip bulbs in Amsterdam in the 1630s, to Florida real estate in the 1920s, to our modern equivalents, cryptocurrencies such as Bitcoin and Ethereum. Each time, there is a sudden surge in prices for assets with apparently unlimited demand, before values reach some previously unimaginable peak and suddenly unwind, often right to where they began.

The South Sea Bubble of 1720 in Britain ironically emerged because of Britain's shift towards stable prosperity after 1688, once the monarchy's tendency to profligate borrowing had been constrained by parliamentary sovereignty. In the early eighteenth century, the costs of borrowing were declining dramatically. But the crown still owed huge amounts of debt it was looking to sell off. It did so by promising its creditors shares in a new royal-backed venture – the South Sea Company – chartered to trade in the South Atlantic. The limits of this venture should have been obvious – the British were banned from these Spanish-controlled waters. But the chance to acquire shares in this venture excited investors enormously, and British financial markets could cater to their demands.

Over the course of a few months in 1720, the value of shares in the company increased tenfold, creating sudden fortunes. This caused some kerfuffle among existing elites. The former Lord Mayor of London, Sir Gilbert Heathcote, lamented that 'great Estates acquired by Miscreants who, twelve Months ago, were not fit to be Valets to the Gentlemen they have ruin'd'. Ruination was in fact quite widespread. By the middle of 1721, prices were below where they had begun.

Had eighteenth-century Englishmen been seized by madness? That's not entirely clear. Many financial firms made fortunes by 'riding the bubble'. While other investors piled in, it made sense to keep hold of the stock. The tricky thing was to know when to let go. Individual self-interest and collective behaviour were in an uneasy dance.

Manias are easier to spot in hindsight than at the time. But if we funnel our money in foolhardily every time a new fad appears, we'll ultimately bankrupt ourselves. Worse, if everyone behaves like this – gets caught up in the excitement of 'this time it's different' – we will end up collectively poorer, as sectors with better fundamentals are starved of funds and money is frittered on the ephemeral.

Manias and their consequent panics provide a very visceral example of the prosperity trap. We all want to make a quick buck. And we can do so immediately, at least if we sell as the market is still rising. But at each point up the rollercoaster, the temptation is to hold on, buy more and see if the price will climb just a little higher. Which, as we all pile in, it does. Until it doesn't. And then our immediate interest is to sell as quickly as we can and get out with our shirts. But as we all do that collectively, the nightmare becomes real, and the panic intensifies. Driven each time by what seems best for us in the short term, we collectively end up with a crash and broken dreams.

Rather pejoratively, this is known as 'herding behaviour'. Not so fast. Herds are sometimes good. There's a reason animals herd. Doing what everyone else does *is* sometimes the right play. For animals it confuses and confounds predators. It helps birds fly in synchrony and stops them crashing into one another.

Even when the choice is arbitrary, sometimes coordination is good. Think about what side of the road to drive on. American and European readers of this book will doubtless agree that driving on the right is best. And I guess a few fellow British, Japanese or Indian readers might make a plea for driving on the left. But regardless of whether one really is 'better' than the other, I think we can all agree that driving on the *same* side of the road is better than us driving down the same street but with different ideas of which the correct lane is.

Coordination thrives on mutual trust. If I assume that you know we need to coordinate and you assume likewise, provided each of us trusts the other, we will all be fine. But if we think someone might slip up, then it can all fall apart. This gets more complicated the more people who are involved. If everyone has to do the same thing, we all have to place our trust in the weakest link.

On the face of it, panics and manias look like coordination problems. As we plough our funds into the same investment, the fact that *all* of us are doing so itself adds value to the investment. In modern economies the 'value' of something comes from how much people are willing to pay for it. So, if everyone is willing to pay huge amounts for tulip bulbs, I guess they really are worth a fortune. After all, that's how we treat diamonds.

This is the rationale behind cryptocurrencies. The most popular cryptocurrency, Bitcoin, is a scarce resource – the number of Bitcoins is limited by algorithm, and it becomes ever more expensive to 'mine' them by solving mathematical problems. But, at its core, Bitcoin is valuable because we agree it's valuable. Just as gold is only valuable as a unit of exchange because we agree on its value. It's finite, sure. But lots of things are finite. Like pretty much everything.

If we all coordinate around something, then we can indeed shape its value. But what if we have some kind of horrible naysayer, some bratty kid who decides the emperor has no clothes? Our coordination evaporates and with it the value of the very thing we all agreed was valuable. Until we didn't. Everybody may be behaving entirely rationally in the short term but it is collectively irrational in the long run. Manias are just an extreme form of the prosperity trap.

We are likely to see more of them because we have been living in an era of very low interest rates. Investors are better off holding fixed assets such as housing or valuable paintings, since the returns on traditional saving are so low. That in turn produces a rush into housing markets, antiques markets and, even now, into the strange world of non-fungible tokens – the right to permanently own a digital work of art, or perhaps non-art in the case of people buying NFTs of tweets and cat gifs.

But the most striking example of speculative new assets is the cryptocurrency market. Cryptocurrencies have political attractions – they promise independence from fiat currencies issued by governments and perhaps also from international financial agencies. But their very volatility can lead us right into the prosperity trap.

In 2021 the President of El Salvador, Nayib Bukele, approved Bitcoin as legal tender in the country. Bukele, a mercurial populist, claimed it would help El Salvadoreans outside the formal economy – each citizen was entitled to a Bitcoin wallet worth $30 to start them off – and make the country a home for innovation. He also invested $21 million that September in Bitcoin for the country's reserves, announcing several more similarly sized purchases over the following months.

It is entirely possible that Bitcoin's long-term future will make this seem a wise move. But in the first few months of 2022 collapses in the value of Bitcoin cost the El Salvadorean treasury tens of millions of dollars of its reserves. The short-term sugar hit of Bitcoin booms could quickly turn into the hangover of cryptocurrency panics, but with huge budgetary implications for a small and relatively poor country. There were also other long-term risks – the Bitcoin wallet used by El Salvadoreans was run privately by unnamed individuals, and international lenders have become increasingly frustrated, demanding an end to Bitcoin convertibility. A short-term gamble could have rather harsh long-run consequences for the country.

20. Escaping the Prosperity Trap

How can we make politics work for the long run? The prosperity trap is set off by short-term temptations distracting us from our long-term goals. If politics is about embedding promises about the future, what types of policies, institutions or norms can secure those promises? We'll need ideas that help us generate wealth and to make sure we use it wisely once we have it. And we'll need to figure out ways to stop ourselves destroying the planet in the process.

Can the government help us get rich? There's a striking tension in the two halves of political economy. Political scientists know that governments are more likely to win elections when the economy is booming. But economists argue that elected governments should have a light touch in the private market and that intervention often backfires in the long run. Governments, in other words, have short-term incentives to intervene in ways that will be harmful over the long haul – a classic statement of the prosperity trap.

But is that still true when we talk about long-term growth and innovation? Most investments that governments make in technology or education take years to come to fruition – hardly the stuff of campaign managers' dreams. So we face the reverse problem – the things that make us rich in the long run aren't good for governments in the short run, something we saw in the solidarity trap. Campaign slogans about 'building back better' or 'levelling up' may sound attractive. But as policies promising goodies to voters they are not ideal – boosting the growth of poorer cities or regions is a slow, gradual process that fits poorly with the electoral calendar.

To get long-term economic growth requires stable, reliable political institutions that prevent politicians from seizing short-term temptations to get elected or, worse, steal public money. We can't rely on the 'magic' of the market alone, if we need stable property rights, reliable courts, widespread education and social trust to make innovation stick. And we certainly can't depend on the platitudes of a 'strong leader' who promises to boost the economy by smashing special interests – before too long, a strong leader without controls will be cutting their own deals and channelling money into Swiss bank accounts. We will need politics. But what kind?

How can we get governments to invest in the types of innovation policies that do produce long-term, widely shared growth? The German model of innovation has often been attractive to policymakers, particularly from the English-speaking world. German firms dominate markets in high-end, mass-produced goods from cars to domestic appliances to machine tools. German brands are a byword for quality. And German growth has been strong over the past two decades, with low unemployment and restrained inequality. When we examined the equality trap we saw that the German model of apprenticeships and training is partly responsible for this success. But there is something just as crucial to this particular 'variety of capitalism' – long-term financial markets.

German banks provide long-term loans, so-called 'patient capital' to German manufacturing firms. As part of this deal, they also insist on seats on the boards of these companies, to make sure their loan is being well used. A long-term horizon allows firms to engage in incremental innovation – gradually improving the quality of manufactured goods. Each Bosch dishwasher or BMW 3 series builds on design and production lessons learned in the previous model. All this, in turn, is built on long-standing vocational-training systems and coordination between trade unions and employers' associations. This thick web of interlinked institutions makes it easier for German firms to plan for the long run and escape the prosperity trap – workers have the certainty they can invest in very specific skills and remain employed; firms can afford to spend the time to continuously improve their products.

It's not possible to simply export the German model into other countries, given the importance of all these complementary institutions. So what more realistic policy options are there for countries that want to promote innovation? One possibility is to develop a public-innovation body that can channel funds or support to innovative businesses – what Mariana Mazzucato thinks of as the 'entrepreneurial state'.

Finland is often put forward as a shining example with its innovation agency, Tekes (now Business Finland), and an innovation fund/ thinktank, Sitra (on whose board Mazzucato sits). When I worked for the British government on education policy, we met with leaders at Tekes who proudly showed us their rooftop sauna, something perhaps a little innovative for fusty British civil servants. Tekes had been founded to fund research and development both at Finnish companies and in the university sector. Tekes funded around one quarter of Nokia's projects in the 1990s, on which Finland's transition to a tech-based economy rested. And once Nokia began to decline, Tekes shifted into funding start-ups at enormous levels, over half a billion euros per annum.

While Tekes was a separate agency it ultimately sat under the Ministry of Employment and the Economy. Sitra is much smaller but is operationally independent from the government – it is funded through an independent endowment of almost one billion euros and explicitly funds start-ups. While any research and development agency may make funding mistakes, the relative independence of these Finnish agencies, along with Scandinavian norms, may have prevented their being captured by failing businesses seeking support. At any rate it surely dampened down political temptations to fund favourite businesses in the short run. By detaching innovation policy from the electoral cycle, policymakers can take the time to plan Finnish industrial strategy over a horizon of decades, not months.

There are some risks, however, with this innovation model. One is that states should not necessarily focus all their energy on the cutting-edge of innovation. Governments make a mistake when they want the 'next Silicon Valley'. The problem with the Valley is that the venture capital funding model on which it is based functions well for huge Google-size players or for super-innovative start-ups but rather poorly for 'tech teens' – companies between five and ten years old. But mega-tech companies and start-ups tend not to be great for local tax revenues – the big guys are based multinationally and start-ups run losses. They are even worse for inequality – large tech firms do much of their production abroad, keeping only well-paid execs in the head office.

Tech teens by contrast need a more patient funding model that allows them to grow and develop locally, hopefully bringing in a wider range of jobs. Even better are the firms that use and incrementally improve rather than invent technologies – such firms from the bicycle company Giant in Taiwan to the machine tool companies of Germany are stable, profitable, long-term employers. Germany again. Once more, we see the value of patient investment and the need for institutional regulation and business norms that encourage long horizons. Just as with cooperation, innovation also needs time.

The *Financial Times* publishes a weekend supplement for its well-to-do readership provocatively titled 'How to Spend It', with a litany of featured luxury foods, goods and properties. Traditionally, countries with resource booms, or rather their leaders, had similar spending habits, with oil wealth expended on speedboats, jewellery and penthouses. As we saw earlier, in recent decades there has been a shift in some of the oil-rich emirates, towards spending on education and infrastructure. But since much of the vast resources of petro-states makes its way with minimal oversight into the hands of relatives of the royal family, luxury spending on London real estate and loss-making soccer clubs remains buoyant.

Surely there must be a better way of managing resource wealth? For a striking counter-example, consider Europe's own petro-state, Norway. Norway was substantially poorer than its Scandinavian neighbour Sweden until the discovery of oil in the mid 1970s. Since that time, the average Norwegian has climbed from being two thirds as rich to 50 per cent richer than the average Swede. That's not of itself surprising – oil finds make citizens richer. What is more noteworthy is that Norway has managed to establish a series of policies that allow it to stably cover around 6 per cent of national income in government spending. In other words, Norway can run a sizeable permanent budget deficit thanks to oil and gas. These are non-renewable resources – they will eventually run out. But because of the way Norway has managed its newfound wealth, this budget bonus will last at least another fifty years.

Norway's model is based on three key policies. The first is very heavy government control and taxation of natural-resource production. Norway has its own oil company, Statoil. It has sovereign ownership of all oilfields – all licences to explore and produce come from the government. And it taxes private energy companies a whopping 78 per cent on their profits. This explains where those budget revenues are coming from. It also ensures that the lion's share of wealth extracted from Norwegian oil- and gas fields goes to the Norwegian public, rather than to the shareholders of foreign energy firms.

Why do these firms still invest, you might ask? Taxation is heavy but it is also transparent and consistent – firms know what they will have to pay, know they will not be arbitrarily expropriated and can make the decision themselves about whether investments are worthwhile. Norwegian politics can make a stable promise to business because Norway is democratic and has secure property rights institutions.

These institutional advantages also underpin the other two key aspects of Norway's model. The first is where the proceeds of energy taxation and Statoil's revenue go. Rather than into the murky coffers of an oil ministry run by the ruling party's or monarchy's clients, Norway's energy wealth goes into a sovereign wealth fund, run by Norges Bank Investment Management (NBIM), which is tasked with investing the money in foreign assets.

This system avoids many political risks. The management of Norway's riches is done at two steps removed from the government and is regularly audited. This works because NBIM is a formally independent institution but also because Norwegian politicians have established informal norms of non-interference. The stipulation that money must be invested abroad also avoids the risks of corruption and special-interest influence that might happen if Norwegian firms could lobby for investment.

The final crucial aspect of Norway's model is how the money is spent. It doesn't just sit indefinitely in a sovereign wealth fund.

Regular Norwegians should benefit from the country's oil riches. But how to avoid the twin risks of highly volatile spending and money being frittered away on white elephants (Norway is not bidding to construct eight new stadiums for a World Cup)? Norway has instituted a fiscal rule that transfers the 'expected real return' of the sovereign wealth fund to the government to pay for Norway's structural budget deficit. The return of about 4 per cent per annum enables Norway to run a deficit of 6 per cent, which means that Norway is essentially financing day-to-day government expenses from the fund. Norway can maintain its cradle-to-grave welfare state – maternity leave at full pay for a year, some of the highest social spending in Europe and some of Europe's top universities.

These stable, long-term policies rely on the consensual nature of Norwegian politics. They may not be easily translated elsewhere. Norway's electoral system means coalition government is the norm. Both parties on the centre left and right broadly agree on the three components of the model. Both are committed to the extensive social services funded by the sovereign wealth fund's contribution to the budget. Both are happy to divest themselves of responsibility for the fund to independent, non-democratic institutions like the NBIM. And both agree on high taxes for energy companies. Ultimately, the success of the Norwegian model depends on the success of Norwegian politics.

But perhaps this praise for Norway's careful management of its resources rather misses the point. Norway's wealth comes from non-renewable fossil fuels – the very resources that are endangering the world's climate. And while we might all agree it's better to manage fossil fuel revenues responsibly than not, this feels a little like praising the executioner for the cleanliness of their axe.

Most countries do not have Norway's luck. But that doesn't mean they don't also have booms. The problem is that many of our recent booms appear built on sand: the early 2000s property boom on the back of subprime mortgages; the web3 boom on the back of unstable cryptocurrencies. Are there ways to prevent such booms from emerging in the first place? One, perhaps unappetizing possibility is simply higher taxes. Clearly, taxes on property transactions and other assets might help slow down speculation. But what I mean here is higher taxes on incomes.

Higher taxes stop runaway credit bubbles. Put simply, higher taxes cramp people's behaviour in two ways. First, the rich are now rather less rich and so can spend less money on these kinds of assets. But there is also a trickle-down effect driven by people's consumption. Or rather, by their propensity to care about other people's consumption. We're often driven to 'keep up with the Joneses'. We look at the consumption of the rich and model our own choices on it. When the rich have less cash in their pocket, that urge is tempered – the Joneses look more like us.

The way inequality translates into conspicuous consumption and credit bubbles depends on taxes. In countries with low taxes, high levels of income inequality spill over very quickly into more borrowing and credit. Witness the enormous housing bubbles in the US, Britain and Ireland in the early 2000s. But where the rich are taxed more heavily this relationship is greatly weakened.

Tax isn't the only answer, you'll be glad to hear. Credit crises aren't an inevitable cost of modern life. Consider each side of the 49th parallel, dividing Canada and the United States. Since 1800 America has suffered fourteen banking crises, whereas Canada had a mere two, with the last in 1839. It's not because Canada has a limited financial sector. In fact, as a proportion of national income, Canada's bank credit was almost double that of the US in 2007.

Instead, the political design of Canada's banking system has underpinned its stability. Both are federal countries. But federalism goes much further in America. In Canada, the federal government acquires any power not delegated directly to the provinces – the opposite of the American system. The federal Canadian government has been able to regulate the Canadian banking system from Ottawa, without having to worry about provincial politicians. In the US, states jealously guarded their power over banking within their borders.

The result was sharply contrasting financial systems. In Canada, a small number of very large national banks came to dominate. This gave them economies of scale and diverse lending portfolios, allowing them to absorb shocks effectively. Although that meant a risk of cartel-like behaviour among a few big banks, a national banking system also meant banks had to follow national regulation and the requirement of the federal Bank Act that banks be rechartered every five years. Canadian banks have been stable and borrowers have had access to cheaper credit than Americans.

By contrast, in America, consumer banking regulation was largely reserved to the states. Each state developed its own rules and was lobbied by its own banks. A protectionist regime emerged, where no truly national bank existed until recent decades. Local 'unit banks' dominated local access to capital and were poorly diversified, making them prone to bank runs, if depositors suddenly feared that their local bank wasn't going to be able to make good on their deposits. But this inefficient system was stable because regulation was also local, which meant banks could preserve their market power by blocking bigger players from entering.

At their core, then, credit crises, manias and panics are built on the successes or failures of political promises. This ought not to surprise us. Credit is about trust. And trust rests on promises about an uncertain future. Canadian banks had greater clarity about what long-term regulation would look like and less ability to buy off local politicians to influence the rules they would follow. Political institutions and norms frame our certainty about what others might do and our incentives to play follow the leader. Even in a global credit market, local differences matter.

Let's return to where we started: climate change. Can we move from a world where we use the proceeds of fossil fuels more responsibly to one where we don't burn them at all? Ultimately, to lower the risks of rising global temperatures we need to reduce the amount of carbon emitted into the atmosphere. We could do that by banning it, taxing it or subsidizing alternatives. What would work best? What kinds of political promises about reducing carbon emissions might be easiest to keep?

To get to net zero – where we add no more carbon to the atmosphere than we remove from it – we have three broad options. The first seems simplest. We tell businesses and consumers that they can't emit carbon. We could do this through regulations, banning the development of coalmines or insisting on mileage standards for new cars for example. This sounds direct and sensible, so what's the problem?

First, these regulations aren't as universal as they may seem – they normally apply just to *new* power plants or cars. That in turn raises the value of the *old* polluting ones still out there – they have been made scarcer. Second, there is a political danger to regulation. It is obviously deeply unpopular with the industries affected, which bear large immediate costs. So they lobby to alter regulations. And nothing is permanent in politics. Governments can't constrain what their successors do, unless they can amend the constitution. President Obama's executive order regulating greenhouse gas emissions was simply overridden by President Trump's Environmental Protection Agency. Finally, regulations are generally inflexible – fixed targets can't respond to subsequent changes in the level of carbon emission. Very fixed promises are often harder to keep.

If regulating fossil fuels has drawbacks, what about subsidizing renewables? Many countries have directly subsidized solar panels or wind energy – Germany's well-known 'feed-in tariffs' – or the purchase of electric vehicles – for example, the UK gives a grant of up to £2,500 per electric car. Subsidies change the incentives facing companies and consumers. They are also less rigid than fixed regulatory targets, since they increase in value the more people invest in or use renewable energy. But they do have some perverse consequences – cheaper energy may mean people use more than before, possibly cancelling out the benefit.

The other problem with subsidies is something we saw with the solidarity trap – it's hard to know for sure who needs to be subsidized and whether the activity the government wants to encourage would have been done even in the absence of a subsidy. This informational problem means over two thirds of purchases might have happened anyway, only now the taxpayer is on the hook. Similarly, seeing a juicy subsidy, firms of dubious financial viability may end up being supported indefinitely by the government.

Economists' preferred response to climate change is neither regulation nor subsidies but – that dreaded word again – taxation. There are essentially two types of environmental taxation – a direct carbon tax per ton of carbon emitted, and a 'cap and trade' system where a cap for total emissions is set, emissions permits are issued and firms trade for the 'right to pollute' within the cap. In the former case, the government sets the price of emitting carbon directly, whereas in the latter the price of emission is set on the market.

The great benefit of both is *any* decision firms or consumers make that involves emitting more carbon should face a cost. This incentivizes people to emit carbon only for the most efficient reasons and to find ways to produce or consume the same energy in a renewable manner. And it avoids setting stringent regulations or subsidizing unviable firms.

We already live in a world where carbon taxes and cap-and-trade systems abound, though their impact on our carbon emissions is embryonic. Carbon taxes have spread widely since Sweden first adopted one in 1991. They vary massively in their size – some are minimal, such as those in Japan, Mexico and Ukraine, which are all under $5 per ton, and some are quite chunky, such as those in Norway and Finland, both over $65 per ton, with Sweden's double that. Cap-and-trade systems are also widespread, from California's state system to the European Union's Emissions Trading Scheme (ETS), which traded 200 billion euros' worth of permits in 2020.

What are the political benefits and challenges of each type of system? Let's begin with cap and trade. The good news is it sounds less like a tax! When we look at public opinion, that's a serious bonus. But there's also bad news. It's hard to set emissions caps effectively. The ETS cap was set at a low level, which may have increased its initial political viability but also meant that the price for carbon it fixed was too low to encourage much abatement.

Cap-and-trade systems are also administratively very complex and require a large bureaucracy to run, something that won't surprise students of the European Union. And even then, like a lost Bitcoin wallet, emissions permits can get out of the hands of legitimate users easily. In 2011 a huge scandal emerged involving the ETS, when hackers seized several million euros' worth of permits from accounts in the Czech Republic, Austria and Estonia. Finally, cap-and-trade systems carry the major political risk that a future government could devalue all existing permits by changing the rules. The market alone can't solve this problem. Cap-and-trade systems rely on companies being certain about the political promises made by governments.

Carbon taxes by contrast avoid many of these administrative problems. They are bottom-up not top-down: they are collected from energy providers at source. The tax is usually transparent and simple. If it changes because of a future government, that only applies to future tax payments, not the value of current permits, so there's less political risk.

In fact, clever carbon tax systems like that in Switzerland are dynamic – they rise if Switzerland fails to meet its emissions targets. This makes the carbon tax a more credible promise – governments can try to make the effects of the tax self-enforcing by having it respond to how well people behave as regards pollution. Almost like a Tit for Tat system of taxation.

Even more attractively, carbon taxes can create their own support base if their proceeds are distributed back to people. The British Columbia carbon tax has been used to provide business tax rebates, a 'low-income climate tax credit' to poorer families and a $100 'climate action dividend' to all residents.

But, at the end of the day, it is still a tax. And taxes face all the problems we saw in our discussions of the equality trap and solidarity trap – in particular, that people do not want to pay taxes for benefits they don't think will apply to them. That's particularly challenging with carbon taxes since the real beneficiaries are not even other people but as yet unborn generations. We may ethically owe these generations, but if people already have difficulty accepting taxes that will benefit their future selves, it's hard to believe that they will feel more inclined to pay for future descendants. We know that environmental cooperation thrives over the long haul. But we are still mortal.

Surveys that try to figure out whether people really will accept carbon taxes are tentatively encouraging. People are more likely to support carbon taxes if they think the revenues will be recycled back either in the form of lower taxes or in spending on mitigation. A slim majority of respondents in France, Germany and the UK do support a carbon tax and this rises substantially when they are told other countries will implement one too. This cuts to the heart of the prosperity trap – people know that climate change is a collective action problem where progress can only be made when multiple, maybe all, countries are willing to take the hit.

This raises the question, though, of whether we need a global carbon tax to make this work. Which is likely to be politically rather challenging. In surveys, there are stark differences across countries in how people feel about a global carbon tax with a uniform international climate dividend given to all global citizens. This idea was, unsurprisingly, much more popular in poorer countries such as India than in the United States. We may all be on the same planet. We're not used to being in the same tax system.

Escaping the prosperity trap requires us to commit to the long term – to tie our hands and prevent ourselves from succumbing to short-term temptations. Sometimes that means institutions, like regulating our banks to prevent the mania of speculation from destabilizing our financial systems. At other times, we can develop norms that help us focus on the long run – from Tit for Tat on the battlefield to reciprocal environmental policy. Long-term promises may be the hardest to keep. But credibility is the heart of prosperity.

How Politics Can Succeed

So, to the title of this book. Why does politics fail? Politics fails when we pretend that we can get along without it. It fails when we don't take it seriously. When we try and repress, smother or banish it. We cannot wish away our differences. Any attempt to do so and replace them with the purity and clarity of a single solution or figurehead is doomed to fail. We will still disagree, but we will have removed our ability to express or act on that disagreement.

There are innumerable books out there arguing that our global problems can be solved by avoiding politics – by better living through technology or markets; by strong leadership or moral improvement. That's not this book. I want to make a plea for the fundamental centrality of politics to achieving our collective goals. But we must go in clear-eyed, acknowledging that the wrong politics, too much or too little of it, might push us ever further from our dreams of the future.

Alternatives to politics will only let us down. There's a brand of techno-libertarianism that views politicians, bureaucrats, even voters as an impediment to progress. If only politicians would stop trying to regulate technology companies, those companies could innovate a way out of our global problems. Global violence could be curtailed by omniscient satellite monitoring. Climate change can be counteracted with geoengineering. Just let smart people figure out a solution.

But technological solutions work better when the object they act on can't answer back. We're still in a world – for now – where people are smarter than computers. Algorithms don't always achieve what they set out to do. People find ways to manipulate them or work around them. Many algorithms also fail to comprehend society – reinforcing existing gender or racial discrimination.

And technological solutions are often anti-democratic – they may try and design out independent human desires and decisions.

Ultimately if humans are still in control, we can't ignore what they want. Politics can still wrap technology back in chains if that's what voters and politicians want. We can't innovate politics away.

Another popular solution is to blame politicians for getting in the way of the market. Climate change a concern? Attach a price to carbon and trade it. Democracy not responding to intense popular grievances? Then allow people to trade and amass multiple votes. The problem is perfect markets rarely exist and not simply because governments 'get in the way'. Many of our conflicts exist in areas where there are unclear property rights, imperfect monitoring, badly affected third parties and so forth. There are ambiguities that contracts can't resolve and that ultimately must rely on political promises.

The past decade has seen the revival of another trend – the desire for a strong leader who can overrule squabbling politicians. Politics as usual is castigated as an elitist plot to stymie and undermine the common citizen. Political promises are there to be broken by a leader who doesn't need to play by the rules.

This urge fundamentally misunderstands democratic politics. It denies the reality of different preferences among the population. And it champions the deconstruction and denouncing of the very political institutions and norms that hold together stable democracies. In the United Kingdom that meant castigating judges as 'enemies of the people' and the unlawful prorogation of Parliament during the Brexit debate. In the United States, the Trump presidency moved from calls to lock up political opponents to the false denunciation of a presidential election and an insurrection on Capitol Hill. Institutions can be fragile things, backed as they are by a state that itself can be turned against them. Norms are even more fragile. Yet together they may be all that keeps us from watching politics fail.

There is also a grand tradition on the left of trying to remove the influence of perceived malign actors from politics. Get business out of politics. Get campaign contributions out of politics. Get selfishness out of politics. Replace them with a benign government that serves what the people want and what they need. But self-interest can't be taken out of politics. Nor is there such a thing as an undebatable 'will of the people'. While we may share common goals, we often differ substantially on how to get there or the exact shape of the end point. These types of disagreements can't be wished away and they're not simply the product of the malign influence of special interests. They're fundamental to collective life.

The false certainties of technologists, of market fundamentalists, of prophets of left or right, can't eliminate our need to make each other promises in an uncertain future. We will need politics for that.

The inevitability of politics

Can politics succeed? It won't always. That's part of the deal. The traps we face are inevitable and we will have to keep our eyes keen to avoid them or escape them. We live in an uncertain world. One where we all disagree and act in our self-interest. But we still have collective goals. And to achieve them we need to make promises to one another. Promises that we can't enforce perfectly. Promises that are inherently political.

How can we make good on those promises? We need to embed our promises somehow. Make them last longer than the breath in which they are uttered. We have to provide structure in uncertainty. The way we can do that is by developing political institutions and norms that make our promises credible.

Institutions are the formal agreements we make. These are not made of titanium – they too can be ignored or broken. But at a cost to trust we may come to regret, when we need the stability those institutions provide. We need to protect institutions from the arrows of populist iconoclasts. They help us to coordinate our behaviour, they set punishments for defecting and they grant rewards for cooperating.

Citizens' assemblies, offline or online, help us to understand where we all agree and commit us to a consensus. Social investment policies and apprenticeships can squeeze down inequality by providing guaranteed paths for non-graduates. Universalist social insurance programmes can tie the middle class into supporting the welfare state. Collective-security agreements can protect vulnerable countries far better than 'ambitions' and 'pathways'. Independent sovereign wealth funds can prevent governments from exploiting the temptations of mineral riches. And flexible climate treaties can bridge the uneasy pathway between environmental anarchy and unenforceable agreements.

These institutions will work best when we nurture norms about how we'll keep promises and develop trust over the long run. For democracy to work we need to learn to debate and discuss with one another so we can find where we agree and ensure that losers don't always lose. For equality, we must be willing to accept a mushy compromise where we balance our equal rights against equal outcomes. For solidarity, we need to nurture a more expansive view of 'us', including our future and our fellow citizens, no matter their ethnicity or religion. For security, we need to be willing to punish those who are meant protect us but exploit us instead. And for prosperity we should encourage longer time horizons to build trust and avoid short-term temptations.

The traps we face often reinforce each other – polarized democracy can worsen inequality; a threadbare social safety net can worsen crime; runaway climate change could threaten global peace. But there are also big solutions that can release us from multiple traps at once.

Consider proportional representation (PR). As an electoral system it may help us escape the democracy trap both because it better represents the diversity of differences among us but also because it encourages cooperation among parties. But PR doesn't only have electoral effects. Countries with PR, such as Sweden and Norway, also seem better able to escape the other traps.

Compare, for example, inequality levels in countries with PR, such as those in Scandinavia or the Netherlands, to those in countries with majoritarian electoral systems, such as Australia, the UK and the USA. Not only is earnings inequality somewhat lower in the PR countries – likely a legacy of high levels of unionization – but inequality in disposable incomes is often dramatically lower because countries with PR have much higher levels of redistribution – in part because they have more left-wing parties in government. Higher taxation and powerful trade unions may not be a price all of us are willing to pay to escape the equality trap, but PR certainly seems to promote them.

Countries with PR also seem better able to escape the solidarity and prosperity traps. They tend to have more generous, visible welfare states that buy in the middle classes and are less prone to dramatic cutbacks during moments of austerity, as is the case in, for example, Britain. Proportional representation also produces more-stable policymaking as more parties need to agree to major changes – hence coalition government lowers the volatility of economic growth. Consensual policymaking is also behind the success Norway achieved investing its North Sea oil windfalls in a sovereign wealth fund – in sharp contrast to the UK, where they were largely used to finance short-term tax cuts, forgoing an estimated £354 billion by not investing them.

Electoral systems cannot, of course, solve all our problems, many of which are global in nature. To escape the security and prosperity traps we will need international cooperation.

Here there is an intriguing contrast. What works for escaping the security trap may not be right for the prosperity trap. The international security trap is typically a problem about *them* – preventing some actor, state or otherwise, with malign intentions from hurting us. The recent Russian invasion of Ukraine suggests that for international cooperation on security to be credible it has to be formal and certain. Ukraine may have had informal agreements to cooperate with NATO, even to be on a glide-path to joining. But it was not a member. Western countries were not compelled, as they would have been with a Russian attack on the Baltic states, to actively intervene. And while sending weapons and aid certainly helped the Ukrainian war effort, it neither deterred Russia nor forced it into a multistate war. To escape the security trap we need to bind ourselves tightly to agreements.

The prosperity trap, however, is a problem about *us*. All of us are tempted to take succour in short-term temptation and avoid the sacrifices required for long-term prosperity. Nowhere is that more striking, or significant, than climate change. But hard, formal rules such as those imposed in the Kyoto Protocol failed. Nobody was willing or able to enforce them. This was not a military alliance but a pollution agreement. In this case, we need to be realistic about what states will do in the absence of real enforcement – we need flexibility and informality. The Paris accords may seem modest and permissive. They may not work. But they are realistic and have brought in all major nations. To escape the prosperity trap we will need to develop norms of reciprocity and forgive occasional trespasses.

These are grand solutions – at the national or international level. None of us alone can bring them into being, though we can of course advocate for them. What can we do on our own? We shouldn't mistake the limits of our individual reach as a call to apathy.

I began this book by talking about the pervasiveness of self-interest. The first thing to acknowledge is that self-interest is inevitable and not immoral, in oneself or others. What prevents us from achieving collective goals is that our individual self-interests clash with one another. So rather than bemoaning self-interest we need to design institutions and follow norms to channel it. That means each of us should not be too quick to denounce the political institutions that surround us as ineffective or corrupt (though sometimes they may be!). Institutions allow us to set our expectations of how others will behave and how we should too. We should be careful before we rip them up – otherwise we may face a much more unconstrained, volatile and perhaps violent world of clashing interests.

And so this is a plea for understanding. We should not be too quick to judge others for self-interested behaviour when we blindly and blithely engage in it ourselves. We should be careful to resist the siren calls of demagogues who ask to drain the swamp and rip down our institutions. Who call for a clean slate but don't recognize that politics still lurks on the other side of every revolution. We live in an imperfect world but those imperfections are often the glue holding it together.

The solutions I've offered in this book won't always work. Quite often they will disappoint us. We will need to put in the hard hours to reshape them for the new challenges we face. Max Weber called politics the 'slow boring of hard boards'. Change is hard. The institutions and norms we built painfully in the past may not always serve our present well. And we'll need to make new political promises again and again.

But the contingent promises of politics are better than the false promises of technologists and populists to fix the deepest and most intractable problems we human beings face. We will always disagree. We need to find solutions that accept that, not ignore it. Politics won't end. But it doesn't have to fail.

Acknowledgements

Writing a book covering the breadth of political economy means incurring a lot of intellectual debts. And debts begin at home.

It is my parents, first and foremost, I must thank for their encouragement, support, generosity and judgement and to whom I dedicate this book. My father, Tony Ansell, has always been an inveterate debater – an incessant, incisive, gadfly-cum-svengali. Much of this book was also written or edited in his basement! Thanks, Dad, for all the arguments and sometimes even agreements. My mother, Penny Ansell, was the social scientist in the family – the teacher of psychology and sociology to generations of miffed A-Level students. Her careful judgement, support, kindness and refusal to let me get away with flip asides have shown me what actually matters in the serious study of why people do what they do. Thanks, Mum.

I could not have written a word of this book without the enormous support of my wife, Jane Gingrich, who made uncountable sacrifices to help me finish this, encouraging me to take time away to get this project finished and carrying the burden of my absences. Thanks and love to you, Jane. My two boys, Theo and Eli, are the joys in my life. Thanks to both of you for being such energetic, wonderful young men.

I'd also like to thank some lifelong friends for their support in the genesis of this book, which happened in part on a narrowboat on the Thames. So thank you, especially, Ed Ansell, Jack Stilgoe, Faith Hummerstone, Tom Edge, Jim McTavish, Rupert Russell and James Shaw (Jas, I'm sorry I didn't use any of your unprintable titles).

I owe great intellectual debts to the people who set me on the path of graduate study and helped in the early part of my academic career. I would never have followed this path, and certainly not in America, if I hadn't met Mark Micale, with whom I studied the social construction of mental illness. Not so close to political economy and yet not so far. At graduate school in political science, three figures were foundational to my interest in political economy and ultimately to my becoming the scholar I am now. My PhD chair, Beth Simmons, got me interested in political economy and first made me take rigorous empirical work seriously. Torben Iversen and David Soskice, whom I met at Harvard, showed me what I wanted to be – their work, always at the nexus of formal elegance and policy relevance, is what I have always aspired to mimic. And all three have supported me more than I deserved as my career took me to exciting and unexpected places.

There are many – too many – other debts incurred to the political science and economics communities, to which I cannot possibly do justice. My co-authors – especially David Samuels, Johannes Lindvall, John Ahlquist and Jane Gingrich – have suffered the challenges of working with me and are my greatest creditors. Thanks for putting up with my untimeliness.

I'm also grateful, among hundreds of political scientists who should be thanked, to Jim Alt, David Art, Pablo Beramendi, David Doyle, Peter Hall, Silja Häusermann, Des King, Jonah Levy, Julie Lynch, Cathie Jo Martin, the late, great Bob Powell, David Rueda, Kathy Thelen, Maya Tudor, Stefanie Walter and John Zysman. Among economists I'd especially like to thank Tim Besley, Paul Johnson and Dani Rodrik for having welcomed me into their world.

I'd like to express my special appreciation to my colleagues at the University of Oxford and Nuffield College. In particular, my heartfelt gratitude goes to Sir Andrew Dilnot, who, along with being the best boss I have had (or likely will ever have), has been an inspiration for connecting academic work to the policy world and to the public.

For their interviews and input into this book I'd specially like to offer my thanks to David Adler, Tom Chivers, Tom Hale, Iain McLean and Yuan Yang. My sincere thanks to Tamsin Mather, who provided incredibly helpful feedback on early drafts.

This book owes its very existence to my agent, Jack Ramm, once upon a time also my potential commissioning editor. Jack, working with you has been one of the great professional experiences of my life.

Nor could this book have been written – or at least made readable – without the fantastic team at Penguin and Viking, especially my editors, Connor Brown and Greg Clowes, whose edits, comments and sound advice made the good bits of the book better and the bad bits scarcer. I was also extremely fortunate to have Mark Handsley copy-editing this book and Ellie Smith managing the production. My gratitude also to Daniel Crewe for taking such an interest in me and this project. John Mahaney at PublicAffairs has also been a wonderful editor, working in sync with Con and Greg and always pulling me to the key question: 'Why does politics fail?' I hope this book has gone a long way to answering that question.

Bibliography

Acemoglu, Daron (2008). *Introduction to Modern Economic Growth*. Princeton University Press.

Acemoglu, Daron, Simon Johnson and James A. Robinson (2001). 'The colonial origins of comparative development: An empirical investigation.' *American Economic Review* 91.5: 1369–401.

Acemoglu, Daron, Simon Johnson and James A. Robinson (2002). 'Reversal of fortune: Geography and institutions in the making of the modern world income distribution.' *The Quarterly Journal of Economics* 117.4: 1231–94.

Acemoglu, Daron, Suresh Naidu, Pascual Restrepo and James Robinson (2019). 'Democracy does cause growth.' *Journal of Political Economy* 127.1: 47–100.

Acemoglu, Daron, and Pascual Restrepo (2020). 'Robots and jobs: Evidence from US labor markets.' *Journal of Political Economy* 128.6: 2188–244.

Acemoglu, Daron, and James A. Robinson (2002). 'The political economy of the Kuznets curve.' *Review of Development Economics* 6.2: 183–203.

Acemoglu, Daron, and James A. Robinson (2006a). *Economic Origins of Dictatorship and Democracy*. Cambridge University Press.

Acemoglu, Daron, and James A. Robinson (2006b). 'Economic backwardness in political perspective.' *American Political Science Review* 100.1: 115–31.

Acemoglu, Daron, and James A. Robinson (2012). *Why Nations Fail: The Origins of Power, Prosperity, and Poverty*. Crown Publishers.

Ackerman, Bruce, and Anne Alstott (1999). *The Stakeholder Society*. Yale University Press.

Adler, David, and Ben W. Ansell (2020). 'Housing and populism.' *West European Politics* 43.2: 344–65.

Aelst, Peter van, and Tom Louwerse (2014). 'Parliament without government: The Belgian parliament and the government formation processes of 2007–2011.' *West European Politics* 37.3: 475–96.

Ahlquist, John S., and Ben W. Ansell (2017). 'Taking credit: Redistribution and borrowing in an age of economic polarization.' *World Politics* 69.4: 640–75.

Ahlquist, John S., and Ben W. Ansell (2022). 'Unemployment insurance, risk, and the acquisition of specific skills: An experimental approach.' Working Paper.

Aidt, Toke, Felix Grey and Alexandru Savu (2021). 'The meaningful votes: Voting on Brexit in the British House of Commons.' *Public Choice* 186.3: 587–617.

Aklin, Michaël, and Matto Mildenberger (2020). 'Prisoners of the wrong dilemma: Why distributive conflict, not collective action, characterizes the politics of climate change.' *Global Environmental Politics* 20.4: 4–27.

Alesina, Alberto, and Edward Glaeser (2004). *Fighting Poverty in the US and Europe: A World of Difference.* Oxford University Press.

Alfani, Guido (2015). 'Economic inequality in northwestern Italy: A long-term view (fourteenth to eighteenth centuries).' *The Journal of Economic History* 75.4: 1058–96.

Alfani, Guido (2017). 'The rich in historical perspective: evidence for pre-industrial Europe (ca. 1300–1800).' *Cliometrica* 11.3: 321–48.

Allen, Robert C. (2003). 'Progress and poverty in early modern Europe.' *The Economic History Review* 56, no. 3: 403–43.

Alstadsæter, Annette, Niels Johannesen and Gabriel Zucman (2019). 'Tax evasion and inequality.' *American Economic Review* 109.6: 2073–103.

Anderson, Christopher J., Andre Blais, Shane Bowler, et al., eds. (2005). *Losers' Consent: Elections and Democratic Legitimacy.* Oxford University Press.

Andrew, Alison, Oriana Bandiera, Monica Costa-Dias and Camille Landais (2021). 'Women and men at work.' *IFS Deaton Review of Inequalities.*

Ansell, Ben W. (2008a). 'Traders, teachers, and tyrants: Democracy, globalization, and public investment in education.' *International Organization* 62.2: 289–322.

Ansell, Ben W. (2008b). 'University challenges: Explaining institutional change in higher education.' *World Politics* 60.2: 189–230.

Ansell, Ben W. (2010). *From the Ballot to the Blackboard: The Redistributive Political Economy of Education.* Cambridge University Press.

Ansell, Ben W. (2014). 'The political economy of ownership: Housing markets and the welfare state.' *American Political Science Review* 108.2: 383–402.

Ansell, Ben W. (2019). 'The politics of housing.' *Annual Review of Political Science* 22.1: 165–85.

Ansell, Ben W., Martin Bauer, Jane Gingrich and Jack Stilgoe (2021). 'Coping with Covid: Two wave survey.' Working Paper, https://rpubs.com/benwansell/729135.

Ansell, Ben W., Laure Bokobza, Asli Cansunar, et al. (2022). 'How do wealth and income affect individuals' attitudes towards redistribution and taxation?' Working Paper.

Ansell, Ben, Asli Cansunar and Mads Andreas Elkjaer (2021). 'Social distancing, politics and wealth.' *West European Politics* 44.5–6: 1283–313.

Ansell, Ben, and Jane Gingrich (2017). 'Mismatch: University education and labor market institutions.' *PS: Political Science & Politics* 50.2: 423–5.

Ansell, Ben, Frederik Hjorth, Jacob Nyrup and Martin Vinæs Larsen (2022). 'Sheltering populists? House prices and the support for populist parties.' *The Journal of Politics* 84.3: 1420–36.

Ansell, Ben W., and Johannes Lindvall (2021). *Inward Conquest: The Political Origins of Modern Public Services.* Cambridge University Press.

Ansell, Ben W., and David J. Samuels (2014). *Inequality and Democratization.* Cambridge University Press.

Ariel, Barak, William A. Farrar and Alex Sutherland (2015). 'The effect of police body-worn cameras on use of force and citizens' complaints against the police: A randomized controlled trial.' *Journal of Quantitative Criminology* 31.3: 509–35.

Arrow, Kenneth J. (1950). 'A difficulty in the concept of social welfare.' *Journal of Political Economy* 58.4: 328–46.

Arrow, Kenneth J. (1951). *Social Choice and Individual Values.* Yale University Press.

Arrow, Kenneth, Partha Dasgupta, Lawrence Goulder, et al. (2004). 'Are we consuming too much?' *Journal of Economic Perspectives* 18.3: 147–72.

Atkinson, Giles, and Kirk Hamilton (2020). 'Sustaining wealth: Simulating a sovereign wealth fund for the UK's oil and gas resources, past and future.' *Energy Policy* 139: 111273.

Austen-Smith, D., and J. Banks (1996). 'Information aggregation, rationality, and the Condorcet jury theorem.' *American Political Science Review*, 90.1: 34–45.

Axelrod, Robert (1984). *The Evolution of Cooperation.* Basic Books.

Axelrod, Robert, and Robert O. Keohane (1985). 'Achieving cooperation under anarchy: Strategies and institutions.' *World Politics* 38.1: 226–54.

Baldwin, Kate, and John D. Huber (2010). 'Economic versus cultural differences: Forms of ethnic diversity and public goods provision.' *American Political Science Review* 104.4: 644–62.

Balkin, Jack (2011). '3 ways Obama could bypass Congress.' CNN website, 28 July 2011. https://edition.cnn.com/2011/OPINION/07/28/balkin.obama.options/.

Barr, Nicholas Adrian (2001). *The Welfare State as Piggy Bank: Information, Risk, Uncertainty, and the Role of the State.* Oxford University Press.

Barr, Nicholas (2012). 'The higher education White Paper: The good, the bad, the unspeakable – and the next White Paper.' *Social Policy & Administration* 46.5: 483–508.

Barry, Brian (1989). *Democracy, Power, and Justice: Essays in Political Theory.* Vol. 1. Oxford University Press.

Bartels, Larry M. (2005). 'Homer gets a tax cut: Inequality and public policy in the American mind.' *Perspectives on Politics* 3.1: 15–31.

Bartels, Larry M. (2016). *Unequal Democracy.* Princeton University Press.

Batson, C. Daniel, M. P. Polycarpou, E. Harmon-Jones, et al. (1997). 'Empathy and attitudes: Can feeling for a member of a stigmatized group improve feelings toward the group?' *Journal of Personality and Social Psychology* 72.1: 105.

Bayley, David H. (1990). *Patterns of Policing: A Comparative International Analysis.* Rutgers University Press.

Bechtel, Michael M., Kenneth Scheve and Elisabeth van Lieshout (2019). 'What determines climate policy preferences if reducing greenhouse-gas emissions is a global public good?' *SSRN* 3472314.

Beramendi, Pablo, Silja Häusermann, Herbert Kitschelt and Hanspeter Kriesi, eds. (2015). *The Politics of Advanced Capitalism.* Cambridge University Press.

Bertrand, Marianne (2020). 'Gender in the twenty-first century.' *AEA Papers and Proceedings* 110: 1–24.

Bidadanure, Juliana Uhuru (2019). 'The political theory of universal basic income.' *Annual Review of Political Science* 22: 481–501.

Binmore, Ken (2004). 'Reciprocity and the social contract.' *Politics, Philosophy & Economics* 3.1: 5–35.

Black, Duncan (1948). 'On the rationale of group decision-making.' *Journal of Political Economy* 56.1: 23–34.

Black, Sandra E., Jeffrey T. Denning and Jesse Rothstein (2020). *Winners and Losers? The Effect of Gaining and Losing Access to Selective Colleges on Education and Labor Market Outcomes.* No. w26821. National Bureau of Economic Research.

Black, Sandra, Paul Devereux, Fanny Landaud and Kjell Salvanes (2022). *The (Un)Importance of Inheritance.* No. w29693. National Bureau of Economic Research.

Bleemer, Zachary (2021). 'Top percent policies and the return to postsecondary selectivity.' *Research & Occasional Paper Series: CSHE* 1.

Bloodworth, James (2018). *Hired: Six Months Undercover in Low-Wage Britain*. Atlantic Books.

Boix, Carles (2003). *Democracy and Redistribution*. Cambridge University Press.

Bolton, Matt (2020). ' "Democratic socialism" and the concept of (post) capitalism.' *The Political Quarterly* 91.2: 334–42.

Bonica, Adam, Nolan McCarty, Keith T. Poole and Howard Rosenthal (2013). 'Why hasn't democracy slowed rising inequality?' *Journal of Economic Perspectives* 27.3: 103–24.

Bränström, Richard, and Yvonne Brandberg (2010). 'Health risk perception, optimistic bias, and personal satisfaction.' *American Journal of Health Behavior* 34.2: 197–205.

Braumoeller, Bear F. (2019). *Only the Dead: The Persistence of War in the Modern Age*. Oxford University Press.

Breen, Richard, and Signe Hald Andersen (2012). 'Educational assortative mating and income inequality in Denmark.' *Demography* 49.3: 867–87.

Brennan, Jason (2017). *Against Democracy*. Princeton University Press.

Breznitz, Dan (2021). *Innovation in Real Places: Strategies for Prosperity in an Unforgiving World*. Oxford University Press.

Breznitz, Dan, and Darius Ornston (2013). 'The revolutionary power of peripheral agencies: Explaining radical policy innovation in Finland and Israel.' *Comparative Political Studies* 46.10: 1219–45.

Buchanan, Neil H., and Michael C. Dorf (2012). 'Nullifying the debt ceiling threat once and for all: Why the president should embrace the least unconstitutional option.' *Columbia Law Review* 112.

Calomiris, Charles W., and Stephen H. Haber (2015). *Fragile by Design: The Political Origins of Banking Crises and Scarce Credit*. Princeton University Press.

Canon, J. (2022). 'Three general wills in Rousseau.' *The Review of Politics*, 84.3: 350–71.

Caplan, Bryan (2011). *The Myth of the Rational Voter*. Princeton University Press.

Cappelen, Cornelius, and Stefan Dahlberg (2018). 'The Law of Jante and generalized trust.' *Acta Sociologica* 61.4: 419–40.

Carattini, Stefano, Steffen Kallbekken and Anton Orlov (2019). 'How to win public support for a global carbon tax.' *Nature* 565.7739: 289–91.

Carozzi, Felipe, Christian A. L. Hilber and Xiaolun Yu (2020). 'On the economic impacts of mortgage credit expansion policies: Evidence from Help to Buy.' *CEPR* Discussion Paper No. DP14620 (April 2020).

Carugati, Federica (2020). 'Tradeoffs of inclusion: Development in ancient Athens.' *Comparative Political Studies* 53.1: 144–70.

Catlin, Aaron C. and Cathy A. Cowan (2015). 'History of health spending in the United States, 1960–2013.' Centers for Medicare and Medicaid Services.

Cavaille, Charlotte, and Jeremy Ferwerda (2022). 'How distributional conflict over in-kind benefits generates support for far-right parties.' *The Journal of Politics*.

Charities Aid Foundation (2016). *Gross Domestic Philanthropy: An International Analysis of GDP, Tax, and Giving*. The Trustees of the Charities Aid Foundation.

Charnysh, Volha, Christopher Lucas and Prerna Singh (2015). 'The ties that bind: National identity salience and pro-social behavior toward the ethnic other.' *Comparative Political Studies* 48.3: 267–300.

Chaudhry, Kiren Aziz (1997). *The Price of Wealth: Economies and Institutions in the Middle East*. Cornell University Press.

Chetty, Raj (2008). 'Moral hazard versus liquidity and optimal unemployment insurance.' *Journal of Political Economy* 116.2: 173–234.

Cobbina-Dungy, Jennifer E., and Delores Jones-Brown (2021). 'Too much policing: Why calls are made to defund the police.' *Punishment & Society*.

Cohen, Gerald A. (1989). 'On the currency of egalitarian justice.' *Ethics* 99.4: 906–44.

Cohen, Gerald Allan (2008). *Rescuing Justice and Equality*. Harvard University Press.

Cohen, Robin, Emily Terlizzi and Michael Martinez (2019). 'Health insurance coverage: Early release of estimates from the National Health Interview Survey, 2018.' National Center for Health Statistics. May 2019.

Colgan, Jeff D., Jessica F. Green and Thomas N. Hale (2021). 'Asset revaluation and the existential politics of climate change.' *International Organization* 75.2: 586–610.

Cook, Lisa D. (2014). 'Violence and economic activity: Evidence from African American patents, 1870–1940.' *Journal of Economic Growth* 19.2: 221–57.

Corden, Warner Max (1984). 'Booming sector and Dutch disease economics: Survey and consolidation.' *Oxford Economic Papers* 36.3: 359–80.

Coyle, Diane (2015). *GDP: A Brief But Affectionate History*, revised and expanded edition. Princeton University Press.

Creemers, Rogier (2018). 'China's social credit system: An evolving practice of control.' Available at SSRN 3175792.

Crepaz, Markus M. L. (1998). 'Inclusion versus exclusion: Political institutions and welfare expenditures.' *Comparative Politics* 31.1: 61–80.

Cullen, Julie Berry, Mark C. Long and Randall Reback (2013). 'Jockeying for position: Strategic high school choice under Texas' top ten percent plan.' *Journal of Public Economics* 97: 32–48.

Dahl, Gordon B., Katrine V. Løken and Magne Mogstad (2014). 'Peer effects in program participation.' *American Economic Review* 104.7: 2049–74.

Dancygier, Rafaela M. (2010). *Immigration and Conflict in Europe*. Cambridge University Press.

de Swaan, Abram (1988). *In Care of the State: Health Care, Education and Welfare in Europe and the USA in the Modern Era*. Oxford University Press.

Dixit, Avinash K., and Barry J. Nalebuff (1993). *Thinking Strategically: The Competitive Edge in Business, Politics, and Everyday Life*. W. W. Norton & Company.

Downs, Anthony (1957). *An Economic Theory of Democracy*. Harper.

Dryzek, John S., and Christian List (2003). 'Social choice theory and deliberative democracy: A reconciliation.' *British Journal of Political Science* 33.1: 1–28.

Duch, Raymond M., and Randolph T. Stevenson (2008). *The Economic Vote: How Political and Economic Institutions Condition Election Results*. Cambridge University Press.

Durkheim, Emile (2019). 'The division of labor in society.' *Social Stratification*. Routledge (originally 1893).

Dworkin, Ronald (1983). 'Comment on Narveson: In defense of equality.' *Social Philosophy and Policy* 1.1: 24–40.

Economist (2015). 'Princes of paperwork', 19 March.

Economist (2019). 'How Argentina and Japan continue to confound macroeconomists', 28 March.

Eeckhaut, Mieke C. W., and Maria A. Stanfors (2021). 'Educational assortative mating, gender equality, and income differentiation across Europe: A simulation study.' *Acta Sociologica* 64.1: 48–69.

Eggers, Andrew C. (2021). 'A diagram for analyzing ordinal voting systems.' *Social Choice and Welfare* 56.1: 143–71.

Eika, Lasse, Magne Mogstad and Basit Zafar (2019). 'Educational assortative mating and household income inequality.' *Journal of Political Economy* 127.6: 2795–835.

Ekberg, John, Rickard Eriksson and Guido Friebel (2013). 'Parental leave – A policy evaluation of the Swedish "Daddy-Month" reform.' *Journal of Public Economics* 97: 131–43.

Ekiert, Grzegorz (1998). 'Liberum Veto.' *The Encyclopedia of Democracy*, ed. Seymour M. Lipset. Congressional Quarterly Books, 1340–46.

Elkjaer, Mads, Ben Ansell, Laure Bokobza, et al. (2022). 'Why is it so hard to counteract wealth inequality? Evidence from England and Wales.' Working Paper.

Elster, Jon (2015). *Explaining Social Behavior: More Nuts and Bolts for the Social Sciences*. Cambridge University Press.

Emsley, Clive (2014). *The English Police: A Political and Social History*. Routledge.

Ermisch, John, Marco Francesconi and Thomas Siedler (2006). 'Intergenerational mobility and marital sorting.' *The Economic Journal* 116.513: 659–79.

Esping-Andersen, Gosta (1990). *The Three Worlds of Welfare Capitalism*. Princeton University Press.

Estevez-Abe, Margarita, Torben Iversen and David Soskice (2001). 'Social protection and the formation of skills: A reinterpretation of the welfare state.' In Hall and Soskice (2001), 145–83.

Farrell, David M., Jane Suiter and Clodagh Harris (2019). ' "Systematizing" constitutional deliberation: The 2016–18 citizens' assembly in Ireland.' *Irish Political Studies* 34.1: 113–23.

Foucault, Michel (1977). *Discipline and Punish: The Birth of the Prison*. Random House.

Fowler, Anthony (2013). 'Electoral and policy consequences of voter turnout: Evidence from compulsory voting in Australia.' *Quarterly Journal of Political Science* 8.2: 159–82.

Frye, Timothy (2022). *Weak Strongman: The Limits of Power in Putin's Russia*. Princeton University Press.

Fukuyama, Francis (2006). *The End of History and The Last Man*. Simon & Schuster.

Fussey, Peter, and Daragh Murray (2019). 'Independent report on the London Metropolitan Police Service's trial of live facial recognition technology.'

Gaikwad, Nikhar, Federica Genovese and Dustin Tingley (2022). 'Creating climate coalitions: Mass preferences for compensating vulnerability in the world's two largest democracies.' *American Political Science Review* 116.4: 1165–83.

Gains, Adrian, Benjamin Heydecker, John Shrewsbury and Sandy Robertson (2004). 'The national safety camera programme – three year evaluation report.' Available at http://speedcamerareport.co.uk/4_year_evaluation.pdf.

Galbiati, Roberto, and Giulio Zanella (2012). 'The tax evasion social multiplier: Evidence from Italy.' *Journal of Public Economics* 96.5–6: 485–94.

Gartzke, Erik (2007). 'The capitalist peace.' *American Journal of Political Science* 51.1: 166–91.

Geiger, Ben Baumberg (2018). 'Benefit "myths"? The accuracy and inaccuracy of public beliefs about the benefits system.' *Social Policy & Administration* 52.5: 998–1018.

Gest, Justin (2016). *The New Minority: White Working Class Politics in an Age of Immigration and Inequality*. Oxford University Press.

Gest, Justin, Tyler Reny and Jeremy Mayer (2018). 'Roots of the radical right: Nostalgic deprivation in the United States and Britain.' *Comparative Political Studies* 51.13: 1694–719.

Gibbard, Allan (1973). 'Manipulation of voting schemes: A general result.' *Econometrica: Journal of the Econometric Society* 41.4: 587–601.

Gibbons, Robert S. (1992). *Game Theory for Applied Economists*. Princeton University Press.

Gilens, Martin (2003). 'How the poor became black: The racialization of American poverty in the mass media.' *Race and the Politics of Welfare Reform*, ed. Sanford F. Schram, Joe Soss and Richard C. Fording, 101–30. University of Michigan Press.

Gilens, Martin (2009). *Why Americans Hate Welfare: Race, Media, and the Politics of Antipoverty Policy*. University of Chicago Press.

Gingrich, Jane (2014). 'Visibility, values, and voters: The informational role of the welfare state.' *The Journal of Politics* 76.2: 565–80.

Gingrich, Jane, and Ben W. Ansell (2014). 'Sorting for schools: Housing, education and inequality.' *Socio-Economic Review* 12.2: 329–51.

Gingrich, Jane, and Ben Ansell (2015). 'The dynamics of social investment: Human capital, activation, and care.' In Beramendi, Hänsermann, Kitschelt and Kriesi, eds. (2015), 282–304.

Goldin, Claudia, and Lawrence F. Katz (2010). *The Race between Education and Technology*. Harvard University Press.

Goldin, Claudia, and Robert A. Margo (1992). 'The great compression: The wage structure in the United States at mid-century.' *The Quarterly Journal of Economics* 107.1: 1–34.

Gondermann, Thomas (2007). 'Progression and retrogression in Herbert Spencer's *Explanations of Social Inequality*.' *History of the Human Sciences* 20.3: 21–40.

Goodin, Robert E., and Kai Spiekermann (2018). *An Epistemic Theory of Democracy*. Oxford University Press.

Graefe, Andreas (2014). 'Accuracy of vote expectation surveys in forecasting elections.' *Public Opinion Quarterly* 78.S1: 204–32.

Greenwood, Jeremy, Nezih Guner, Georgi Kocharkov and Cezar Santos (2014). 'Marry your like: Assortative mating and income inequality.' *American Economic Review* 104.5: 348–53.

Grogan, Colleen M., and Sunggeun Park (2017). 'The racial divide in state Medicaid expansions.' *Journal of Health Politics, Policy and Law* 42.3: 539–72.

Haas, Linda, and C. Philip Hwang (2019). 'Policy is not enough – the influence of the gendered workplace on fathers' use of parental leave in Sweden.' *Community, Work & Family* 22.1: 58–76.

Habyarimana, James, Macartan Humphreys, Daniel Posner and Jeremy Weinstein (2007). 'Why does ethnic diversity undermine public goods provision?' *American Political Science Review* 101.4: 709–25.

Hacker, Jacob S. (1999). *The Road to Nowhere: The Genesis of President Clinton's Plan for Health Security*. Princeton University Press.

Hacker, Jacob, Ben Jackson and Martin O'Neill (2013). 'The politics of predistribution: Jacob Hacker interviewed by Ben Jackson and Martin O'Neill.' *Renewal* 21.2–3: 54–65.

Hacker, Jacob S. and Paul Pierson (2005). *Off Center: The Republican Revolution and the Erosion of American Democracy*. Yale University Press.

Haerpfer, Christian, Ronald Inglehart, Alejandro Moreno, et al., eds. (2022). *World Values Survey: Round Seven – Country-Pooled Datafile Version 4.0.* JD Systems Institute & WVSA Secretariat. doi.org/10.14281/18241.18.

Hale, Thomas (2020). 'Catalytic cooperation.' *Global Environmental Politics* 20.4: 73–98.

Hall, Peter A., and David Soskice, eds. (2001). *Varieties of Capitalism: The Institutional Foundations of Comparative Advantage*. Oxford University Press.

Harrison, Kathryn (2013). 'The political economy of British Columbia's carbon tax.' *OECD Environment Working Papers* 63.

Heinrich, Tobias, Yoshiharu Kobayashi and Kristin A. Bryant (2016). 'Public opinion and foreign aid cuts in economic crises.' *World Development* 77: 66–79.

Herrmann, Michael, Simon Munzert and Peter Selb (2016). 'Determining the effect of strategic voting on election results.' *Journal of the Royal Statistical Society: Series A (Statistics in Society)* 179.2: 583–605.

Herzog, Lisa (2018). 'Durkheim on social justice: The argument from "organic solidarity".' *American Political Science Review* 112.1: 112–24.

Hill, Terrence D., Catherine E. Ross and Ronald J. Angel (2005). 'Neighborhood disorder, psychophysiological distress, and health.' *Journal of Health and Social Behavior* 46.2: 170–86.

Hills, John (2017). *Good Times, Bad Times: The Welfare Myth of Them and Us*. Policy Press.

Hillygus, D. Sunshine, and Sarah A. Treul (2014). 'Assessing strategic voting in the 2008 US presidential primaries: The role of electoral context, institutional rules, and negative votes.' *Public Choice* 161.3: 517–36.

Hix, Simon, Ron J. Johnston and Iain McLean (2010). *Choosing an Electoral System*. The British Academy.

Hoffman, Mitchell, Gianmarco León and María Lombardi (2017). 'Compulsory voting, turnout, and government spending: Evidence from Austria.' *Journal of Public Economics* 145: 103–15.

Holden, Steinar (2013). 'Avoiding the resource curse the case Norway.' *Energy Policy* 63: 870–76.

Hopkin, Jonathan, and Mark Blyth (2012). 'What can Okun teach Polanyi? Efficiency, regulation and equality in the OECD.' *Review of International Political Economy* 19.1: 1–33.

Hoppit, Julian (2002). 'The myths of the South Sea Bubble.' *Transactions of the Royal Historical Society* 12: 141–65.

Horowitz, Michael C. (2019). 'When speed kills: Lethal autonomous weapon systems, deterrence and stability.' *Journal of Strategic Studies* 42.6: 764–88.

Horton, Chris (2018). 'The simple but ingenious system Taiwan uses to crowdsource its laws.' *MIT Technology Review*, 21 August 2018.

Hotelling, Harold (1929). 'Stability in competition.' *The Economic Journal* 39.153: 41–57.

Howard, Christopher (1999). *The Hidden Welfare State: Tax Expenditures and Social Policy in the United States*. Princeton University Press.

Huntington, Samuel P. (1993). *The Third Wave: Democratization in the Late Twentieth Century*. University of Oklahoma Press.

Hurwicz, Leonid (2008). 'But who will guard the guardians?' *American Economic Review* 98.3: 577–85.

Intergovernmental Panel on Climate Change (2019). *Global Warming of 1.5°C*. Scientific report.

International Social Survey Program: Role of Government (2016).

International Social Survey Program: Social Inequality (2019).

Irwin, Douglas A., and Randall S. Kroszner (1996). 'Log-rolling and economic interests in the passage of the Smoot–Hawley Tariff.' *Carnegie–Rochester Conference Series on Public Policy*: 173–200 45 NBER.

Iversen, Torben (2010). 'Democracy and capitalism.' *The Oxford Handbook of the Welfare State* ed. Francis G. Castles, Stephan Liebfried, Jane Lewis, et al., 183–95. Oxford University Press.

Iversen, T., and P. Rehm (2022). *Big Data and the Welfare State: How the Information Revolution Threatens Social Solidarity*. Cambridge University Press.

Iversen, Torben, and David Soskice (2001). 'An asset theory of social policy preferences.' *American Political Science Review* 95.4: 875–93.

Iversen, Torben, and David Soskice (2006). 'Electoral institutions and the politics of coalitions: Why some democracies redistribute more than others.' *American Political Science Review* 100.2: 165–81.

Jacobs, Alan M. (2011). *Governing for the Long Term: Democracy and the Politics of Investment*. Cambridge University Press.

Jacobs, Lawrence R. (2019). *The Health of Nations*. Cornell University Press.

Johnston, Norman Bruce (2000). *Forms of Constraint: A History of Prison Architecture*. University of Illinois Press.

Jones, Calvert W. (2015). 'Seeing like an autocrat: Liberal social engineering in an illiberal state.' *Perspectives on Politics* 13.1: 24–41.

Jones, Calvert W. (2017). *Bedouins into Bourgeois: Remaking Citizens for Globalization*. Cambridge University Press.

Keohane, Robert O., and Michael Oppenheimer (2016). 'Paris: Beyond the climate dead end through pledge and review?' *Politics and Governance* 4.3: 142–51.

Kim, Taeho (2019). 'Facilitating police reform: Body cameras, use of force, and law enforcement outcomes.' *Use of Force, and Law Enforcement Outcomes*, 23 October.

Kim, Taeho (2022). 'Measuring police performance: Public attitudes expressed in Twitter.' *AEA Papers and Proceedings* 112: 184–7.

Kinder, Donald R., and Cindy D. Kam (2010). *Us Against Them: Ethnocentric Foundations of American Opinion*. University of Chicago Press.

Klein, Ezra (2020). *Why We're Polarized*. Simon & Schuster.

Kleven, Henrik, and Camille Landais (2017). 'Gender inequality and economic development: Fertility, education and norms.' *Economica* 84.334: 180–209.

Kohler-Hausmann, Julilly (2007). ' "The crime of survival": Fraud prosecutions, community surveillance, and the original "welfare queen".' *Journal of Social History* 41.2: 329–54.

Korpi, Walter, and Joakim Palme (1998). 'The paradox of redistribution and strategies of equality: Welfare state institutions, inequality, and poverty in the Western countries.' *American Sociological Review* 63.5: 661–87.

Kremer, Michael (1993). 'The O-ring theory of economic development.' *The Quarterly Journal of Economics* 108.3: 551–75.

Krueger, Alan (2012). 'The rise and consequences of inequality.' *Presentation Made to the Center for American Progress, January 12th.*

Kurlansky, Mark (2011). *Cod: A Biography of the Fish That Changed the World.* Vintage Canada.

Kuznets, Simon (1955). 'Economic growth and income inequality.' *American Economic Review* 45.1: 1–28.

Kydd, Andrew H. (2015). *International Relations Theory.* Cambridge University Press.

Kymlicka, Will (2002). *Contemporary Political Philosophy: An Introduction.* Oxford University Press.

Lake, David A., and Matthew A. Baum (2001). 'The invisible hand of democracy: Political control and the provision of public services.' *Comparative Political Studies* 34.6: 587–621.

Leeson, Peter T. (2007). 'Better off stateless: Somalia before and after government collapse.' *Journal of Comparative Economics* 35.4: 689–710.

Leeson, Peter T. (2009). 'The laws of lawlessness.' *The Journal of Legal Studies* 38.2: 471–503.

Leonard, Andrew (2020). 'How Taiwan's unlikely digital minister hacked the pandemic.' *Wired,* 23 July.

Levenson, Eric (2020). 'These GOP governors long resisted mask mandates and coronavirus rules. Now their states are in crisis.' CNN website, 17 November. Available at https://lite.cnn.com/en/article/h_ac45098a5d54038d61449dcf93727488.

Levitsky, Steven, and Lucan A. Way (2002). 'Elections without democracy: The rise of competitive authoritarianism.' *Journal of Democracy* 13.2: 51–65.

Levitsky, Steven, and Daniel Ziblatt (2018). *How Democracies Die.* Broadway Books.

Lewis, William Arthur (1954). 'Economic development with unlimited supplies of labour.' *The Manchester School* 22.2: 139–91.

Lewis, W. Arthur (1976). 'Development and distribution.' *Employment, Income Distribution and Development Strategy: Problems of the Developing Countries,* 26–42, Palgrave Macmillan.

Lieberman, Evan S. (2003). *Race and Regionalism in the Politics of Taxation in Brazil and South Africa*. Cambridge University Press.

Lijphart, Arend (1999). *Patterns of Democracy: Government Forms and Performance in Thirty-Six Countries*. Yale University Press.

Lindert, Peter H. (2004). *Growing Public: Social Spending and Economic Growth since the Eighteenth Century*, Vol. 1: *The Story*. Cambridge University Press.

List, Christian, and Robert E. Goodin (2001). 'Epistemic democracy: Generalizing the Condorcet jury theorem.' *Journal of Political Philosophy* 9.3: 227–306.

Locke, Richard M. (2001). 'Building trust.' *Annual Meetings of the American Political Science Association, Hilton Towers, San Francisco, California*.

Lum, Kristian, and William Isaac (2016). 'To predict and serve?' *Significance* 13.5: 14–19.

Lupu, Noam (2016). 'Latin America's new turbulence: The end of the Kirchner era.' *Journal of Democracy* 27.2: 35–49.

Lynch, Julia (2020). *Regimes of Inequality: The Political Economy of Health and Wealth*. Cambridge University Press.

Maddison, Angus (2006). *The World Economy*. OECD Publishing.

Maskin, Eric, and Amartya Sen (2014). *The Arrow Impossibility Theorem*. Columbia University Press.

Matthews, Dylan (2019). 'Bernie Sanders's most socialist idea yet, explained.' *Vox*, 29 May.

Mazzucato, Mariana (2011). 'The entrepreneurial state.' *Soundings* 49: 131–42.

McCarty, Nolan, Keith T. Poole and Howard Rosenthal (2016). *Polarized America: The Dance of Ideology and Unequal Riches*. MIT Press.

McGann, Anthony J. (2006). *The Logic of Democracy: Reconciling Equality, Deliberation, and Minority Protection*. University of Michigan Press.

McInnes, Roderick (2021). 'Pensions: International comparisons.' House of Commons Briefing Paper. Number CBP00290, 9 April.

McLean, Iain (2002). 'William H. Riker and the invention of heresthetic (s).' *British Journal of Political Science* 32.3: 535–58.

McLean, Iain (2010). *What's Wrong with the British Constitution?* Oxford University Press.

McLean, Iain, and Fiona Hewitt, eds. (1994). *Condorcet: Foundations of Social Choice and Political Theory*. Edward Elgar Publishing.

Meltzer, Allan H., and Scott F. Richard (1981). 'A rational theory of the size of government.' *Journal of Political Economy* 89.5: 914–27.

Messer, Lynne C., Jay S. Kaufman, Nancy Dole, et al. (2006). 'Violent crime exposure classification and adverse birth outcomes: A geographically-defined cohort study.' *International Journal of Health Geographics* 5.1: 1–12.

Mettler, Suzanne (2011). *The Submerged State: How Invisible Government Policies Undermine American Democracy*. University of Chicago Press.

Michener, Jamila (2018). *Fragmented Democracy: Medicaid, Federalism, and Unequal Politics*. Cambridge University Press.

Miguel, Edward, and Mary Kay Gugerty (2005). 'Ethnic diversity, social sanctions, and public goods in Kenya.' *Journal of Public Economics* 89.11–12: 2325–68.

Milanovic, Branko (2016). *Global Inequality: A New Approach for the Age of Globalization*. Harvard University Press.

Milanovic, Branko, Peter H. Lindert and Jeffrey G. Williamson (2011). 'Pre-industrial inequality.' *The Economic Journal* 121.551: 255–72.

Miyajima, Takeru, and Hiroyuki Yamaguchi (2017). 'I want to but I won't: Pluralistic ignorance inhibits intentions to take paternity leave in Japan.' *Frontiers in Psychology* 8: 1508.

Morris, Norval, and David J. Rothman, eds. (1998). *The Oxford History of the Prison: The Practice of Punishment in Western Society*. Oxford University Press.

Morse, Yonatan L. (2012). 'The era of electoral authoritarianism.' *World Politics* 64.1: 161–98.

Mueller, Dennis C. (2003). *Public Choice III*. Cambridge University Press.

Müller, Miriam (2005). 'Social control and the hue and cry in two fourteenth-century villages.' *Journal of Medieval History* 31.1: 29–53.

Murr, Andreas Erwin (2011). '"Wisdom of crowds"? A decentralised election forecasting model that uses citizens' local expectations.' *Electoral Studies* 30.4: 771–83.

Murr, Andreas E. (2015). 'The wisdom of crowds: Applying Condorcet's jury theorem to forecasting US presidential elections.' *International Journal of Forecasting* 31.3: 916–29.

Murr, Andreas E. (2016). 'The wisdom of crowds: What do citizens forecast for the 2015 British general election?' *Electoral Studies* 41: 283–8.

Murray, Charles (2016). *In Our Hands: A Plan to Replace the Welfare State*. Rowman & Littlefield.

Nietzsche, Friedrich Wilhelm (1974). *The Gay Science: With a Prelude in German Rhymes and an Appendix of Songs*. Vol. 985. Vintage (originally 1882).

Nooruddin, Irfan (2010). *Coalition Politics and Economic Development: Credibility and the Strength of Weak Governments*. Cambridge University Press.

North, Douglass C., and Barry R. Weingast (1989). 'Constitutions and commitment: The evolution of institutions governing public choice in seventeenth-century England.' *The Journal of Economic History* 49.4: 803–32.

OECD Income Distribution Database (2015). Accessed July 2022. https://stats.oecd.org.

Okun, Arthur M. (2015). *Equality and Efficiency: The Big Tradeoff.* Brookings Institution Press (originally 1975).

Olson, Mancur (1965). *The Logic of Collective Action.* Harvard University Press.

Olson, Mancur (1993). 'Dictatorship, democracy, and development.' *American Political Science Review* 87.3: 567–76.

Olson, Mancur, and Richard Zeckhauser (1966). 'An economic theory of alliances.' *The Review of Economics and Statistics* 48.3: 266–79.

Ornston, Darius (2013). 'Creative corporatism: The politics of high-technology competition in Nordic Europe.' *Comparative Political Studies* 46.6: 702–29.

Owen, John M. (1994). 'How liberalism produces democratic peace.' *International Security* 19.2: 87–125.

Parijs, Philippe van (2017). *Basic Income.* Harvard University Press.

Pasotti, Eleonora (2010). *Political Branding in Cities: The Decline of Machine Politics in Bogotá, Naples, and Chicago.* Cambridge University Press.

Pew Research Center (2016). 'Partisanship and Political Animosity in 2016.' Available at https://www.pewresearch.org/politics/2016/06/22/partisanship-and-political-animosity-in-2016/.

Pfeffer, Fabian T., and Nora Waitkus (2021). 'The wealth inequality of nations.' *American Sociological Review* 86.4: 567–602.

Piketty, Thomas (2014). *Capital in the Twenty-First Century.* Harvard University Press.

Piketty, Thomas, Emmanuel Saez and Gabriel Zucman (2018). 'Distributional national accounts: Methods and estimates for the United States.' *The Quarterly Journal of Economics* 133.2: 553–609.

Pinker, Steven (2011). *The Better Angels of Our Nature: The Decline of Violence in History and Its Causes.* Penguin Books.

Pontusson, Jonas (1993). 'The comparative politics of labor-initiated reforms: Swedish cases of success and failure.' *Comparative Political Studies* 25.4: 548–78.

Pontusson, Jonas (2005). *Inequality and Prosperity: Social Europe vs. Liberal America.* Cornell University Press.

Pontusson, Jonas, and Sarosh Kuruvilla (1992). 'Swedish wage-earner funds: An experiment in economic democracy.' *ILR Review* 45.4: 779–91.

Portes, Jonathan (2016). 'What do the people really want? The Condorcet paradox and the referendum.' *LSE Brexit Vote Blog*, 15 June. https://blogs.lse.ac.uk/brexit/2016/06/15/what-do-the-people-really-want-the-condorcet-paradox-and-the-referendum/.

Posner, Eric A., and E. Glen Weyl (2018). *Radical Markets: Uprooting Capitalism and Democracy for a Just Society*. Princeton University Press.

Pritchett, Lant (1997). 'Divergence, big time.' *Journal of Economic Perspectives* 11.3: 3–17.

Putnam, Robert D. (1992). *Making Democracy Work: Civic Traditions in Modern Italy*. Princeton University Press.

Putnam, Robert D. (2000). *Bowling Alone: The Collapse and Revival of American Community*. Simon & Schuster.

Quistberg, D. Alex, Leah L. Thompson. James Curtiu, et al. (2019). 'Impact of automated photo enforcement of vehicle speed in school zones: Interrupted time series analysis.' *Injury Prevention* 25.5: 400–406.

Rachman, Gideon (2022a). 'Russia and China's plans for a new world order.' *Financial Times*, 23 January.

Rachman, Gideon (2022b). *The Age of the Strongman: How the Cult of the Leader Threatens Democracy around the World*. Random House.

Reeves, Richard V. (2018). *Dream Hoarders: How the American Upper Middle Class is Leaving Everyone Else in the Dust, Why That is a Problem, and What to Do About It*. Brookings Institution Press.

Reich, Rob, Mehran Sahami and Jeremy M. Weinstein (2018). *System Error: Where Big Tech Went Wrong and How We Can Reboot*. Hodder & Stoughton.

Riker, William H. (1986). *The Art of Political Manipulation*. Yale University Press.

Rodrik, Dani (2000). 'Institutions for high-quality growth: What they are and how to acquire them.' *Studies in Comparative International Development* 35.3: 3–31.

Romer, Paul (2010). *Technologies, Rules, and Progress: The Case for Charter Cities*. No. id: 2471.

Ross, Michael L. (2001). 'Does oil hinder democracy?' *World Politics* 53.3: 325–61.

Ross, Michael L. (2008). 'Oil, Islam, and women.' *American Political Science Review* 102.1: 107–23.

Rothstein, Bo (1998). *Just Institutions Matter: The Moral and Political Logic of the Universal Welfare State*. Cambridge University Press.

Rothstein, Bo (2020). 'Why no economic democracy in Sweden? A Counterfactual Approach.' *Paper in Conference: Democratizing the Corporation*.

Rousseau, Jean-Jacques (2018). *The Social Contract and Other Later Political Writings*. Cambridge University Press (originally 1762).

Rubin, Ashley T. (2021). *The Deviant Prison: Philadelphia's Eastern State Penitentiary and the Origins of America's Modern Penal System, 1829–1913*. Cambridge University Press.

Rueda, David, and Jonas Pontusson (2000). 'Wage inequality and varieties of capitalism.' *World Politics* 52.3: 350–83.

Russett, Bruce (1994). *Grasping the Democratic Peace: Principles for a Post-Cold War World*. Princeton University Press.

Saez, Emmanuel, Joel Slemrod and Seth H. Giertz (2012). 'The elasticity of taxable income with respect to marginal tax rates: A critical review.' *Journal of Economic Literature* 50.1: 3–50.

Saez, Emmanuel, and Gabriel Zucman (2019). 'Progressive wealth taxation.' *Brookings Papers on Economic Activity* 2019.2: 437–533.

Saez, Emmanuel, and Gabriel Zucman (2020). 'The rise of income and wealth inequality in America: Evidence from distributional macroeconomic accounts.' *Journal of Economic Perspectives* 34.4: 3–26.

Sagar, Rahul (2016). 'Are charter cities legitimate?' *Journal of Political Philosophy* 24.4: 509–29.

Satterthwaite, Mark Allen (1975). 'Strategy-proofness and Arrow's conditions: Existence and correspondence theorems for voting procedures and social welfare functions.' *Journal of Economic Theory* 10.2: 187–217.

Scheidel, Walter (2017). *The Great Leveler: Violence and the History of Inequality from the Stone Age to the Twenty-first Century*. Princeton University Press.

Schelling, Thomas C. (2006). *Micromotives and Macrobehavior*. W. W. Norton & Company (originally 1978).

Scheve, Kenneth, and David Stasavage (2009). 'Institutions, partisanship, and inequality in the long run.' *World Politics* 61.2: 215–53.

Schumpeter, Joseph A. (2013). *Capitalism, Socialism and Democracy*. Routledge (originally 1942).

Schwartz, Christine R. (2010). 'Earnings inequality and the changing association between spouses' earnings.' *American Journal of Sociology* 115.5: 1524–57.

Schwartz, Christine R. (2013). 'Trends and variation in assortative mating: Causes and consequences.' *Annual Review of Sociology* 39: 451–70.

Scott, James C. (2008). *Seeing Like a State: How Certain Schemes to Improve the Human Condition Have Failed*. Yale University Press.

Scott, James C. (2010). *The Art of Not being Governed: An Anarchist History of Upland Southeast Asia*. Yale University Press.

Seamans, Robert (2021). 'Tax not the robots.' *Brookings Institute*, 25 August. https://www.brookings.edu/research/tax-not-the-robots/.

Sen, Amartya (1982). *Poverty and Famines: An Essay on Entitlement and Deprivation*. Oxford University Press.

Sen, A. (1985). *Commodities and Capabilities*. North-Holland.

Sen, Amartya (1995). *Inequality Reexamined*. Harvard University Press.

Shaw, T. M., and United States (2015). *The Ferguson Report: Department of Justice Investigation of the Ferguson Police Department*. New Press.

Shepsle, Kenneth A., and Barry R. Weingast (1981). 'Structure-induced equilibrium and legislative choice.' *Public Choice* 37.3: 503–19.

Silverman, Bertram (1998). 'The rise and fall of the Swedish model: Interview with Rudolf Meidner.' *Challenge* 41.1: 69–90.

Simas, Elizabeth N., Scott Clifford and Justin H. Kirkland (2020). 'How empathic concern fuels political polarization.' *American Political Science Review* 114.1: 258–69.

Singh, Prerna, and Matthias vom Hau (2016). 'Ethnicity in time: Politics, history, and the relationship between ethnic diversity and public goods provision.' *Comparative Political Studies* 49.10: 1303–40.

Sloman, Peter (2018). 'Universal basic income in British politics, 1918–2018: From a "Vagabond's Wage" to a global debate.' *Journal of Social Policy* 47.3: 625–42.

Sorge, Arndt, and Wolfgang Streeck (2018). 'Diversified quality production revisited: Its contribution to German socio-economic performance over time.' *Socio-Economic Review* 16.3: 587–612.

Standing, Guy (2017). *Basic Income: And How We Can Make It Happen*. Penguin Books.

Stavins, Robert N. (2019). 'Carbon taxes vs. cap and trade: Theory and practice.' Harvard Project on Climate Agreements Discussion Paper ES 19–9.

Surowiecki, James (2005). *The Wisdom of Crowds: Why the Many are Smarter Than He Few*. Anchor.

Teele, Dawn Langan (2018). *Forging the Franchise: The Political Origins of the Women's Vote*. Princeton University Press.

Temin, Peter, and Hans-Joachim Voth (2004). 'Riding the South Sea Bubble.' *American Economic Review* 94.5: 1654–68.

Tetlock, Philip E. (2017). *Expert Political Judgment: How Good is It? How Can We Know?* Princeton University Press.

Thelen, Kathleen (2004). *How Institutions Evolve: The Political Economy of Skills in Germany, Britain, the United States, and Japan*. Cambridge University Press.

Thomasson, Melissa A. (2003). 'The importance of group coverage: How tax policy shaped US health insurance.' *American Economic Review* 93.4: 1373–84.

Tiebout, Charles M. (1956). 'A pure theory of local expenditures.' *Journal of Political Economy* 64.5: 416–24.

Tilly, Charles (1975). 'Reflections on the history of European state-making.' Charles Tilly, ed. *The Formation of National States in Western Europe*. Princeton University Press, 3–89.

Tilly, Charles (1998). *Durable Inequality*. University of California Press.

Tomz, Michael R., and Jessica L. P. Weeks (2013). 'Public opinion and the democratic peace.' *American Political Science Review* 107.4: 849–65.

Tufte, Edward R. (1978). *Political Control of the Economy*. Princeton University Press.

Uslaner, Eric M. (2017). *The Historical Roots of Corruption: Mass Education, Economic Inequality, and State Capacity*. Cambridge University Press.

Valentino, Lauren, and Stephen Vaisey (2022). 'Culture and durable inequality.' *Annual Review of Sociology* 48: 109–29.

Wallace, Danielle, Michael D. White, Janne E. Gaub and Natalie Todak (2018). 'Body-worn cameras as a potential source of depolicing: Testing for camera-induced passivity.' *Criminology* 56.3: 481–509.

Wang, Xin Yuan (2019). 'China's social credit system: The Chinese citizens' perspective.' *Anthropology of Smartphones and Smart Ageing Blog* UCL, 9 December. Available at https://blogs.ucl.ac.uk/assa/2019/12/09/chinas-social-credit-system-the-chinese-citizens-perspective/.

Weitzman, Martin L. (2017). 'Sustainability and technical progress.' *The Economics of Sustainability*, ed. John C. V. Pezzey and Michael A. Toman, 329–41. Routledge.

Weyland, Kurt (2014). *Making Waves: Democratic Contention in Europe and Latin America since the Revolutions of 1848*. Cambridge University Press.

Wilkinson, Richard G., and Kate Pickett (2009). *The Spirit Level: Why More Equal Societies Almost Always Do Better*. Allen Lane.

Wolff, Jonathan (1998). 'Fairness, respect, and the egalitarian ethos.' *Philosophy & Public Affairs* 27.2: 97–122.

Yang, Dali L. (1996). *Calamity and Reform in China: State, Rural Society, and Institutional Change since the Great Leap Famine*. Stanford University Press.

Notes

Introduction

The prescient *New York Times* article by Waldemar Kaempffert can be found at https://www.nytimes.com/1956/10/28/archives/science-in-review-warmer-climate-on-the-earth-may-be-due-to-more.html.

On estimates for best-case scenario warming of 1.5°C, see Intergovernmental Panel on Climate Change (2019). On the IPCC estimates for 2040, see https://www.ipcc.ch/report/ar6/wg1/figures/summary-for-policymakers.

Support for democracy comes from the World Values Survey: question 238, 2017–22 wave: Haerpfer, Inglehart, Moreno, et al. (2022). Data on differences in income are from the International Social Survey Program (2019) on social inequality: questions v21, v22, v26. Support for government role in healthcare comes from International Social Survey Program (2016) on the role of government: question v23. Support for security over freedom and trust in the police come from the World Values Survey: questions 150 and 69, 2017–22 wave. The estimate of 2016 being the most violent year on record comes from Braumoeller (2019). Data on having a better life than parents and protecting the environments come from the World Values Survey: questions 56 and 111, 2017–22 wave.

On education and self-interest, see Ansell (2008a, 2008b, 2010). An excellent summary of the Cod Wars can be found in Kurlansky (2011).

Part I: Democracy

1. Westminster

Iain McLean's book on the British constitution is McLean (2010). His analysis of differing electoral systems in the British context is in Hix, Johnston and McLean (2010).

2. What is Democracy?

Support for democracy comes from the World Values Survey: question 238, 2017–22 wave. Schumpeter's definition of democracy comes from Schumpeter (2013, originally 1942).

On outcomes in democracies versus autocracies, see Lake and Baum (2001) for infant mortality, immunization and literacy. See Ansell (2010) on public spending on education, and Ansell and Lindvall (2021) on the development of primary education systems worldwide. On the rarity of famine in democracies, see Sen (1982). On the successes and failures of authoritarian countries in economic growth, see Rodrik (2000). The current consensus is that democracy does directly cause higher economic growth – an increase of around 20 per cent in the long run – see Acemoglu, Naidu, Restrepo and Robinson (2019).

On female enfranchisement, women over the age of thirty in the United Kingdom were granted the vote in 1918, but the voting age was not equalized with men at twenty-one until 1928. See Teele (2018) for a comprehensive and insightful analysis of female enfranchisement. On ancient Athens, see Carugati (2020). On waves of democracy, the classic exposition is Huntington (1993) – see also Weyland (2014). Fukuyama's 'end of history' argument is laid out in Fukuyama (2006). On electoral authoritarianism, see Morse (2012) and Levitsky and Way (2002) – on risks it produces democratic collapse, including in America, see Levitsky and Ziblatt (2018).

3. The Democracy Trap

Jean-Jacques Rousseau develops the idea of the *volonté générale* in Book 2 of the *Social Contract*: Rousseau (2018, originally 1762). There is some debate about whether he viewed the general will as the decision being made collectively, or the process of deliberation to get there; see Canon (2022). On the Polish *Sejm* and the liberum veto, see Ekiert (1998). On losers' consent more generally and the case of the Spanish Popular Front, see Anderson, Blais, Bowler, et al. (2005), p. 4.

On Condorcet's jury theorem, see Goodin and Spiekerman (2018), or for a popular account Surowiecki (2005). In the spirit of this chapter there is debate about whether there is even a rational basis for the jury theorem to hold, since members will not vote sincerely, see Austen-Smith and Banks (1996). On Condorcet's paradox, see McLean and Hewitt (1994). On Brexit and Condorcet's paradox, Portes (2016) suggested this was likely to be a problem even before the referendum's results were known. Eggers (2021) shows how different voting systems applied to the public's preferences would have produced distinct outcomes between Deal, No Deal and Remain. Arrow (1950) is his first statement of the impossibility theorem. Maskin and Sen (2014) is an excellent retrospective set of essays. My favourite proof of the theorem is in Mueller (2003).

The classic solution to the problem of cycling is 'structure-induced equilibria' – that is, institutions that limit some aspects of pure democracy; see Shepsle and Weingast (1981). On the Belgian government formation process, see Van Aelst and Louwerse (2014). The proof that strategic voting is inevitable when you have at least three options, no restrictions on preferences and no dictator comes from Gibbard (1973) and Satterthwaite (1975) and is called the Gibbard–Satterthwaite theorem. The finding that strategic voting often backfires comes from Herrmann, Munzert, and Selb (2016). The 'logrolling' explanation of the Smoot–Hawley tariff comes from Irwin and Kroszner (1996). Aidt, Grey and Savu (2021) provide an interesting analysis of the meaningful votes on Brexit.

Anthony Downs (1957) is the key statement on the median-voter theorem and party positioning, drawing from Hotelling's argument about firm location (1929). Single-peaked preferences were developed by Black (1948) and Arrow (1951). The concept of 'off-centre' politics comes from Hacker and Pierson (2005). The growth in polarization in the US Congress comes from McCarty, Poole and Rosenthal (2016). For a readable popular take, see Klein (2020).

The poll citing partisans' views of the other party as a threat to the nation is discussed in Pew Research Center (2016).

The polls on attitudes to children marrying a member of the opposite party are (for the United States) at https://today.yougov.com/topics/politics/articles-reports/2020/09/17/republicans-democrats-marriage-poll, and (for the UK) at https://yougov.co.uk/topics/lifestyle/articles-reports/2019/08/27/labour-voters-more-wary-about-politics-childs-spouse.

Jack Balkin's platinum coin plan was first mentioned in Balkin (2011) and is discussed in Buchanan and Dorf (2012). An excellent discussion of recent

Argentinian politics is Lupu (2016). The Kuznets quote comes from the *Economist* (2019). Brian Barry developed his argument about shifting majorities in Barry (1989).

4. Escaping the Democracy Trap

The pronouncement of a 'new world order' led by China and Russia comes from Rachman (2022a). Rachman (2022b) provides an excellent book-length treatment. For books arguing voters are too irrational or ill-informed to vote, see Caplan (2011) and Brennan (2017). On democracy and technology, see Reich, Sahami and Weinstein (2021). On elite capture, see Hacker and Pierson (2005). On markets in democracy, quadratic voting and many other intriguing market innovations, see Posner and Weyl (2018).

On the epistemic theory of democracy and its connection to Condorcet's jury, see List and Goodin (2001). On Mao's Great Leap Forward, see Yang (1996, p. 65). On the wisdom of crowds versus experts, see Tetlock (2017). On the wisdom of crowds and election prediction, see Murr (2011, 2015, 2016) and Graefe (2014). On deliberation helping to resolve multi-peaked preferences, see Dryzek and List (2003). On citizens' assemblies in Ireland, see Farrell, Suiter and Harris (2019). On vTaiwan and Audrey Tang, see Horton (2018) and Leonard (2020).

On empathy and stigmatized groups, see Batson, Daniel, Polycarpou, Harmon-Jones, et al. (1997). On empathy and higher polarization, see Simas, Clifford and Kirkland (2020). On strategic voting in US primaries, see Hillygus and Treul (2014). On compulsory voting in Austria, see Hoffman, León and Lombardi (2017), and in Australia see Fowler (2013). On Lincoln and the concept of heresthetics, see Riker (1986) and McLean (2002).

On the benefits of proportional representation for securing minority interests *because of* cycling, see McGann (2006). On PR systems having higher public spending and left-wing governments, see Crepaz (1998) and Iversen and Soskice (2006). On PR and lower inequality, see Lijphart (1999), though with the caveat that Scheve and Stasavage (2009) find this pattern does not hold up before the Second World War. On PR and higher policy stability, see McGann (2006) and Nooruddin (2010).

Part II: Equality

5. Jeff Bezos Goes to Space

The BBC quote about Bezos's salary as a multiple of the median Amazon employee's salary comes from Kim Gittleson, the BBC New York business correspondent, at https://www.bbc.co.uk/news/business-45717768. James Bloodworth's compelling book *Hired* recounts his experience in the Rugeley Amazon fulfilment centre (Bloodworth (2018)). Data on the top 1 per cent and bottom 50 per cent of earners come from Piketty, Saez and Zucman (2018). Data on the wealth held by the top 0.1 per cent come from Saez and Zucman (2020, p. 10).

6. What is Equality?

Dworkin develops his concept of the 'egalitarian plateau' in Dworkin (1983). Kymlicka provides a comprehensive account of theories of egalitarianism in Kymlicka (2002), with the quote taken from pp. 3–4. Amartya Sen sets out the relationship between impartiality and equality, along with the core question 'equality of what?' in Sen (1995). Spencer's obsession with physiognomy comes from Gondermann (2007). The Nietzsche quote comes from Nietzsche (1974, p. 377, originally 1882). Evidence on the various benefits of lower inequality comes from Wilkinson and Pickett (2009, Chapters 6, 8, 10): note this data is simply correlational at the country level – establishing whether changes in inequality within countries cause better outcomes is much more challenging. See Lynch (2020) for a state-of-the-art analysis of inequality and healthcare. Data on inequality before and after taxes come from the OECD Income Distribution Database (2022). Data on wealth inequality come from Pfeffer and Waitkus (2021).

Scheidel develops his idea of the 'great disequalization' in Scheidel (2017), which also provides evidence on hunter-gatherer inequality (p. 37), along with the claims that war, famine and plague are the 'great levelers'. Data on ancient and medieval inequality come from Milanovic, Lindert and Williamson (2011), who develop the concepts of the 'inequality possibility frontier' and 'inequality extraction ratio', which measure how unequal societies could be and how close they got to that point. On rising inequality in the medieval period as living standards improved, see Alfani (2015, 2017). The classic argument about economic development increasing inequality, partly through urbanization, comes from Kuznets (1955) – an interesting formalization of this is in Acemoglu and Robinson (2002). Kuznets also argued inequality would eventually decline with development, which did occur during the twentieth century. But he did not predict its consequent rise once more, as noted in Piketty (2014). W. Arthur Lewis made a related argument about urbanization and inequality in Lewis (1954, 1976) – inequality rises because incomes shoot up in the developed core but stagnate elsewhere.

Goldin and Margo (1992) develop the idea of the Great Compression. Scheve and Stasavage (2009) argue that wars and economic depressions are the chief causes of declines in inequality, an argument also made in Scheidel (2017). Goldin and Katz (2010) is the classic book-length treatment on the opposite effects of education and technological innovation on inequality. Rueda and Pontusson (2000) provide evidence on wage-bargaining and inequality. Data on the top 1 per cent's share of income across countries come from the World Inequality Database: https://wid.world. Milanovic provides a very readable account of inequality and globalization in Milanovic (2016).

7. The Equality Trap

The trade-offs inherent in democratic capitalism are nicely summarized in Iversen (2010). The Meltzer–Richard model is developed in Meltzer and Richard (1981). The 'Robin Hood paradox' is developed in Lindert (2004). G. A. Cohen developed his idea of the 'egalitarian ethos' in Cohen (1989) and expanded it in Cohen (2008). Jonathan Wolff provides an excellent analysis in Wolff (1998). Okun (2015, originally 1975) develops the 'leaky bucket' analogy of the alleged trade-off between efficiency and equality. Hopkin and Blyth (2012) provide a helpful critique and suggest the possibility of 'trade-ins' as well as trade-offs. The lack of 'Laffer curve'-type inefficient taxation situations where higher taxes reduce revenues in real-world taxes is explored in Saez, Slemrod and Giertz (2012). The 'off-centre' push of right-wing parties can be seen in Hacker and Pierson (2005) and McCarty, Poole and Rosenthal (2016); and Bonica, McCarty, Poole and Rosenthal (2013) argue that this has produced a gridlock effect, making expansions of the welfare state challenging. 'Opportunity-hoarding' was developed by Charles Tilly in Tilly (1998) and popularized in Reeves (2018) – an excellent discussion is in Valentino and Vaisey (2022).

Bernie Sanders's quote about Scandinavia and democratic socialism is from https://edition.cnn.com/2016/02/17/politics/bernie-sanders-2016-denmark-democratic-socialism/. A useful discussion of democratic socialism and its emphasis on workers owning firms, as opposed to just redistribution, is in Bolton (2020). The Rehn–Meidner model and the Meidner Plan are discussed in an interview with Meidner in Silverman (1998), and in Pontusson (1993), Pontusson and Kuruvilla (1992) and Rothstein (2020). Sanders's advocacy of employee ownership is from Matthews (2019). The 'Great Gatsby' curve was developed by Alan Krueger (2012). The high regulation of Italian markets comes from Hopkin and Blyth (2012) and the role of *notaios* from the *Economist* (2015). The suppression of African American innovators is from Cook (2014).

The redistributivist model of democratization refers to Boix (2003) and Acemoglu and Robinson (2006a). The argument that instead we should expect democratization to occur when inequality is *higher* is from Ansell and Samuels (2014). The level of inequality in nineteenth-century China is from Milanovic, Lindert and Williamson (2011). The discussion of oligarchs' fate under Putin is from Frye (2022, p. 9).

Kleven and Landais (2017) and Bertrand (2020) provide an excellent analysis of female employment participation rates and the gender gap in salaries across countries. On the gender gap by country, gaps in household work, the shock to pay after childbirth and the effects of COVID, see the comprehensive review by Andrew, Bandiera, Costa-Dias and Landais (2021). On parental leave for Swedish men, see Haas and Hwang (2019) and Ekberg, Eriksson and Friebel (2013); for Norway, see Dahl, Løken and Mogstad (2014); and for Japan see Miyajima and Yamaguchi (2017). The estimate that American inequality would be 25–30 per cent lower in the absence of growing assortative mating comes from Greenwood, Guner, Kocharkov and Santos (2014) and assortative mating's reduction of intergenerational mobility comes from Ermisch, Francesconi and Siedler (2006). Assortative mating in Denmark comes from Breen and Andersen (2012), and in Denmark, Germany, Norway and the UK from Eika, Mogstad and Zafar (2019). The comparison of Eastern Europe to Scandinavia comes from Eeckhaut and Stanfors (2021). The quote from Christine Schwartz is from Schwartz (2010, pp. 1524–5). Schwartz (2013) provides an excellent overview of assortative mating.

8. Escaping the Equality Trap

The stand-off between Larry Summers and Emmanuel Saez occurred at the Peterson Institute for International Economics biennial meeting 'Combatting Inequality' on 17 October 2019, where I had presented earlier that day. Video of the fascinating exchange can be seen at https://www.piie.com/events/combating-inequality-rethinking-policies-reduce-inequality-advanced-economies. Saez and Zucman (2019) set out their 'radical' wealth tax plan alongside those of Warren and Sanders and provide estimates of billionaires' wealth under the various policies. Sweden's high wealth inequality can be seen in Pfeffer and Waitkus (2021). Piketty's global wealth tax is discussed in Piketty (2014, Chapter 15). Larry Bartels's analysis of public opinion and the Bush tax cuts is in Bartels (2005, 2016). The 2015 British poll asking about the fairness of various taxes was by YouGov, https://yougov.co.uk/topics/politics/articles-reports/2015/03/19/inheritance-tax-most-unfair. My own study of inheritance tax preferences is Elkjaer, Ansell, Bokobza, et al. (2022). On the proportion of British estates that incur inheritance tax, see: https://www.gov.uk/government/statistics/inheritance-tax-statistics-commentary/inheritance-tax-statistics-commentary. The online laboratory experiment on income versus wealth taxation is Ansell, Bokobza, Cansunar et al. (2022). The small proportion that inheritances contribute to lifetime inflows of money comes from Black, Devereux, Landaud and Salvanes (2022).

The perils and promise of a robot tax are discussed in Seamans (2021). Evidence on robots replacing workers is in Acemoglu and Restrepo (2020). The concept of 'predistribution' comes from Jacob Hacker, see Hacker, Jackson and O'Neill (2013). An excellent discussion of social investment versus social consumption is in the introduction of Beramendi, Häusermann, Kitschelt and Kriesi (2015), and my chapter on the politics of social investment with Jane Gingrich is Gingrich and Ansell (2015). On the slant of higher-education spending, see Ansell (2008a, 2008b, 2010). On mismatched graduates, see Ansell and Gingrich (2017). On the German apprenticeship system and the importance of complementary institutions, see Hall and

Soskice (2001); and in comparison to the UK, see Thelen (2004). The quote from David Soskice comes from https://www.ft.com/content/f8bacb60-d640-11e4-b3e7-00144feab7de.

Part III: Solidarity

9. Obamacare

News reports of the slurs cast at congressmen Lewis, Carson and Cleaver are from CBS: https://www.cbsnews.com/news/rep-protesters-yelled-racial-slurs/; and, with a longer quote from Cleaver's office, from *The New York Times*: https://prescriptions.blogs.nytimes.com/2010/03/20/spitting-and-slurs-directed-at-lawmakers/. Clyburn's quote about not having heard such slurs since 1960 comes from https://www.politico.com/story/2010/03/dems-say-protesters-used-n-word-034747. Data on the US and other countries' healthcare expenses come from the World Bank DataBank, available at https://data.worldbank.org: indicators SH.XPD.CHEX.PC.CD and SH.XPD.GHED.GD.ZS. Data on the percentage uninsured come from Cohen, Terlizzi and Martinez (2019) and https://www.census.gov/library/publications/2021/demo/p60-274.html. On the history of the development of the US healthcare system and the role of tax benefits, see Thomasson (2003) and Catlin and Cowan (2015). On the failure of the Clinton healthcare plan, see Hacker (1999). On the origins of Medicare in the USA and the NHS in the UK, see Jacobs (2019). On the Medicaid expansion and public opinion by race, see Grogan and Park (2017) and Michener (2018).

10. What is Solidarity?

Emile Durkheim developed his concepts of organic and mechanical solidarity in Durkheim (2019, originally 1893). An interesting analysis of its connection to social justice is in Herzog (2018). Classic accounts of the various components of the welfare state and how they were developed are in Esping-Andersen (1990) and de Swaan (1988). On the rich potentially supporting social insurance, see Moene and Wallerstein (2001) and Iversen and Soskice (2001). 'Decommodification' was developed in Esping-Andersen (1990). Data on social spending come from the OECD Social Expenditure

Database (SOCX) for 2017: available at https://www.oecd.org/social/ expenditure.htm. Data the charitable giving come from Charities Aid Foundation 2016. Data on pension generosity come from McInnes (2021). Information on unemployment benefit rights can be found, country by country, at https://ec.europa.eu/social/main.jsp?catId=858&langId=en. The history of solidarity draws on de Swaan (1988) and Ansell and Lindvall (2021), who develop the idea of 'inward conquest'. Tilly's quote comes from Tilly (1975). An excellent account of the growth of social spending is Lindert (2004).

11. The Solidarity Trap

On optimism bias and health risks, see Bränström and Brandberg (2010). On credit constraints and higher-education access, see Barr (2012). Barr (2001) provides an excellent introduction to the political economy of the welfare state, including adverse selection and moral hazard. John Hills's wonderful book on benefits and costs of the welfare state over a lifetime is Hills (2017). The example of FDR and Social Security comes from Jacobs (2011, Chapter 5). Tony Blair's 'baby bonds' were influenced by the 'stakeholder society' argument, a rival of the UBI, which foresaw granting Americans $80,000 at birth; see Ackerman and Alstott (1999).

An interesting account of Linda Taylor is Kohler-Hausmann (2007). Martin Gilens's analysis of racial politics in America's welfare system is in Gilens (2003, 2009). The political-economy literature on ethnic diversity and social spending is enormous. See Alesina and Glaeser (2004), Lieberman (2003), Habyarimana, Humphreys, Posner and Weinstein (2007), and Singh and vom Hau (2016). Miguel and Gugerty (2005) examine public-school fundraising in Kenya. On the connection between ethnic diversity and the income of groups, see Baldwin and Huber (2010). On ethnic diversity and welfare 'in kind', see Dancygier (2010); and for the Viennese case of public housing, see Cavaille and Ferwerda (2022). Schelling's famous model of segregation is in Schelling (2006, originally 1978). Kinder and Kam (2010) is the key work on ethnocentrism and public opinion, including over Social Security and foreign aid in the US. On European attitudes to foreign aid, see Heinrich, Kobayashi and Bryant (2016). On civic nationalism and the Indian map flag, see Charnysh, Lucas and Singh (2015). On voting behaviour of white working classes and support for the radical right, see Gest (2016) and Gest, Reny and Mayer (2018).

On the Panama papers and Norwegian tax evasion, see Alstadsæter, Johannesen and Zucman (2019). The loss of £6 billion of COVID support to fraud in the UK is reported at https://www.theguardian.com/world/ 2022/feb/11/hmrc-accused-of-ignorance-and-inaction-over-6bn-covid. The enormous Oklahoma COVID fraud is at https://www.justice.gov/opa/ pr/woman-pleads-guilty-438-million-covid-19-relief-fraud-scheme. The overestimates of benefit fraud in the UK come from Geiger (2018). Estimates of obesity and its relation to death come from the WHO Global Health Observatory and the IHME, Global Burden of Disease 2019, respectively; see https://ourworldindata.org/obesity. On the degree to which moral hazard explains the connection between unemployment generosity and length on benefits, see Chetty (2008). The positive relationship between unemployment benefit generosity and employment rates across countries is in Pontusson (2005). The positive connection between unemployment benefit generosity and investing in skills is from Estevez-Abe, Iversen and Soskice (2001). My experimental analysis of this claim is in Ahlquist and Ansell (2022). The failure of the British Help to Buy model is analysed in Carozzi, Hilber and Yu (2020). On school choice and sorting in England and Wales, see Gingrich and Ansell (2014). On sorting more generally, the classic piece is Tiebout (1956).

12. Escaping the Solidarity Trap

On Universal Basic Income, the best introductory book, which includes cases of early schemes, including Dauphin, MB, is by a major supporter of the policy, Standing (2017). Bidadanure (2019) provides a very thoughtful discussion of the political theory of UBI. Sloman (2018) has an interesting discussion of UBI in the UK and beyond. The key originator of UBI is Philippe van Parijs – a good retrospective is Van Parijs (2017). A conservative plan for a UBI which explicitly replaces the welfare state can be found in Murray (2016). The danger of artificial intelligence and big data for existing insurance models is well laid out in Iversen and Rehm (2022).

Korpi and Palme's paradox of redistribution was developed in Korpi

and Palme (1998). The most extensive and convincing support for universalism and its ability to 'buy in' the middle class is Rothstein (1998). The
estimate of American childcare costs can be found at https://www.epi.
org/child-care-costs-in-the-united-states/#/MA. The 'submerged' nature
of the American welfare state is in Mettler (2011) and its 'hidden' form in
Howard (1999). Gingrich (2014) shows how the 'visibility' of welfare states
helps citizens connect them to electoral politics. Bleemer (2021) finds the
California ELC increased UC attendance by lower-income and minority
students. The finding that students pulled into the UT system had better
education and income outcomes is in Black, Denning and Rothstein
(2020). The finding that parents moved to different schools to advantage
their kids in getting into university is in Cullen, Long and Reback (2013).

Part IV: Security

13. Lockdown

My thanks to David Adler and Yuan Yang for recounting their COVID experiences. Death totals attributed to COVID-19 in China, Italy and the USA are
from the World Health Organization: https://covid19.who.int. Kristi Noem is
quoted in Levenson (2020). The *New York Times* report on Sturgis is available at
https://www.nytimes.com/2020/11/06/us/sturgis-coronavirus-cases.html. My
survey conducted on COVID vaccine hesitancy and social distancing is Ansell,
Bauer, Gingrich and Stilgoe (2021). The analysis of cross-national social distancing behaviour is Ansell, Cansunar and Elkjaer (2021).

14. What is Security?

On neighbourhood disorder and negative mental effects, see Hill, Ross and
Angel (2005). The finding that pre-term births were more common in areas
with high crime is in Messer, Kaufman, Dole, et al. (2006). Olson's 'stationary bandit' concept is from Olson (1993). On the concept of 'hue and cry',
see Müller (2005). On the origins of policing and prisons, and the quote
from Defoe, see Ansell and Lindvall (2021, p. 68). The mysterious book on
prisons in my office is Johnston (2000). The best comparative analysis of the
history of prisons is Morris and Rothman (1998). The punishment statistics

from the early nineteenth century are from Ansell and Lindvall (2021, p. 97). On Eastern State Penitentiary, see Rubin (2021). Michel Foucault's analysis of the spectacle of early modern punishment is in Foucault (1977).

Good overviews of the origin of policing are Bayley (1990) and Emsley (2014). The sniffy quote from the *Daily Universal Register* and the origins of police forces are from Ansell and Lindvall (2021, Chapter 3). Pinker makes his case for ever-greater peace in Pinker (2011), and Braumoeller responds in Braumoeller (2019).

15. The Security Trap

The game theory argument about a circle of guardians is due to Binmore (2004). The O-Ring thing was popularized in Kremer (1993). Democracy as a solution to this problem is due to Hurwicz (2008). The report of the Department of Justice on Ferguson, MO, can be read in Shaw and United States (2015). Quasi-moral norms are explored in Elster (2015). Antanas Mockus's mayorship of Bogotá is examined in Pasotti (2010). Peter Leeson's analysis of Somalia is in Leeson (2007). Numbers on Somali refugees since the beginning of the civil war are from the United Nations; see https://www.un.org/development/desa/pd/content/international-migrant-stock. Jante as underpinning Danish social equality is from Uslaner (2017). The Norwegian sociologists who found Jante made people less trusting are Cappelen and Dahlberg (2018). Robert Putnam develops his theory of social capital in Putnam (1992, 2000).

The distaste of existing elites for technological change is in Acemoglu and Robinson (2006b). Schumpeter developed 'creative destruction' in Schumpeter (2013, originally 1942). Yes, the same book in which he defined 'democracy'! James C. Scott's analysis of how states make citizens 'legible' is in Scott (2008) and his analysis of the hill people of Zomia is in Scott (2010, p. 9). The chief evangelist for charter cities has been Paul Romer in Romer (2010). Sagar (2016) has a thoughtful critique of their legitimacy.

16. Escaping the Security Trap

The reduction in UK traffic injuries attributed to speed cameras is in Gains, Heydecker, Shrewsbury and Robertson (2004). The reduction in Seattle speeding in school safety zones is in Quistberg, Thompson, Curtin, et al. (2019). The independent review of London's facial-recognition technology is Fussey and Murray (2019). Yuan Yang of the *Financial Times* provided me with a very helpful guide to what China's social credit system can and cannot accomplish. Xin Yuan Wang's interviews with Chinese citizens about social credit are recorded in Wang (2019). Rogier Creemers has an excellent discussion of social credit at Creemers (2018). The problem of predictive policing leading to 'state dependence' is in Lum and Isaac (2016).

The year-long study of body-worn cameras in Rialto is covered in Ariel, Farrar and Sutherland (2015). The evidence that body-worn cameras could restrain whole police departments is in Kim (2019), and the relationship between cameras and social media coverage in Kim (2022). James Comey gave his speech expressing concern about depolicing at the University of Chicago Law School on 23 October 2015. The study in Spokane of depolicing is Wallace, White, Gaub and Todak (2018). A useful analysis of the arguments for 'defunding the police' is Cobbina-Dungy and Jones-Brown (2021).

Various versions of the democratic peace exist, including Russett (1994), Owen (1994), and Tomz and Weeks (2013). The 'capitalist peace' is due to Gartzke (2007). The discussion of Ukraine and NATO builds on Frye (2022, pp. 162–3). An excellent analysis of LAWS is in Horowitz (2019).

Part V: Prosperity

17. Paris

My thanks to Thomas Hale for discussing his experience of the Paris climate accords. The Laurent Fabius quote that 'states are no cold monsters' is at https://www.ft.com/content/c2a54a0e-89fb-11e5-90de-f44762bf9896. The comparison of the draft report to apartheid is from https://mg.co.za/article/2015-10-20-south-africa-compares-global-climate-plan-to-apartheid/. Data on emissions as a percentage of global emissions are from Climate-Trace: https://climatetrace.org/. The effectiveness of the Paris Agreement in terms of its discretion and vagueness is due to Keohane and Oppenheimer (2016).

18. What is Prosperity?

Coyle (2015) provides an entertaining and informative history of GDP, including the story about Italy's informal sector. She also discusses at length what GDP omits. Up-to-date measures of the Big Mac index can be found at https://www.economist.com/big-mac-index. You can look at how PPP varies across countries using the IMF's interactive map at https://www.imf.org/external/datamapper/PPPPC@WEO/OEMDC/ADVEC/WEOWORLD. Angus Maddison's historical estimates of GDP are at Maddison (2006). Sen's capabilities approach was developed in Sen (1985). Kuznets' prosperity index is discussed in Coyle (2015). The incentives for politicians to boost economic growth before elections are in Tufte (1978), and Duch and Stevenson (2008). NNP is discussed in Weitzman (2017). Arrow and colleagues' concern about sustainability is in Arrow, Dasgupta, Goulder, et al. (2004).

The Malthusian Trap is discussed in Allen (2003). Growth rates come from Maddison (2006) and Pritchett (1997). A useful discussion of the various eras of growth theory is in Acemoglu (2008). Acemoglu, Johnson and Robinson (2001, 2002) develop the reversal-of-fortune argument. Acemoglu and Robinson (2012) develop the idea of inclusive versus extractive institutions. The story of the Glorious Revolution and credible constraints is due to North and Weingast (1989).

19. The Prosperity Trap

Excellent introductions to game theory include Gibbons (1992) and Kydd (2015). A popular introduction is Dixit and Nalebuff (1993). Tax evasion in southern Italy is from Galbiati and Zanella (2012). Tit for Tat comes from Axelrod (1984). The *Leges Marchiarum* are discussed in Leeson (2009). Lengthening the shadow of the future was a major topic of discussion in 1980s international relations; see Axelrod and Keohane (1985). Olson developed his theory of collective action in his seminal Olson (1965), one of the great books of political economy. The argument about NATO and collective action is due to Olson and Zeckhauser (1966). The parable of buffalo mozzarella is from Locke (2001). The argument that climate change is a distributive – not a collective action – problem is from Aklin and Mildenberger (2020) and Colgan, Green and Hale (2021). 'Catalytic cooperation' comes from Hale (2020).

The classic analysis of the 'Dutch Disease' is Corden (1984). On the Saudi Arabian tax department, see Chaudhry (1997). Ross (2001) provides the classic account of the political-resource curse. On lower spending on education in oil-rich countries, see Ansell (2010). Ross (2008) argues that it is oil not Islam that is responsible for lower female political participation in the Middle East. The attempts of some Gulf states to modernize through education and spectacle are covered in Jones (2015, 2017). The South Sea Bubble and the possibility of riding it are covered in Temin and Voth (2004). The quote from Sir Gilbert Heathcote is from Hoppit (2002). The experience of El Salvador with Bitcoin is covered at https://www.nytimes.com/2021/10/07/world/americas/bitcoin-el-salvador-bukele.html.

20. Escaping the Prosperity Trap

On German 'diversified quality production', see Sorge and Streeck (2018). Mazzucato develops her idea of the 'entrepreneurial state' in Mazzucato (2011). An excellent analysis of innovation policy in Finland and elsewhere in Scandinavia is Ornston (2013), as well as in Breznitz and Ornston (2013). Breznitz (2021) discusses the importance of 'tech teens' to development and the success of Giant. The success of the Norwegian model of resource management is well explained in Holden (2013). The 'tax' solution to inequality and credit bubbles comes from Ahlquist and Ansell (2017). The relative experience of Canadian and American banks is due to Calomiris and Haber (2015). On carbon taxes versus cap-and-trade systems there is a vast debate, of which Stavins (2019) is a useful summary. The British Columbia carbon tax and its effectiveness are examined in Harrison (2013). Popular support for a carbon tax, when told other countries will also introduce one, can be seen in Bechtel, Scheve and van Lieshout (2019). How to create support for a carbon tax is explored in Gaikwad, Genovese and Tingley (2022). The survey analysis of a global carbon tax is from Carattini, Kallbekken and Orlov (2019).

How Politics Can Succeed

The ancillary benefits to proportional representation are discussed at length in McGann (2006). The loss to the United Kingdom of not adopting a sovereign wealth fund is calculated in Atkinson and Hamilton (2020).

Index

Index

United States of America (USA)
  affirmative action in 176–7
  American Civil War (1861–5) 69, 70,
    88, 153
  Bush tax cuts (2001) 116–17
  childcare in 173–4
  civil rights and 18, 33, 54, 101, 131, 155
  climate change and 1, 2, 234–5, 236,
    237
  Congress 12, 45, 55, 68, 131, 133
  COVID-19 and 183, 185, 186, 188
  debt ceiling 55–6
  democracy, history of within 32–3
  democracy, popularity of within 5
  election turnout 39
  filibuster rule 18–19
  foreign-aid spending 159
  Great Compression, twentieth-
    century 87–8
  healthcare in 7, 131–5, 145, 151, 163,
    171, 172, 174
  inequality in 75–8, 83, 84, 86, 87, 88,
    97, 101, 103, 107, 111, 114–17
  inheritance taxation 116–17
  NATO and 257–8
  obesity rates 163
  polarization in 53, 54–6, 68
  police in 8, 204–6, 221, 224
  political donors in 78
  political parties *see individual political
    party name*
  presidential election (1936) 153
  presidential election (1964) 51–2
  presidential election (2000) 40–41, 64
  presidential election (2016) 54, 188
  presidential election (2020) 41, 53,
    66, 76–7, 114, 284
  school bussing 166
  security in 183, 186, 197, 198, 200,
    201, 202, 205–6, 209, 212, 219, 220,
    221, 224, 225, 226, 229
  Senate 18–19, 45, 48, 76
  6 January 2021 insurrection 35, 41
  slavery and 33, 69–70, 107, 246
  Social Security 7, 51–2, 120, 140,
    144, 153, 158–9, 172
  social spending as a percentage of
    national income 139
  solidarity in 131–5, 139, 144, 145,
    146, 151, 154–6, 158–9, 162, 163,
    166, 170–72, 173–5, 176
  state pension 140
  Supreme Court 18, 41, 67, 135, 235
  swing voters 52
  UBI in 170–72
  universal suffrage in 32–3
  voting choice in 29
  voting rights in 32–4
  voting systems in 48
  welfare in 7, 51–2, 76, 135, 139, 144,
    145, 146, 151, 154–6, 158–9, 162,
    163, 166, 170–72, 173–5, 176,
    224
Universal Basic Income (UBI) 168–73,
  179
universal suffrage 29, 32–3
universalism 81, 146, 172–5, 178,
  285–6
University of California (UC)
  176–7
University of Texas Austin (UT
  Austin) 177
utility 11
Utopia 79

venture capital 272
veto 29, 39–40, 47, 59
Vietnam War (1955–75) 43
vocational education 124–7, 271
volatility 56, 72, 97, 237, 261–3, 268,
  275, 287, 288
volonté générale ('general will') 38